Modern Critical Views

Modern Critical Views

TOM WOLFE

Edited and with an introduction by
Harold Bloom
Sterling Professor of the Humanities
Yale University

CHELSEA HOUSE PUBLISHERS
Philadelphia

Printed and bound in the United States of America

10 9 8 7 6 5 4 3 2 1

∞ The paper used in this publication meets the minimum
requirements of the American National Standard for
Permanence of Paper for Printed Library Materials,
Z39.48-1984

Library of Congress Cataloging-in-Publication Data

Tom Wolfe / editor, Harold Bloom.
      p. cm.
    Includes bibliographical references and index.
    ISBN 0-7910-5916-2 (alk. paper)
    1. Wolfe, Tom — Criticism and interpretation.
    I. Bloom, Harold.

    PS3573.O526 Z88   2000
    818'.5409—dc21   00-060321
                                          CIP

Chelsea House Publishers
1974 Sproul Road, Suite 400
Broomall, PA 19008-0914

The Chelsea House World Wide Web address is
http://www.chelseahouse.com

Contributing Editor: Janyce Marson

Produced by: Robert Gerson Publisher's Services, Santa Barbara, CA

Contents

Editor's Note

My Introduction centers upon *A Man in Full*, Tom Wolfe's immensely popular novel of 1998, which seems to me more Hemingway than Balzac, and a period piece, though its invocation of Epictetus as a sage for America seems to me a masterstroke.

Ronald Weber begins the chronological sequence of criticism by asserting that Wolfe's celebration of the Cultural Revolution is more authentic than most realize.

Mas'ud Zavarzadeh meditates upon the non-fiction novel, as composed by Wolfe and Norman Mailer, and concludes with them that our values are no longer centered.

For A. Carl Bredahl, the difference between Wolfe and Ken Kesey is that Wolfe never loses sight of context while, for Richard A. Kallan, Wolfe's New Journalism belongs to the Television Age, rather than the Print Era.

Thomas L. Hartshorne, reflecting upon Wolfe as chronicler of the 1960s, sees him as carrying the moral values of Richmond, Virginia, into a New York City context, after which Barbara Lounsberry intimates that Wolfe's negativity masks a nostalgia for the impossible quest his subjects undertake.

Ed Cohen, in a analysis much in Foucault's wake, sees Wolfe as exposing the power structure (though I cannot see that Wolfe declines it), while James N. Stull regards Wolfe as deliberately dominating his own gamesmanship.

The Bonfire of the Vanities (1987) is analyzed by James F. Smith as a transfer of the Dreiser novel into the 1980s, after which Tom Wolfe himself gives us a manifesto for his attempt to write the "New Social Novel," in the spirit of Balzac, Zola, and Theodore Dreiser.

Rand Richards Cooper, meditating on *A Man in Full*, wryly defends Wolfe's dark speculation that the inner self is a fiction, while Joshua J. Masters concludes this volume by returning us to *The Bonfire of the Vanities*, and to its nightmare image of "a new urban struggle, sure to be just as terrifying as the last."

Introduction

There are enough reviews out on *A Man in Full* so that I can spare myself, and my readers, any plot summary. Tom Wolfe is, as he deserves to be, a hugely successful "popular novelist," comparable to the recent Toni Morrison of *Beloved*, *Jazz*, and *Paradise* (not the more impressive Morrison of the earlier *Sula* and *Song of Solomon*). We are, these last few years, in a rich era of authentic prose fictions: Philip Roth's *Sabbath's Theater* and *American Pastoral*, Don de Lillo's *Underworld*, Thomas Pynchon's *Mason & Dixon*, and the Border Trilogy of Cormac McCarthy. McCarthy's *Blood Meridian* of 1985 seems to me clearly the major aesthetic achievement of any living American writer. Wolfe is a fierce storyteller, and a vastly adequate social satirist, but both *Bonfire of the Vanities* and *A Man in Full* come short of Wolfe's high ambitions: to be our Victor Hugo, Balzac, and Zola as we ooze into Millennium. The protagonists of *A Man in Full* are extravagant cartoons or ideograms, as were the principal persons of *Bonfire*. Wolfe's characters remain names on a page; the author's preternatural exuberance is invested elsewhere. His sharp reportorial eye sees everything: suits, cars, female anatomies, and above all the way things are in government, finance, business, prison—everything and everywhere in Gingrich-Clinton America. Wolfe is a grand entertainer, a true moralist, and a very intelligent and perceptive journalist. That is not Balzac, but is still very impressive indeed.

Yet there is something more, and it moves me most about *A Man in Full*: the book espouses a Neo-Stoicism, a very unlikely philosophy for the contemporary United States, where the American Religion rages wildly, two centuries into its romance with the American God (who loves only Republicans) and the American Christ (who loves each and every one of us, on a personal and individual basis). Some reviewers have seen *A Man in Full*'s forays into the Stoic Epictetus (A.D. 50–130) as the largest of Wolfe's jokes; perhaps it began as such, but to my aged critical ears Wolfe takes his Epictetus straight, even if he expects (and wants) to convert no one. If we are to have a national moralist, let it be Tom Wolfe and not the unspeakable William Bennett (surely a fictional character, invented by Gore Vidal in the absence of Nathanael West). An immense dose of Epictetus would do all of us a great deal of good, and I am grateful (beyond irony) to Tom Wolfe for reviving Epictetus and making him available to the hundreds of thousands whom Wolfe will reach.

Stoicism goes back to about 300 B.C., and included among its luminaries such estimable Romans as Seneca and Marcus Aurelius. A highly pragmatic doctrine (and thus applicable to Americans), Stoicism is most clearly set forth by Epictetus, who had endured slavery and emerged from it with wisdom:

> Do not seek to have events happen as you want them to, but instead want them to happen as they do happen, and your life will go well.

That sounds both easy and impossible, but has its nuances. What upsets us, according to Epictetus, is not so much what happens to us; but our judgments upon those happenings. We have been assigned roles in a play; we can be good or bad actors, but not choose another assignment. As for the other actors, we need not fret about them, even if they are the usual rabblement of fools, knaves, and ideologues who delight in misrepresenting us:

> When someone acts badly toward you and speaks badly of you, remember that he does or says it in the belief that it is appropriate for him to do so. Accordingly he cannot follow what appears to you but only what appears to him, so that if things appear badly to him, he is harmed in as much as he has been deceived.

I am grateful to Wolfe for reminding me of this, which is excellent advice for any author enduring irrational reviewers. Wolfe's Epictetus finds his American apostle in Conrad Hensley, who emerges from our prison system to convert the "man in full," Charlie Croker, to the Stoic persuasion. Hensley is rather pallid, as a literary character, but Croker has a certain negative splendor, superior to anyone in *Bonfire*, and Croker may presage a further development in Wolfe's drive to become at least a Zola, if not quite a Balzac. Baudelaire remarked that, in Balzac, even a janitor could be a genius. Charlie Croker is not always very smart, but he has something of Wolfe's own daemonic will in him, and he is very likable (unlike everyone in *Bonfire*). The novel's first paragraph gives us conglomerate Charlie just before his Fall into physical and financial crippling:

Charlie Croker, astride his favorite Tennessee walking horse, pulled his shoulders back to make sure he was erect in the saddle and took a deep breath . . . Ahhhh, that was the ticket . . . He loved the way his mighty chest rose and fell beneath his khaki shirt and imagined that everyone in the hunting party noticed how powerfully built he was. Everybody; not just his seven guests but also his six black retainers and his young wife, who was on a horse behind him near the teams of La Mancha mules that pulled the buckboard and the kennel wagon. For good measure, he flexed and fanned out the biggest muscles of his back, the latissimi dorsi, in a Charlie Croker version of a peacock or a turkey preening. His wife, Serena, was only twenty-eight, whereas he had just turned sixty and was bald on top and had only a swath of curly gray hair on the sides and in back. He seldom passed up an opportunity to remind her of what a sturdy cord—no, what a veritable *cable*—kept him connected to the rude animal vitality of his youth.

Wolfe is too sly not to be aware that he parodies Hemingway, the Hemingway who was already a self-parody. Croker, aging vitalist, is emblematic of all those representative men who populate American life and American fiction, powerful men who will be destroyed: by themselves, by their women, by the American system, or simply by entropy. Shrewdly, Wolfe does not allow Charlie Croker to be annihilated. In a mode that is splendidly wild and charmingly improbable, Charlie is converted by Conrad Hensley to the Stoic philosophy of Epictetus, and thus is saved. Wolfe, both parodying the American religion and offering his own alternative, concludes with Croker pursuing a new career as a Stoic evangelist, a notion crazy enough to be rather sublime.

I pass over the minor but frequent pleasures of *A Man in Full*, including its politically incorrect portraits of rascals both black and white. Wolfe's Atlanta is bad news, but then what part of the United States is anything else, in the age of Gingrich, Trent Lott, and all of our other splendors? Let us amiably rejoice in Tom Wolfe, who entertains all those of whom he rightly disapproves. I have read him during an otherwise bad week, and again thank him for returning me to Epictetus, to whom I give the last word.

Whoever wants to be free, therefore, let him not want or avoid anything that is up to others. Otherwise he will necessarily be a slave.

RONALD WEBER

Tom Wolfe's Happiness Explosion

"Kesey's saving grace was that he never got serious when he could say it just as well with a cosmic joke."

After his first book Dwight Macdonald dismissed Tom Wolfe as a fad, part and parcel of his famous girl-of-the-year piece on Baby Jane Holzer; there's nothing, Macdonald forecast, so dead as last year's mannerist. But Wolfe hasn't yet faded into the netherworld of yesterday's celebrities; with the exception of Mailer, no writer has more ambitiously sought the frazzled style of the time, and few writers have shown a defter skill in developing their territory, in continuing to work the topical scene while extending their range and keeping a surprisingly fresh touch. The point is that Tom Wolfe's work merits more than passing attention, and attention not so much directed to the dots-and-exclamation-points style or the self-proclaimed role as a founding father of the New Journalism but, less noticed, to his consistently shaped portrait of an assertive and mocking new sensibility alive in a new America.

"I don't mean for this to sound like 'I had a vision' or anything," he begins the introduction to *The Kandy-Kolored Tangerine-Flake Streamline Baby*, but that, suddenly inspired or not, is what he has—a vision of modern America, of styles and attitudes reshaping the country in strange ways. The starting point for the vision is money, the massive infusion of money into

From *Journal of Popular Culture* 8, no. 1 (Summer 1974). © 1974 by Ray B. Browne/Bowling Green State University.

every level of American society since World War II. One result of the new affluence—as Wolfe picks up the story in the early Sixties—was that lots of "lower class creeps" and "rancid people," flush with money for the first time in their lives, found themselves able to build monuments to their peculiar styles of life, styles that up to that time had been practically invisible in the society as a whole. They began pouring feverish attention and piles of money into such things as custom cars and rock music, stretch pants and decal eyes— and into Las Vegas. Las Vegas became the "super hyper-version" symbol of the new money dynamism in mass America, created by war money and by gangsters, "the first uneducated prole-petty-burgher Americans to have enough money to build a monument to their styles of life." But Las Vegas still was just the symbol of a whole prole culture on the march, rising out of the vinyl deeps of invisibility and neglect, creating gaudy, free-form styles that most Americans considered vulgar and lower-class awful but that were charged with the genuine energy of the time.

The new prole styles, Wolfe argues, were not only worth recording in themselves but were significant because they influenced the life of the entire country. Just as Detroit was paying watchful attention to the baroque custom car designers on the west coast and cashing in on the enthusiasm for southern dirt-track racing, so too crossroads America was busy imitating the skyline of Las Vegas, and New York socialites, lacking natural and aristocratic styles of their own, were lapping up teenage music and clothes and the pop tastes of the bohemian undergrounds. Hence the phenomenon of Baby Jane Holzer, a Park Avenue socialite and wedded to a real estate heir yet an Andy Warhol starlet who "comprehends what the Rolling Stones *mean*."

Elsewhere Wolfe explains the Baby Jane syndrome as a renewal of nineteenth-century *nostalgie de la boue*—a longing on the part of the upper classes to "recapture the raw and elemental vitality of the lower orders." This aping of Low-Rent fads and fashions is in part a way for the beautiful people to separate themselves from the well-heeled middle classes, since money alone can no longer maintain a buffer. The one thing the upper-classes still have going for them is confidence to be shocking and get away with it, while the middle classes, locked into gentility, lack the nerve to be anything but decorously respectable. Prole culture then is not only where the action is in contemporary America, offering kandy-kolored styles alive with vitality, but it provides aristocratic types, indulging in *nostalgie de la boue*, with a means for staying out front in a society in which money is plentiful.

Yet there is more to the new money situation than just lower-class monument building and its influence on high society. Particularly in *The Pump House Gang* and *The Electric Kool-Aid Acid Test* Wolfe began looking at the ways in which various kinds of people, including middle-class dropouts like Ken Kesey's Merry Pranksters and the La Jolla surfers, were creating total "statuspheres" for themselves. There was enough money floating around not only to allow kids to buy Hobie Alter surfboards at $140 a crack but to live *The Life*, an age-segregated total culture that had no truck with the black panthers (not *the* Panthers but the black street-shoe set, the middle-age square world) and the whole "hubby-mommy you're-breaking-my-gourd scene." Because of the available money the kids were not just hanging around together on street corners but establishing "whole little societies for themselves."

And these societies, these statuspheres, defined themselves not only by various internal rules (dress, hair-length, age) but by their rejection of the traditional black-panther status world, the fear of getting "sucked into the ticky-tacky life with some insurance salesman sitting forward in your stuffed chair on your wall-to-wall telling you that life is like a football game and you sit there and take that stuff." From Harvey's Drive-In to Leicester Square Wolfe found kids discovering ways to "drop out almost totally from the conventional class-job system into a world they control."

And not only kids but, increasingly, adults. Enter Hugh Hefner, the "King of the Status Dropouts," another profound symbol. With his Playboy millions Hefner has abandoned conventional status competition— "the old feudal, patrimonial idea of status hierarchies, the being seen, meeting the right people and all of that"—holed up in his electronic mansion, created a statusphere ("contemporary recluse") all his own. For Wolfe the quality of Hefner's statusphere matters little; what does matter is that Hefner has started his own league, invented his own rules, managed to "*split* from *communitas*."

"Community" has about the same place in the Wolfe lexicon as black panther, work-a-hubby and arteriosclerotic: it refers to the straight job-class world of good gray status competition, and seems to imply for Wolfe the same kind of pervasive unfulfillment Emerson had in mind when he observed that "Society everywhere is in conspiracy against the manhood of every one of its members." The community, Wolfe observes, "has never been one great happy family for all men"; typical community status systems have in fact been "games with few winners and many who feel like losers." And so large numbers of people, with Hefner as classic example, are now busy liberating themselves physically and psychologically from dependence on communitas by setting up their own often esoteric statuspheres, and they are doing so not from traditional motives of alienation or rebellion but simply because they "want to be happy winners for a change."

In the introduction to *The Pump House Gang* Wolfe tells about taking part with Günter Grass and Allen Ginsberg in a Princeton symposium on

"The Style of the Sixties" that quickly bogged down in such heavy matters as police repression and Gestapo tactics. Relates Wolfe: "I couldn't believe what was happening, but there it was. 'What are you talking about?' I said. 'We're in the middle of a . . . Happiness Explosion!'" In the middle of a happiness explosion apocalyptic talk is out of place; what is called for is fun, joy, pleasure. Says Bob Scull, the pop art collector: ". . . you know what my philosophy is? My Philosophy is, Enjoy." That's the basic Wolfian point about prole-culture monument building and all the weird statuspheres spinning off by themselves; that's what the new money is really allowing many people to do for the first time in their lives: enjoy. Wolfe comments on Bob Scull's comment: "What struck me throughout America and England was that so many people have found such novel ways of doing just that, *enjoying*, extending their egos way out on the best terms available, namely, their own."

But all this, he adds, all this ego-extending happiness explosion is going unnoticed by serious thinkers and cultural custodians. Like Grass and Ginsberg at Princeton, learned voices persist in telling us how miserable things are; indeed, they seem to relish calamity as the "ancient ego-crusher," a whip to keep people in line, noses and spirits to the old moral grindstones. The war in Vietnam, poverty in America, alienation in students—all welcome as fuel for "the old restraints, the old limits." But the joke is on them. While they play their soulful political and intellectual games, vast hordes of people gaily thumb their noses and on their Harley-Davidson 74-XAs roar off "in precisely the opposite direction, through God's own American ozone"—off to enjoy!

That's the underlying point of Wolfe's piece on McLuhan, "What If He Is Right?" That McLuhan may turn out to be for real, the Delphic seer of the electronic future, doesn't matter much; what excites Wolfe is his capacity to turn society on its head, to say of most of its cherished arrangements and structures: you are irrelevant. And made irrelevant by that darling of lowlife culture, the damnable TV set. Even more to Wolfe's liking is the fact that much of the McLuhan attack has been directed against the literary intellectuals and their two overriding concerns, books and moral protest, as well as their tendency to retreat in the face of developments in the physical and social sciences and run up the flag of "values." The literary intellectuals, like the black panthers and all the straight work-a-hubbies, are turned to the past, devoted to the "preservation of sacred values" and dire forecasts of the future, and consequently oblivious to what is really going on in the country, the happiness explosion. McLuhan, on the other hand, knows something radically new is afoot and is generally cheery in his predictions, picturing the end of social, economic and political parochialism, a more tactile existence, man made whole again. At the same time he has found his own statusphere, absorbed everything into his theory, emancipated himself from the conventional intellectuality and moralism of the EngLit establishment just as Hefner has freed himself from conventional high-society status competition.

That's likewise the point, or one of them, of Wolfe's lengthy report on Kesey and the Pranksters. Though Wolfe may be finally ambivalent about the success of the acid experiments and Kesey's role as charismatic leader, familiar themes appear in the book: the creation of special statuspheres of liberation and enjoyment, the exotic extensions ("Everybody's life becomes more fabulous, every minute, than the most fabulous book. It's phony, goddam it . . . but *mysto* . . . and after a while it starts to infect you, like an itch, the roseola"), the concomitant rejection of traditional moral, political and intellectual concerns ("transcending the bullshit"). Though the book ends on a note of defeat with the failure of the acid graduation, Wolfe seems fully to accept the validity of the Pranksters' search for fresh insights and a higher consciousness, and to view it as the far, freaky edge of the happiness explosion ("where it was scary, but people were whole people"), a natural elaboration of the special dropout worlds first created by the surfers and the car kids.

Radical Chic & Mau-Mauing the Flak Catchers renders Wolfe's version of the times in the most explicit form yet. The first of the two long pieces describes an adventure in fashionable politics by fashionable people, and as such is a new manifestation of an old aristocratic syndrome observed before: *nostalgie de la boue*, the upper-class fascination with Low-Rent styles as a means of asserting distance from prosaic middle-class life. In the case of Radical Chic in fashionable New York in the late Sixties *nostalgie de la boue* involved a fascination with revolutionary political styles as a way of demonstrating emancipation from the cautious consensus, the humdrum majority. But of course this emancipation is not *real* emancipation, not part of the ego-extending happiness explosion, but a familiar game played within the confines of traditional high-society status competition.

At times Wolfe's Radical Chic figures, thrown into momentary confusion, confess the truth. A Park Avenue matron, confronted by a particularly intense Maoist type, is gleefully quoted as saying: "He's a magnificent man, but suppose some simple-minded schmucks take all that business about burning down buildings *seriously*?" Radical Chic, growing out of a period of great confusion among the liberal intellectuals and their followers, is despite appearances to the contrary merely an expression of the world of traditional values; it is a radicalism of style only for "in its heart it is part of Society and its traditions."

Radical Chic provides Wolfe with the occasion for full-blast irony; as a flighty, romanticized aspect of the Leavis-Empson-*New York Review of Books* moralism that he pillors in the McLuhan essay, it is that side of traditional and unhappy communitas that appears to touch him most directly (" . . . I had been through the whole Ph.D. route at Yale, in American Studies and everything") and that calls forth a deeply personal style of attack. The article focuses on a fund-raising party given by Leonard Bernstein and his wife in their plush penthouse for a group of (real) Black Panthers. The Bernstein party, dramatized in precise and savage detail, was in turn part of a series of Radical Chic events in hip New York society that followed a massive party thrown by Assemblyman Andrew Stein on his father's Southampton estate for California grape workers. The social season of 1969 was filled with Radical Chic parties—for *Ramparts* magazine, the Chicago Eight, G.I. coffee houses, Friends of the Earth, Bernadette Devlin. But the Bernsteins' fund-raiser was special for it brought the fashionable guests into contact with the most notorious of radical groups, the Panthers, and "if there was ever a group that embodied the romance and excitement of which Radical Chic is made, it was the Panthers."

But as useful as the party itself for Wolfe's lethal irony is the burlesque aftermath. *The New York Times* originally reported the story as a society item, calling attention to Leonard Bernstein's Black Watch trousers, neck piece, and repeated refrain of "I dig it" in response to the Panther philosophy, then sent it out over its wire service where it became an international page-one story. Two days later the *Times* followed up with an editorial taking the Bernsteins and their guests to task for "elegant slumming," and thereupon columnists and editorial writers everywhere jumped on the bandwagon. But still there was more: bitterness between Jews and blacks that involved Panther support for the Arabs against Israel, an issue the Bernsteins apparently had been oblivious to, suddenly flared about the unhappy hosts and they began getting hate mail from Jewish Defense League types. Perhaps the final whacky upshot occurred when Jewish pickets in Miami forced a movie house to withdraw a film of Bernstein conducting the Israel Philharmonic on Mount Scopus in celebration of Israel's victory in the Six-Day War.

In the wake of the Bernstein disaster Radical Chic made a strategic withdrawal. Plans for future Panther parties were hurriedly abandoned, interest turned to such safe causes as The Friends of the Earth. "Politics, like Rock, Pop, and Camp, has its uses," Wolfe wryly concludes, "but to put one's whole status on the line for *nostalgie de la boue* in any of its forms would be unprincipled."

Radical Chic as a form of elegant slumming was a sitting duck for Wolfe, but there is more to the attack than the vulnerability of the target. It illustrates his notion of the impoverishment of high society in the face of raw-vital energy emanating from prole culture, in this case the Panthers; yet even more to Wolfe's point, the ultimate horse laugh running through the article, is not the feeble social climbing and marginal differentiation involved in Radical Chic but that the fashionable culturati and liberal intellectuals take the moral protest-civil libertarian stance seriously at all. If Radical Chic were just a case of vain strivings in high society it would be funny, but that its advocates really care about their causes (to the extent of course that they care for any causes beyond their own) is a delicious *joke*.

Bernstein is portrayed not only as pompous but foolishly serious in the same way that Grass and Ginsberg were foolishly serious at the Princeton symposium. He misses the fact that the Panthers are engaged in an elaborate game of mau-mauing the white liberals (a game they themselves only half know they are playing) and instead tries to involve them in heavy dialogue. He makes reference to *The New York Review of Books* (Mrs. Bernstein quotes from *The New Yorker*), worries about Panther threats against established black community leaders, guiltily wonders if the Panthers are embittered by the luxury of his apartment, finally draws a connection between the rejection experienced by the Panthers and the fact that almost *everyone* in the room has had "a problem about being unwanted." It's the last incredible straw:

> Lenny is unbeatable. . . . He has done it. He has just steered the Black Panther movement into a 1955 Jules Feiffer cartoon. Rejection, Security, Anxiety, Oedipus, Electra, Neurosis, Transference, Id, Superego, Archetype and Field of Perception, that wonderful 1950's game, beloved by all educated young men and women in the East who grew up in the era of the great cresting tide of Freud, Jung, Adler, Reik & Reich, when everyone either had an analyst or quoted Ernest Dichter telling Maytag that dishwashing machines were bought by women with anal compulsions.

The real comedy for Wolfe is the archaic style of Bernstein's thought and the old-fashioned concern for moral protest, however fragile, lingering behind all the Radical Chic events. Bernstein is portrayed as the "Village Explainer, the champion of Mental Jotto, the Free Analyst, Mr. Let's Find Out," and what he takes with such humorless seriousness isn't serious at all but an exercise in ritualistic mau-mauing. By way of contrast, note the way Kesey and the Pranksters respond, with Wolfe's apparent blessing, to a Vietnam Day Committee rally in Berkeley: as a pathetic charade to be treated as such, an occasion to dress up in military duds, paint the bus the color of dried blood, and for Kesey, never one to be serious when a joke will do, to finally get up on the speaker's platform and say: "There's only one thing to do . . . there's only one thing's gonna do any good at all. . . . And that's everybody just look at it, look at the war, and turn your backs and say . . . Fuck it. . . ."

In "Radical Chic" the tactic of mau-mauing is subordinated to Wolfe's delight in cutting up the hip socialites—even the Panthers have tough going upholding their image in the face of Radical Chic concern—but in "May-Mauing the Flak Catchers" it takes over center stage. The article brilliantly treats the routine practice of minority group intimidation of bureaucrats in the San Francisco poverty program. The bureaucrats talk "ghetto" all the time but of course don't know what to do about it, so come to depend on confrontations:

> They sat back and waited for you to come rolling in with your certified angry militants, your guaranteed frustrated ghetto youth, looking like a bunch of wild men. Then you had your test confrontation. If you were outrageous enough, if you could shake up the bureaucrats so bad that their eyes froze into iceballs and their mouths twisted up into smiles of sheer physical panic, into shit-eating grins, so to speak—then they knew you were the real goods. They knew you were the right studs to give the poverty grants and community organizing jobs to. Otherwise they wouldn't know.

The mau-mauing act is seldom conducted in the presence of top bureaucrats but rather flak catchers, Hush Puppy civil-service lifers who take the rhetorical beating and report back to their protected superiors. It's the whole game-like, madly choreographed quality of the mau-mauing that Wolfe delights in. The flak catchers are rarely in more actual physical danger than their bosses because the "brothers understood through and through that it was a tactic, a procedure, a game." The term mau-mauing itself suggested to its practitioners the "put-on side of it. . . . It was like a practical joke at the expense of the white man's superstitiousness."

It's the comic, light-hearted, transcending-the-bullshit side to mau-mauing that fits with Wolfe's vision of the times and links itself to the happiness explosion. At the same time it's an individualistic, idiosyncratic game and so part of the free-wheeling ego extension and esoteric statusphere building that are the distinguishing marks of the new sensibility. Wolfe views the ghettos as alive with individualists, brothers "with their own outlook, their own status system"; no single group represents the ghettos because everybody has "his own angle and his own way of looking at black power."

Special attention is given to brothers who ingeniously get their own things going in exploiting the poverty programs—Chaser, Dudley, and especially Bill Jackson. He hits upon a perfect bureaucratic put on, the equivalent of the Pranksters and Kesey at the Vietnam Day Committee rally. All on his own he shows up in the City Hall lobby one morning with sixty ghetto kids in tow, all carrying the "greatest grandest sweetest creamiest runniest and most luscious mess of All-American pop drinks, sweets, and fried foods ever brought together in one place." The San Francisco City Hall has a magnificent marble lobby; for the functionaries and lifers who work in the building it's a "Golden Whore's Dream of Paradise," the ceremonial seat of government and power, and for Jackson to bring his kids in there and defile it with all that messy kid crud and no one able to lay a finger on them was the ultimate in confrontation, enough to bring the mayor out of hiding, ready to talk. Bill Jackson had forever proven himself to be "a brilliant man and a true artist, a rare artist, of the mau-mau." Not Leonard Bernstein but Bill Jackson—an inspired creator of a "cotton-candy and M & M riot," a true artist of the happiness explosion.

For most of the Haight-Ashbury heads described in *Acid Test* ("still playing the eternal charade of the middle-class intellectuals") Ken Kesey was finally too real; he insisted on preaching the need to move beyond acid and, worse, he had an odd relation with genuine outlaws, the Hell's Angels. The chief Prankster really *meant* it about getting to Edge City. Which suggests a question, not to be passed over lightly in any consideration of Tom Wolfe: does *he* really mean it? Does he truly think public concerns so meaningless, conventional intellectuality and traditional moral protest so bankrupt, ordinary social arrangements so out of tune with the assertive sensibility arising out of the vinyl deeps? Does he actually believe in his vision of a happiness explosion and his avowed message, enjoy?

Reviewers have contended that it's useless to ask what moral or intellectual position Wolfe really speaks from because his method proliferates points of view and implies attitudes that are frequently contradicted or thrown away. Similarly it has been argued that Wolfe is basically uncommitted to his materials, that in his work acceptance is always neatly balanced by rejection, and that appropriately McLuhanesque his medium is more important than his message, his manner more important than his matter. Nevertheless, there remains an insistent vision of modern America running through all of Wolfe's work that derives from a repeated mocking of the styles and concerns of traditional culture and a celebration of the comic, pleasure-seeking, self-centered modes of the happiness explosion. Whether he means it or not he has consistently dramatized a cultural situation in which the received culture appears on its last feeble legs, about to give way under a popular assault based on the new styles and attitudes of widespread affluence.

Indeed, even to ask if Wolfe really means it is perhaps to miss the ultimate mockery of his mocking vision, for to the advocates of the happiness explosion questions of meaning are simply part of the old-culture game, the Bernstein game. Maybe it misses the final Wolfian point to ask what Las Vegas *means*. Or what The New Thang means.

"The New Thang?"

That's what the mayor of San Francisco asks during a City Hall meeting with a new ghetto group shortly after his confrontation with Bill Jackson and his kids. He's told by Ronnie, the group's leader:

> "That's right, The New Thang."
>
> The Mayor looked wigged out, as if the lights had gone out in his skull.
>
> "Thang," said Ronnie. "That's Thing in African."
>
> "Oh," said the Mayor. There wasn't even the faintest shade of meaning in his voice.

MAS'UD ZAVARZADEH

The Contingent Donnée:
The Testimonial Nonfiction Novel

The "monumental disproportions" of events—to use Norman Mailer's comment on his own eyewitness stance in *The Armies of the Night*—have aroused suspicions about the epistemological authority of any omniscient interpreter of reality. In contemporary writing, "The literary tones are those of voices paying witness to the fantastic." The dominance of the testimonial narrative situation in recent American literature manifests a "common sense of crisis and a common feeling of having been conned about it." The witness stance assumes that the only authority on appearance and existence is the witness himself—a kind of solipsism imposed on the contemporary consciousness by fabulous reality. By adopting this narrative posture, the nonfiction novelist further rejects the very notion of a monolithic, separable reality beyond sense experience which might be discovered through the patterning of life impressions or the exercise of the fictive imagination. The testimonial nonfiction novel, in other words, enacts the epistemological belief that in an extreme situation the only authentic way to deal with outside phenomena is to report them as they register themselves on one's participating senses.

This participation has seemed to many critics an active, personal interference with events and an implicit, private totalization of reality which charges the neutral actuality with values and meaning. However, the nature

From *The Mythopoeic Reality: The Postwar American Nonfiction Novel.* © 1976 by Mas'ud Zavarzadeh.

of the involvement of the witness participant in this type of nonfiction novel differs from the conventional fictive eyewitness narrative situation. In the testimonial nonfiction novel, the participation is "instrumental," not "projectional": although a person participates in events and reports in his own individual voice from the inside circle of action, the ensuing subjectivity is that of the involved people themselves, not a "projection" of the writer's personal feeling onto them for the purpose of totalizing the experience. The witness-participant-narrator is more a medium, an instrument, an articulating voice through which the interiority of events experienced by people is registered. Tom Wolfe compares such a participant narrator to a "method actor"—one who gets inside the emotions and passions of people, rather than projecting his own emotions into them. "It is a matter," he maintains, "not of projecting your emotions into the story but of getting inside the emotions, inside the subjective reality of the people you are writing about." The witness-narrator usually maps the interior landscape of the psyche by means of intensive "saturation reporting" and long periods of living with, talking to, and observing his subjects. Chapter XXI of Tom Wolfe's *The Electric Kool-Aid Acid Test* is an extended "interior monologue." The interiority, however, is Ken Kesey's. The witness-narrator Tom Wolfe serves only as an instrument through which Kesey's mind registers its feelings, fears, and flow of sensations. The chapter is "constructed completely from diaries, letters, tapes, and interviews with Kesey." John Sack's *m* is a nonfictive narrative almost entirely in the form of "interior monologue" which follows a company through its tour of duty in Vietnam. Sack also serves as a reflecting instrument which registers the soldiers' emotions.

The degree of participation of the witness in the actions he registers varies from total immersion (*The Armies of the Night*) to detached observation (*The Electric Kool-Aid Acid Test*): in briefer terms, from "generator" to "reflector" of feelings. The two roles are closely related in *Armies*, where Mailer is both "generator" and "reflector" of reported actions and emotions. Significantly, the ideas and acts of Mailer the "generator" of events are registered by Mailer the "reflector" of events from a third-person point of view. This narrational schizophrenia of *Armies* is in itself a direct acting out of the schizoid nature of the actualities in which Mailer is trapped. Here we see another instance of the differences between modernist and supramodernist aesthetics. Modernist poetics requires that the schizophrenic reality be stylized from a proper aesthetic distance: you do not behave like a schizophrenic if you are trying to write about the schizoid behavior of reality or its agents. In supramodern literature, Yvor Winters's "imitative fallacy" is in fact an operative aesthetic principle. What most critics have found objectionable in Wolfe's stylistic devices are aspects of this principle of imitative form: attempts to approximate the haze that envelops the mental atmosphere in which persons of the book receive actuality.

The testimonial nonfiction novel, then, is the narrative of encounter between the author—the historical person whose name appears on the title page, not a fictional "second self"—and the brute psychic or physical facts. Like other types of nonfiction novel, the testimonial too relies on public records, documents, interviews, and other information sources, but, unlike the exegetical nonfiction novel, the voice of the narrator-participant-witness is one important constituent of the narrative axis of the book. Indeed in some cases the author's participation in and witnessing of the events forms in itself a kind of public document. The involvement of Norman Mailer in the March on the Pentagon, the culmination in the late 1960s of dissenting voices gathering momentum since the Civil War, is now an inseparable part of the history of the March. Historians will utilize the active protest of writers such as Mailer and Lowell to describe and evaluate the postwar American public consciousness. The testimonial nonfiction novel may emphasize essentially public occurrences or the primarily private domain of experience. In either case, the belief that only the reality-tested part of actuality can be trusted by the individual informs the narrative.

Ken Kesey's bus trip across the United States in 1964 (which, as Tony Tanner observes, is in a sense his third novel, an attempt like Mailer's New York City mayoral campaign "to move beyond writing") forms the central episode of Wolfe's nonfiction novel, *The Electric Kool-Aid Acid Test* (1968). Wolfe's transcription of Kesey's trip represents an attempt to deal with that zone of consciousness which emerges from the tension between the "factual" and the "fictional" levels of experience. In order to liberate themselves from the fictions imposed on their minds in the name of reality, the Merry Pranksters, as Kesey and his followers call themselves, attempt to construct a counter-reality. They neutralize a fictitious reality by releasing their wildest fantasies. The official reality in which contemporary man tries to relate to his fellows and society at large cannot endure the pressures of the live sur-fiction invented by the Pranksters. Once tested by their planned fiction, official reality collapses into fragments no less fictitious than that invented by the Pranksters. Kesey and his cohorts are aware of the nature of their actions and of the fiction they externalize with their actions. Their intention is to bring everybody into their "movie"—their own fiction—or, put another way, their own reading of reality. Once a person is brought into the "movie," he realizes the fictitiousness of the more encompassing assumptions accepted in the outside world as reality. The two "fictions" clash, the mind is freed, and the individual nears "Edge City"—the ever-expanding frontiers of consciousness. Out of the tension between the two versions of reality, the "on the bus" and "off the bus" versions, the "fictual" zone of experience emerges. Wolfe captures this area of experience in his book, which Elizabeth Hardwick calls an "extraordinary, imaginative achievement . . . one of those rare, strange books that is not like any other book."

> Then I pick up my telephone and he picks up his—and this is truly Modern Times. We are all of twenty-four inches apart, but there is a piece of plate glass as thick as a telephone directory between us. We might as well be in different continents, talking over Videophone.

Here Tom Wolfe himself, not his fictional persona, registers his first meeting with Ken Kesey, the historical man who up to the time of this conversation had written *One Flew over the Cuckoo's Nest* (1962) and *Sometimes a Great Notion* (1964), set up an acid commune in La Honda, California, been arrested twice for possession of marijuana (April, 1965, and January, 1966), and, at the time of the phone conversation, following capture by the FBI on the Bayshore Freeway south of San Francisco, was jailed in Redwood City, San Mateo County, California. The glass-partitioned, phone-connected, first meeting of Wolfe and Kesey gradually loses its literalness and gains a metaphorical significance. Strangely charged with the horror associated with political polemics-caricature-propaganda, the scene captures in a single visual image the life of contemporary caged man, his attempt to reach out, and his final subjugation and abandonment. It could have been lifted from plays by Adamov, Ionesco, or van Itallie. Wolfe merely records the scene, and the transcription reads like an energized fiction—an absurd playlet.

Wolfe recalls this scene while waiting at the Warehouse, the Pranksters' headquarters, for the "Chief's" release. The double layer of surrounding reality is signaled here by Wolfe's disclosure that Kesey has two names: "Chief," when traveling to "Edge City," and "Kesey," when operating within the circle of ordinary life. The two names are used according to the *niveau* of meaning he is involved in. Kesey, the "straight" successful man, and "Chief," the spiritual guru, work like two terms of the dialects of an identity fading into a flow of actions-thoughts-feelings, partly man, partly the projection of a mythical figure. In one of the acid festivals Kesey appears as the "Space Man" in a silver space suit complete with a big bubble space helmet.

The Warehouse, situated on Harriet Street, between Howard and Folsom, is a storehouse of objects as well as projected images and masks, a collage of the factual and fictional, a reverse image of a middle-class house, a place in which people wearing white coveralls sewn over with American flag patches do their own things. Theater scaffolding, curtainlike blankets, and "whole rows of uprooted theater seats" line the walls. As the newly arrived Wolfe tries to orient himself to this scene, a blanket curtain moves, and a little man wearing a sort of World War 1 aviator's helmet vaults down from a platform about nine feet high. He tells Wolfe: "I just had an eight-year-old-boy up there." Wolfe's new acquaintance is the "Hermit." All the Pranksters have allegorical names, like characters in medieval morality plays. Wolfe also meets Mountain Girl, Cool Breeze, Black Maria, and, as if to complete the range of fictual personages, Neal Cassady, who behaves as though he has just walked out of *On the Road*. The solidity of identity begins to crack, and the sense of "reality" recedes and merges with some version of fantasy as Wolfe discovers in the center of the room-garage a curious *objet d'art*: "A school bus . . . glowing orange, green, magenta, lavender, chlorine blue, every fluorescent pastel imaginable in thousands of designs, both large and small, like a cross between Fernand Leger and Dr. Strange, roaring together and vibrating off each other as if somebody had given Hieronymous Bosch fifty buckets of Day-Glo paint and a 1939 International Harvester school bus and told him to go to it." This is the bus used by the Pranksters to invade towns and cities all over the country to disturb the deep sleep of the citizens.

The registration of the trip is one of the main blocks of narrative in the book. The destination sign on the bus reads: "Furthur." From the outside, the bus looks "freaking lurid"; inside it possesses a sophisticated communications system to proclaim its message, verbally as well as visually, to the outside world. The journey acquires the form and significance of an initiation rite into a "separate reality," a "nonordinary reality" to use Castaneda's term. An element of playfulness, however, redeems the counter-reality of the Pranksters from becoming a self-righteous, substitute reality. The Pranksters know their version of "reality" is only another "game"; although a dynamic and flowing "movie," their counter-reality is a "fiction"— another reading of reality and, as such, an imposition of a model of values on the experiential continuum. The ultimate objective is to "transcend the bullshit"—to attain self-liberation and emancipate the consciousness of others by juxtaposing charged levels of reality.

The trip moves toward the de-totalization of commonly accepted models of reality, but Wolfe's recording of this ongoing "movie" refuses to enter and totalize its de-totalization. *The Electric Kool-Aid Acid Test* maintains a complex relationship with the experiential world. Ostensibly an intimate mapping of the contours of a particular gesture by a group of people toward accepted reality, its actual informing theme is not the Pranksters' "movie" but the fictuality of contemporary experience. In the book, the two basic approaches to the external world mentioned in Chapter 1 are combined. Kesey's "movie"—his nonverbal, action novel—is an "over-totalization" of reality, a parallel fiction very much like the transfictions of Barthelme, Nabokov, Barth, Pynchon, and others. Wolfe's approach to Kesey's "movie," on the other hand, is nontotalizing. Wolfe's methodology is often similar to that of the exegetical nonfiction novel. He supplements his actual witnessing of parts of the "group adventure and personal exploration" of the Pranksters, such as the acid graduation ceremonies, with a forty-hour movie, tapes, written statements, and other records kept in the "Prankster Archives." As the book opens, the events of the past are retrieved, then the present is registered directly by Tom Wolfe, the testifier.

Through meticulous recording, the book reveals how Kesey and the Pranksters transform the trip into a collective parable. As the parable progresses, the bus, its riders, the space in which they move, all become metaphorical components of an "action allegory." Each person is fully aware of his part in a parable—not only have they gone through a baptismal rite of adopting new names, but they behave and talk as actors of the ongoing movie, literally shot by Hagen "like this was some crazed adventure in cinema verite." Kesey is the psychic force which animates the Pranksters' counter-environment. His statements, as the events unfold, become more cryptic, metaphorical, and aphoristic: "You're either on the bus or off the bus," "feed the hungry bee," "Nothing lasts," "See with your ears and hear with your eyes." Gradually they form an elaborate interpretative pattern for a metaphorical ordering of reality approaching the complexity of Yeats's extended metaphor, *A Vision*. The key concept in Kesey's thought system is "fantasy." The aim of the "fantasy" is to actualize the allegory of the trip to reach Edge City. One of the Merry Prankster signs reads: "Hail to the Edges." It symbolizes the quest for the absolute NOW which the Pranksters are trying to achieve through drugs. The only authentic mode of being is existence in the moment itself, for "any attempt to plan, compose, orchestrate, write a script, only locked you out of the moment, back in the world of conditioning and training where the brain was a reductive value." But Kesey admits there is always a sensory lag, the lag between the time your senses receive something and your reaction—one thirtieth of a second, if you're the most alert person alive—and he acknowledges that ". . . we are all of us doomed to spend our lives watching a *movie* of our lives—we are always acting on what has just finished happening." He accepts that NOW is always a movie of the past, but sees the destination as "Furthur," toward a liberated consciousness, away from one's own "snug-harbor dead center, out of the plump little game of being ersatz alive, the middle-class intellectual's game, and move out to . . . Edge City . . . where it was scary, but people were whole people."

Those moving toward Edge City are "on the bus"; those trapped in what Kesey has called (in *One Flew over the Cuckoo's Nest*) the "combine" or "system" are "off the bus." The last phrase need not be taken literally. Sandy, one of the Pranksters, is physically on the bus but reserved, detached, not "out front," and therefore "off the bus." The allegorical quality of the trip and the significance of the bus metaphors are most clearly revealed in what might be called "The Boy and the Bus" exemplum:

> And in Boise they cut through a funeral or wedding or something . . . and a kid—they have tootled *his song*, and he likes it, and he runs for the bus and they all pile on and pull out, just ahead of him, and he keeps running for the bus, and Kesey keeps slowing down and then pulling out just out of his reach, six or eight blocks this way, and then they speed up for good, and they can still see him floating away in the background, his legs still running, like a preview—
> —allegory of life—
> —of the multitudes who very shortly will want to get on the bus . . . themselves. . . .

Those "on the bus" can formulate their own version of reality and protect themselves from other people's "movies." The term "movie" refers both to the literal forty-hour film shot by the Pranksters on their trans-American trip and to various metaphorical readings of reality. The collective parable works here too: the Pranksters try to absorb all America into their movie (the literal-metaphorical movie) before America puts them in its movie (the metaphorical movie). The refusal to play other people's games, to let them entrap him in their movies lies behind Kesey's "fouling up" of a Vietnam rally held at Berkeley. While awaiting his turn to speak, Kesey becomes convinced that the antiwar rally is modeled on a war rally, and that the rhetoric of the pacifist is patterned after the rhetoric of the warmonger. He decides that the peace people are actors in the military's movie and, once on the platform, urges them to free themselves: "You know, you're not gonna stop this war with this rally, by marching. . . . That's what they do. . . .They hold rallies and they march . . . and that's the same game you're playing . . . their game." And he takes out his harmonica and plays "Home on the Range."

To invent one's own "fantasy" and to shoot one's own "movie" is the route to "Edge City," an expedition into the innermost circle of one's unique reality—to move with its "flow." "Going with the flow" is the ability to "transcend the bullshit," to see through the surfaces and discover the movement of reality behind appearance. The Pranksters are reluctant to verbalize the meaning of "flow" and other concepts for fear of limiting their meaning: Mountain Girl at the annual California Unitarian Church Conference at Asilomar shouts at the minister: "Do It!" She expresses the basic Prankster outlook—don't explain it; do it!

This firmly rooted belief in action rather than explanation is embodied in the Pranksters' most famous reality-disturbing device—the Prank. The idea behind the Prank is to perform great public put-ons to dislodge the established official reality and project a liberating fiction, which will enlarge people's concept of the real. The Pranksters' clothes, their Day-Glo colors, their behavior at the Vietnam rally and the Beatles performance, are all part of this great public put-on. The Pranks should shock and free observers and actors, since the very process of performing pranks is in itself emancipating. This double liberation of observer and actor is one of the differences between the Prank and the Modernist efforts to shock the dull middle-class, *épater le bourgeois*. The latter is usually a one-way affair, with the artist firmly convinced of the superiority of his own values. The Pranks reveal how much the consciousness is inhibited by societal conditioning, and how much Blakean innocence has been lost. To overcome the damage, one must act, be "out front," confess "hang-ups." To remain inhibited and to think rather than to act is to go with the old middle-class intellectual game, to continue one's existence as a "shit kicker"—a state of consciousness not dissimilar to acting with "bad faith." To overcome the "bad faith" and live "out front" with absolute self-transparency, the Pranksters undertake a series of almost ritualistic acts, aimed at dislodging the mind from its habitual mode of thinking and transposing it to a higher order of reality. These rituals, like most tribal rites, are performed with some consciousness-expanding, mind-opening potion. Drugs and multimedia manipulation of ordinary experience expand, if not completely annihilate, the boundaries of the uptight ego, and "*Ego* and *Non-Ego* start to merge." Sense impressions also merge: "a sound became . . . a color! blue . . . colors became smells, walls began to breathe like the underside of a leaf. A curtain became a column of concrete and yet it began rippling . . . the entire harmonies of the universe . . . all flowing together in this very moment." More startling is the cultivation of "intersubjectivity," the crushing of the private, individual reality by collective reality. One way the Pranksters try to achieve this is through "rapping"—a kind of surreal monologue—which Wolfe describes as a "form of free association conversation, like a jazz conversation, or even a monologue, with everyone, or whoever, catching hold of words, symbols, ideas, sounds, and winging them back and forth and beyond . . . the walls of conventional logic."

The emerging verbal flow creates a surreal reality, as though the Prankster consciousnesses open up and flow together. In one of the "briefing" sessions we hear Cassady speaking about "Blue noses, red eyes . . ."; the phrase is modulated to "God is red," and then, "God is dead," and finally, into a flow of mystical contemplation that "God is not dead, God is red, God is the bottled-up red animal inside all of us, whole, all feeling, complete, out front, only it is made dead by all the lags. . . ."

The Pranksters see themselves as liberators. They want to extend the range of their projected fiction and bring everyone else into their movie: "Suddenly it seemed like the Pranksters could draw the whole universe into . . . the movie." To accomplish this, they organize their Acid Test festivals. The typical Acid Test offered music, Prankster movies, acid, and *the strobe!* "To people standing under the mighty strobe everything seemed to fragment. Ecstatic dancers—their hands flew off their arms, frozen in the air—their glistening faces came apart—a gleaming ellipse of teeth here, a pair of buffered highlit cheekbones there—all flacking and fragmenting into images as in an old flicker movie—a man in slices!" The strobes, projectors, mikes, tapes, amplifiers, the variable-lag Ampex are all part of the arsenal of technological gadgetry the Pranksters employ to further subvert the official reality with their private, empirical sur-fiction. The acceptance of the "gadget" as an inseparable element of present-day experience endows the Pranksters' "trip" with a quality uniquely American and unmistakably "technetronic"; it also sharply contrasts Kesey and Timothy Leary, another guru figure in the book, who advocates a trip from the technological reality of contemporary America to an agrarian dreamland. The Acid Tests are a head-on confrontation with contemporary experience in what Mailer disparagingly calls "technology land." The participants in these sacraments, by means of the resistance-crushing pressures generated by drugs, decompose and neutralize the seemingly solid reality through which society has shaped their vision of themselves and the outside world. *The Electric Kool-Aid Acid Test*, however, is not a study of the nature of psychedelic experience. The narrative, like Warhol's *a*, takes the drug experience as its *donnée* and registers the pressures of a fictual reality as it is translated in the actions and thoughts of people attempting to reestablish contact with reality through drugs. The fictivity of the sur-fiction generated by means of chemicals, in other words, is part of the larger fictional reality of postwar America, which has made drugs necessary for finding an epistemological anchor for the self in a discontinuous culture.

When Kesey's drug quest for "super identity" in an alternative reality encounters opposition from the law, he accepts a new identity as an outlaw. In a mock ritual of death by water, Kesey leaves a note mixed in tone and

hallucinatory, and disappears into Mexico—"the land of competent Outlaws."
But the "Acid Tests" continue, culminating in an unusual Acid Festival in
Watts on Lincoln's Birthday, February 12, 1966. The evening begins with
films of Furthur, the bus, and its riders. Then some slides of flowers and
patterns. Afterward everyone is invited to help themselves to Kool-Aid in a
large, plastic trash can. Clair Brush, a "novice," describes her initiation:

> . . . it was being served in paper cups, and since Kool-Aid is a
> staple in the homes of . . . friends of mine, I thought it quite a
> natural thing to serve . . . had a cup, and another, wandered and
> talked for a while, had another . . . suddenly I began to laugh
> . . . and laugh . . . and the laugh was more primitive, more gut-
> tearing, than anything I had ever known. It came from
> somewhere so deep inside that I never felt it before . . . and it
> continued . . . and it was uncontrollable . . . and wonderful.
> Something snapped me back and I realized that there was
> nothing funny . . . nothing to laugh about . . . someone came up
> to me and I shut my eyes and with a machine he projected images
> on the back of my eyelids . . . and nothing was in perspective,
> nothing had any touch of normalcy or reality. . . .

In Mexico, Kesey gradually develops the idea of going beyond the
drug-induced state of consciousness toward a permanent alternative reality
attainable without the help of external agents. "There is no use opening the
door and going through it and then always going back out again," Kesey says
of the drug experience. "We've got to move on to the next step." The drug-
aided projected fiction of the Pranksters, originally an anti-environment
created to neutralize the official reality, has now become a static reality,
almost another ordinary environment. Kesey now wants to project an anti-
reality into the reality which was originally an anti-reality itself. The
technetronic culture's power to absorb counter-environments into the matrix
environment has transformed the Prankster's drug-induced, counter-
environment into an accepted part of public reality.

After returning to California, Kesey announces plans for a public
ceremony and reveals his vision of a new sur-fiction with which to
go beyond the official reality and keep the anti-environment vibrant
and dynamic. The "current Fantasy" is to be a Prankster Fugitive
Extraordinaire—the bringer of the message on the run. But he is in the
cops' movie now, and the acid heads regard his new vision as a betrayal of
the psychedelic cause, rather than a further step toward nonordinary
reality. Kesey finds himself alienated from both the police, the guardians of

the agreed values, and the acid people, the guardians of the now-emaciated projected fiction. Convinced of the creativity of his "current fantasy," Kesey schedules the Acid Test Graduation for Winterland on Halloween night. The Prankster bus, bearing a sign reading ACID TEST GRADUATION, wheels through Haight-Ashbury, downtown San Francisco, North Beach, and Berkeley, advertising the world's biggest convocation of all the heads. The ceremony is promoted in prankish tones:

> Kesey for Governor!
> A man of convictions!
> He stands on his record!
> The idiot's choice!
> A joint in every stash!
> No hope without dope!

Mountain Girl's shouts from the touring bus create a Prankster version of the Brown-Reagan gubernatorial campaign. Prevented from having the festival at Winterland, Kesey holds it in the Pranksters' Warehouse on the same Halloween night. The Pranksters, dressed in American Flag coveralls, dance under a "huge orange-and-white parachute," which is "the very same parachute . . . that astronauts use on reentry for the splashdown." Kesey appears, "bare chested, wearing only white leotards, a white satin cape tied at the neck, and a red, white, and blue sash running diagonally across his chest. It's . . . Captain America! The Flash! Captain Marvel!" At the height of the frenzy, the lights go out, the music stops, and a single spotlight glares on the center of the floor. Kesey steps into the light and describes his new sur-fiction. But from now on Kesey's trip toward supra-reality is a lonely one; most friends stay behind, trapped in what originally was a fiction invented to cancel the official reality. The final celebration in The Bar, a psychedelic nightspot in Scotts Valley, ten miles from Santa Cruz, is, as Hagen says, more like a "wake." The juncture of realities—the agreed reality, the tamed fiction of the acid heads, and the new supra-reality toward which Kesey is groping— proves unsuccessful. The fear of the new supra-reality moves even the Pranksters who have followed Kesey to The Barn to drift off. Finally, only Kesey (on electric guitar) and Babbs (on the electric bass) remain in the center of the vast gloom of the barn singing a "song" which ends in the incantatory refrain "WE BLEW IT."

In *The Electric Kool-Aid Acid Test*, Wolfe ostensibly transcribes the projected live fiction of the Merry Pranksters, but the actual area of experience reflected in the book is the zone of consciousness created in contemporary America by the pressure of the technetronic culture and the bizarre, baffling behavior of its various sub-cults. Wolfe's narrative strategies are all aimed at capturing the live fiction of the Pranksters not only in terms of its heterogeneous elements but also, to use Wolfe's own words, its "mental atmosphere" and "subjective reality." The concept of "subjectivity" should not be understood in its conventional sense—the writer's private reading of reality and the projection of his own emotions. "Subjectivity" here is Wolfe's attempt to transcribe the inwardness and feel of events as they register themselves on the minds of people whose lives or actions he is recording. Of *The Electric Kool-Aid Acid Test*, Wolfe has said: "I was not at all interested in presenting *my* subjective state when confronted with the Pranksters or whatever they had done. It was rather to try to get Kesey's completely" (emphasis is Wolfe's). Wolfe's book is a registration of the Pranksters' emotional involvement in their actions and of the emotive layer of their experience, which seems for them to be the only reliable reality.

To register the Pranksters' adventures, Wolfe employs an imitative form in a supramodernist manner. Robert Scholes's comment that "Wolfe's chameleon styles are more reflective of his material than himself" sums up the characteristics of Wolfe's linguistic style and his overall narrational strategies. *The Electric Kool-Aid Acid Test* is one of the most technically rich and innovative nonfiction novels written in the postwar years. Its narrative methods vary from a mostly discursive section on the nature of religious vision and "the experience of the holy," with density of reference to authorities and comparative religion (Chapter XI, "The Unspoken Thing"), to a type of extended interior monologue (Chapter XXI, "The Fugitive").

The book combines the retrieved past and the experienced present. The most important source for the recovery of the past is the Pranksters' Archives, which contain tapes, diaries, letters, photographs, and the forty-hour movie of the bus trip. The recaptured past is framed between two narrative blocks which are a direct registration of the present. The first segment, told from a witness stance by Wolfe, registers his first contact with Kesey, the Pranksters, and the Warehouse. Then follows his record of the past, based on the Archives as well as oral and written testimony from various participants. The third narrative block is an eyewitness account of the acid graduation ceremony. Wolfe first thinks of Kesey in terms of conventional reality categories and decides to do a piece on him entitled "Young Novelist, Real-Life Fugitive." But, when he finds himself within the centripetal movement of the Pranksters' circle, he realizes the inadequacy of his approach and, abandoning his original project, becomes instead the scribe of past and present events which are constituents of a myth in formation.

Wolfe's witnessing is usually signaled by the use of the first person pronoun; although sometimes the pronoun acknowledges private feelings ("That hurt, Doris Delay, but I know you meant it as a kindly suggestion"), it primarily reports, without intervention, the sense data to testify to what has been observed by the reporter. The epistemological effect of the typographical presence of the "I" is the owning of a "self," and thus a warning to the reader that everything is told by a single man with his unique, acknowledged limitations. The book opens with Tom Wolfe's shy voice talking from the back of a pickup truck which is "Bouncing along. Dipping and rising and rolling on these rotten springs like a boat." He is being given a lift to the Warehouse, where he will see the "Chief." The contrast between his own clothing style and that of the Pranksters makes him aware of the difference in their attitudes toward life in general and toward the projected fiction of the Pranksters in particular. He becomes self-conscious, and the tone of narration curves toward apology for his "Black Shiny FBI Shoes." This tone reinforces the presence of a feeling person whose testimony of events will be presented in the book. The owning of the "ego" becomes clearer in the exchange between Wolfe and Black Maria:

> "When is your birthday?
> "March 2."
> "Pisces," she says. And then: "I would never take you for a Pisces."
> "Why?"
> "You seem too . . . *solid* for a Pisces."

Wolfe adds: "But I know she means stolid. I am beginning to feel stolid." Wolfe records his own reactions to the situations—a technique developed to its full potentialities by Mailer in *The Armies of the Night*. This voice sometimes becomes more obviously reflexive: "Oh christ, Tom, the thing was fantastic, a freaking mind-blower. . . ." But in most cases, the "I" is used to report what Wolfe has seen or heard: "Kesey stares at a spiral notebook he has and then starts talking in a voice so soft I can hardly hear him at first. . . ." Though frequently typographically visible, the "I" is sometimes not foregrounded: "Late in the afternoon in the Warehouse—Christ, it's dismal in here!" When Wolfe uses someone else's testimony to recover the past, Wolfe's voice becomes a linking device between the original witness, Wolfe, and the reader. For example, Wolfe quotes Clair Brush on her acid experience: "'I think what decided me'—Clair is recalling it for me—" Sometimes the "I" informs the reader of events yet to take place: "Nobody every knew his real name at all until a few months later when, as I say, the police would get technical about it. . . ." This use of "I" to tell the reader about future events is similar to Capote's use of the omniscient narrator, since it is based on research, not the imaginative authority of the writer.

The Electric Kool-Aid Acid Test is based on a dual perspective or a double mode of narration which counterpoints the "factual" with the "fictional," and releases the "fictuality" of the total experience. The counterpointing in the book takes a complex form, because the book deals with two layers or circles of "reality." The immediate "reality" which Wolfe depicts is itself a cultivated fiction which attempts to reveal and discredit the thinness of the accepted common reality. In Truman Capote's *In Cold Blood*, the depicted "reality" was the circle of the common reality (albeit a reality so charged with fictivity that its mere transcription produced a strange fictual narrative). The counterpointing in Capote's book was between the experiential reality (facts) and the inherent fiction (bizarreness of facts) in that "reality." In Wolfe's book, the counterpointing is more complicated. Wolfe records a layer of reality which is deliberately "fictional" in the traditional sense of the word. But this fiction, projected by the Pranksters, is located in the tangible reality—which the Pranksters consider a deceptive public fantasy. Both circles of "reality" are part of the recordable outside world and thus form the axis of external reference in *The Electric Kool-Aid Acid Test*. The fictuality which emerges from Wolfe's book, therefore, results from a complex interaction between experiential reality and the invented fiction of the Pranksters on one hand, and the factual registration of this dialectic on the other. Something close to this interaction among layers of experience is present in *The Armies of the Night* where Mailer, the Scribe, records the actions of Mailer, the Beast (Prankster of intellect?) in a book which is a factual registration of both.

The function of the core of documentation in the book, like that of any other nonfiction novel, is to authenticate the events as actual occurrences, not invented components of an interpretation of reality in the narrative. In *The Electric Kool-Aid Acid Test* the core of documents establishes the "facts" about the "fiction" of the Pranksters and thus makes the two components of the external field (the Pranksters' fiction and the daily reality) a unified field of external reference whose constituent events have, at various levels of reality, "happened," and, therefore, become "verifiable." Such events as the trans-American bus trip of the Pranksters are easily verifiable, because they drew a great deal of attention and are now matters of public record. Less publicly known events, such as details of a particular "rap session" or an "acid party," are related in full detail and usually tied to a well-known person (Allen Ginsberg, Timothy Leary, Hunter Thompson) for further possible verification. Such incidents as the Pranksters' visit to Esalen Institute and its director, Gestalt psychologist

Fritz Perls, as well as Kesey's appearance, while still a fugitive, on San Francisco television station KGO, the local ABC outlet, also serve as elements of the verifiable out-referential field.

The blurring of "fact" and "fiction"—the cracking up of the seemingly solid reality and the release of its inner fictivity—is much more obvious in *The Electric Kool-Aid Acid Test* than in the nonfiction novels discussed before. But within the book there are moments when the emerging fictuality is so heightened that it transcends its immediate context and gathers a prototypical resonance for contemporary experience. The disappearance of rational markers for locating the self under the pressure of a new force of reality emerges from Wolfe's record of the trans-sensory experience of Beauty Witch on the bus trip. Her going "stark raving mad" embodies in itself the condition of her generation, for whom the only authentic means for finding a real interior space in which to achieve a sense of self has become the experience of madness and nervous breakdown. The scene of the take-over by the developers of the Bohemian living quarters at Stanford is another case of the clash between two orders of actuality which heightens itself into a mythical pattern of the displacement of contemporary man. Like other aspects of contemporary experience, the "tragic" is embedded in the "comic" and an undertone of black humor pervades the whole episode, which has a deep psychic resonance to it:

> The papers turned up to write about the last night on Perry Lane, noble old Perry Lane, and had the old cliché at the ready, End of an Era, expecting to find some deep-thinking latter-day Thorstein Veblen intellectuals on hand with sonorous bitter statements about this machine civilization devouring its own past.
>
> Instead, there were some kinds of *nuts* out here. They were up in a tree lying on a mattress, all high as coons, and they kept offering everybody, all the reporters and photographers, some kind of venison chili, but there was something about the whole setup . . . and it was hard as hell to make the End of an Era story come out right in the papers, with nothing but this kind of freaking Olsen & Johnson material to work with,
>
> but they managed to go back with the story they came with, End of an Era, the cliché intact, if they could only blot out the cries in their ears of *Ve-ni-son Chi-li—*

The acid graduation festival in the Warehouse has the overtones of a pagan feast tinged with a Kafkaesque sense of persecution and, with the appearance of the police, assumes the extra dimension of a ritual of chase such as one finds in a modern detective story.

Some of the sketches of persons in the book read so much like fiction that some readers have approached Wolfe's book as a "novel" and criticized him for not "developing" his "characters." If real people seem to behave as fictional characters, it is because they are actors in the extended allegory of their own life style. They have adopted a new life pattern and symbolically rebaptized themselves with allegorical names in response to the pressures of the freakish current reality. Like allegorical characters, they are frozen in their single role in parody of the roles they had to play in their "actual" lives: "They were all now characters in their own movies or the Big Movie. They took on new names and used them. Steve Lambrecht was Zonker. Cassady was Speed Limit. Kesey was Swashbuckler. Babbs was Intrepid Traveler . . . George Walker was Hardly Visible. And Paula Sundsten became . . . Gretchen Fetchin the Slime Queen. . . ." Neal Cassady, the Dean Moriarity, Denver Kid, of *On the Road*, consciously behaves as a person who has walked out of one fiction into another. His new name, Speed Limit (with a pun), refers to his new function as the Driver of the Bus, destination "Furthur." They all deliberately suppress other aspects of their personalities and act as two-dimensional, "flat characters" in order to parody the very flatness imposed by common reality on the multifarious, spontaneous human life.

The Electric Kool-Aid Acid Test, like other nonfiction novels, contains a great deal of "discursive" discourse. It brings into the narrative conceptual modes of discourse and incorporates what conventional aesthetics rejects as "chunks of raw life." Chapter XI, "The Unspoken Thing," is a good example of this mixed mode used throughout the book.

The most controversial aspect of *The Electric Kool-Aid Acid Test* as a nonfiction novel, a book which purports to be a registration of happened events, is its style and linguistic maneuvering. The main question is not whether Wolfe's style is "affected," but whether his linguistic pyrotechnics are epistemologically appropriate to the task they undertake. As Robert Scholes has demonstrated in his review of the book, Wolfe succeeds. Describing Wolfe's style as "chameleon," Scholes sees it as "more reflective of his material than of himself." The style of the book is based on what the Modernist aesthetics would denounce as the "imitative fallacy." Tom Wolfe's linguistic transcendences capture the psychic transcendences of the Pranksters' extended trip; their immediate medium is "drugs," Wolfe's is language.

What first strikes the reader about Wolfe's style is, of course, its visual aspect; its iconic typography tries to mimic the ambience of the events. The most visible elements of this typographical concretism are the unexpected use of dashes, periods, exclamation marks, and question marks, nonsense lexical items, punctuation points rarely used in the language (for example :::::) and onomatopoeic words. Such use of the print medium tries to revivify the experience of a "history cut up in slices" by the Pranksters. To do so, Wolfe seems to be aiming at the stylistic equivalent of what the Pranksters call "Sura-Medium." In describing the early experiments with drugs at Perry Lane, Wolfe uses the layout of his page to convey the feel of a "high":

> But then—soar. Perry Lane, Perry Lane.
>   Miles
>   Miles
>   Miles
>   Miles
>   Miles
>   Miles
>   Miles
>   under all that good
> vegetation from Morris Orchids and having visions of
> Faces
>   Faces
>   Faces
>   Faces
>   Faces
>   Faces
>   Faces
>   so many faces
> rolling up behind the eyelids, faces he has never seen
> before. . . .

Or to describe Beauty Witch—the girl who went mad on the bus:

> She keeps coming up to somebody who isn't saying a goddamn thing and looking into his eyes with the all-embracing look of total acid understanding, our brains are one brain, so let's *visit*, you and I, and she says: "Ooooooooh, you really *think* that, I know what you mean, but do you-u-u-u-u-u-u-ueeeeeeeeeeeeeeeeeeeeeeee"—finishing off in a sailing tremolo laugh as if she has just read your brain and it is the weirdest of the weird shit ever, your brain eeeeeeeeeeeeeeeeeeeeeeee eeeeeeeeeeee—

The total impact of all these devices in conveying a moment can be seen in "The Fugitive" chapter where Wolfe describes Kesey's growing paranoia. The tribal consciousness present in a "rap" is captured by internal and end rhymes and staccato rhythm. To combine images, Wolfe may write them together: "Unfreakingbelievable," or use a recurring phrase.

The most innovative section of the narrative is the chapter entitled "The Fugitive." Here Wolfe expands the range of technical possibilities of the in-referential axis of the narrative so the nonfiction novel can contain the most bizarre cacophonies of reality. The dominant narrative device in the chapter is "interior monologue" with suggestions of "stream of consciousness." The technical rationale for the use of such narrational devices in the nonfiction novel is the treatment of the subjectivity of the situation or person portrayed, as distinguished from the projected subjectivity (empathy) of the fictive novelist. The consciousness transcribed in this chapter is the layer of awareness experienced and articulated by Kesey. The techniques for obtaining such interior information are essentially those used in the exegetical nonfiction novel—interviews and documents. The interviewing, however, is directed less at the subject's opinions and ideas than at his "thoughts and emotions." Elaborating on this type of interviewing, another observer adds: "If I were interviewing Tom Wolfe, I would ask him what he *thought* in every situation where I might have asked him in the past what he did and said. I'm not so interested in what he did and said as I am interested in what he *thought*. And I would quote him in the way I was writing as that he *thought* something."

The voice that speaks in the opening "Interior monologue" is reflexive: Kesey addressing Kesey, remembering the past. Gradually the voice modulates. The typography signals the movements of the voice of a man who is going through an acute phase of paranoia, half seeing, half imagining police coming to arrest him. Kesey's voice is then contextualized by a straightforward description of the room in which he is sitting:

> . . . with his elbow on a table and his forearm standing up perpendicular and in the palm of his hand a little mirror, so that his forearm and the mirror are like a big rear-view mirror stanchion on the side of a truck and thus he can look out the window and see them but they can't see him.

The description is then punctured by Kesey's hysterical voice:

> COME ON, MAN, DO YOU NEED A COPY OF THE SCRIPT TO SEE HOW THIS MOVIE GOES? YOU HAVE MAYBE 40 SECONDS LEFT BEFORE THEY COME GET YOU

The time then corresponds to the rhythm of Kesey's movements and is echoed in the pace of the narrative. The chronometric movement is a countdown:

40 seconds left . . .
You have maybe 35 seconds left . . .

so on down to:

ZERO::::::::000000000::::::::RUN!

And Kesey, with one mad dash, jumps out the window and runs into the jungle. The scene is indeed fictitious, even embellished with the "surprise ending" element (Black Maria appears on the scene. The reader realizes that Kesey had taken her footsteps for those of the FBI agents!). But the events have actually happened.

Through the use of "interior monologue" and empirical omniscient point of view, Chapter XXI blends three levels of "reality." All three are clearly distinguished on the first page, but the first two (the inner world of the paranoid Kesey and his interpretation of the outside events) blend into one level which is contrasted with the researched reality the omniscient author brings into the chapter. The omniscient author is at all times alert to the minutest details. Through him we learn about Kesey's state of mind—how he has "hooked down five dexedrines," how he was hidden "in the back of Boise's old panel truck" while crossing into Mexico. The Mexican landscape is carefully depicted. To convey this, Wolfe, like Capote, uses flashback, and this brings to the texture of the prose two tenses: the past and the historical or actual present. This flexibility of tense operates as a very effective mimesis of the fluidity of the "real" in the mind of Kesey and the other Pranksters who somehow participate in the journey to Mexico.

The chronometric rhythm continues to the middle of the chapter, then gives way to a series of interjectory markers to signal the rhythm of Kesey's movement:

WHAZZAT? . . .
PLUNGE—
SHHHHHHHHHHHWAAAAAAAAAP—
WHOP! . . .

When Kesey's movements slow, the rhythm of the mimetic style slows and acquires a meditative mood:

> . . . the rush lowers in his ears, he can concentrate, pay total
> attention, an even, even, even world, flowing into *now*, no past
> terrors, no anticipation of the future horror, only *now*, *this*
> movie. . . .

Wolfe employs a range of narrative techniques whose sophistication enables
him to render the current fictuality. Any other approach, such as the
dramatic treatment of a fictive novelist, would be reductive.

In reviewing one of Tom Wolfe's earlier books, Richard Hoggart, using
the famous typology of American writers first formulated by Philip Rahv,
refers to Wolfe as "substantially a Paleface pretending to be a Redskin."
Norman Mailer is a Redskin through and through who, for reasons discussed
at the opening of this chapter, sounds like a self-searching Paleface in *The
Armies of the Night*. In many instances, his voice is indistinguishable from the
Paleface Robert Lowell whom he portrays in the book. It is no coincidence
that the sudden spread of "confessional poetry" after Lowell's *Life Studies*
(1959) should parallel the development of the testimonial nonfiction novel.
The two literary kinds seek to reestablish a direct relationship between man
and experience. Like other supramodern works, both types reject the
concepts of "aesthetic distance" and "fictional persona" and try to become
transparent media for people eager to talk to other people about the places
they have been and the experiences they have suffered. In a culture lacking
in externally reliable frames of reference for verifying individual experience,
sensory data become the ultimate authority, and sincerity and confession the
last act of regaining elusive selfhood.

Philip Rieff in *The Triumph of the Therapeutic* notes the changing
sensibility in postwar America: "We are, I fear, getting to know one another.
Reticence, secrecy, concealment of self have been transformed into social
problems. . . ." Mailer's so-called egotism and exhibitionism—the observation
has been made that he thinks even his bowel movement has a national
significance—relates to this changing sensibility. The publicization of the
private is not an empty, playful gesture but the last attempt of the pressured
self to retain contact with the outside world. In a society with moral and
valuational consensus rooted in established and shared norms, the individual
feels little need to validate cultural realities by testing them against his or her
own perceptions and experiences. But the individual engulfed in the ever
enclosing and splintering technetronic culture must discover reality by
himself for himself. The glaring "I" in testimonial nonfiction novels and
confessional poetry, far from being the result of an arrogant personality, is
the cry of a lonely, anguished man who must be his own Columbus without

any value markers or cultural compasses. Stephen Stephanchev sees this fragmentation of sensibility dominating the works of postwar American poets: "Feeling secure only when dealing with personally tested facts, they render the loneliness and terror of contemporary life with the terseness and immediacy of a diary record. They permit no evil of 'objective correlatives' to hang between them and their readers, they distrust 'aesthetic distance' and 'anonymity'. . . ." The artist no longer orders the sensory world; rather, the sensory world shapes the work of art.

Nowhere is the schizoid nature of the contemporary sensibility and the need for absolute transparency, both caused by the pressure of the crisis situation in contemporary America, more powerfully enacted than in Mailer's *The Armies of the Night*—a puzzling book both in its generic status and in its aesthetic mode of being. Most critics, reading the book in terms of its surface patterns and the interpretation which seems present in the foreground, have considered *Armies* an extended private reading of recent American reality. From such a point of view the book is, of course, anything but a nonfiction novel. That there is "interpretation" and an attempt to understand, synthesize, and reach conclusions about American experience in the book is beyond question. Every page piles metaphor upon metaphor—the main carriers of personal vision and value-markers—and scrutinizes the experiential *données* received by the narrator. But the ultimate determination of the generic status of the book will depend not merely on the presence or absence of "interpretation," but on the way in which that "interpretation" is used. The question is not unlike the relationship between the use of empirical reality (facts) in a naturalistic novel (e.g., *An American Tragedy*) and their use in a nonfiction novel. The mere presence of empirical data in a naturalistic novel does not make it a nonfiction novel; it remains a fictive conception of reality which uses the commonly known set of facts to solidify its conclusions and interpretations. Mailer's use of "interpretation" in *Armies* transforms its very nature so that even calling his rumination "interpretation" would be misleading. He employs a type of discourse which reads on the surface like "interpretation" but is in fact "meta-interpretation." It brings out the absurdity and arbitrariness of the usual "interpretation," and thus transcends its meaning-imposing function to reach a state in which interpretations are interpreted. Thus the ostensible interpretation is turned into an anti-interpretation; a negation of the proposed reading of reality.

The transformation of one state into meta-state, verbally or actionally, occurs throughout the book. The Ambassador Theater incident represents such an actional change: Mailer compulsively scrutinizes in public his "forty-five second" piss in the darkness of the men's room, and, in the process, he and the audience transcend the conventions of a political rally and reach a meta-rally, which is a curious fictual combination of politics, vaudeville, and an acknowledgment of the helplessness of the individual confronted with a baffling reality. The political rally from that moment is no longer a means of a redefinition of reality; it is a recognition of the impenetrability of reality. A similar transformation takes place with Mailer's verbal "interpretations" of the reality he is dealing with. Analysis of isolated passages is pointless, because the verbal transcendence is a cumulative process, each instance of interpretation building on previous instances so that by the end, "The Metaphor Delivered," the whole string of "interpretations" is transformed into meta-interpretation.

An example of a single verbal "interpretation" which approaches such transcendence is the section entitled, "Grandma with Orange Hair." Mailer gazes into the faces of the Federal Marshals, seeing them collectively as an index of American reality which he then starts to analyze. The analysis, however, cannot stand the pressure of the fictual reality which gradually emerges from Mailer's own probing of America. The "interpretation" disintegrates into a bizarre tableau which transforms the whole episode into a meta-interpretation, a transformation which acknowledges the impossibility of a coherent and sustained decoding of reality or a total patterning of it. Mailer seems like a surgeon who is himself affected by the anaesthetic he is using for his operation. A brooding immobility accompanies the unfolding analysis, and his "interpretation" not only fails to clarify the "meaning" of contemporary reality, but even envelops the particular incident under scrutiny in a haze. The Private Scribe in the book acknowledges this loss of focus by pointing out the lack of correspondence between the interpretation and the data being interpreted.

The meta-interpretation (or meta-situation) can therefore be characterized as an interpretation which ostensibly aims at providing a pattern of meaning, but its aim is undermined by the tension which develops between the data to be interpreted and the conceptual model imposed on them to yield meaning. Mailer's strategy is to let his "actant" Participating self interpret the data of American reality and his "actee" Scribal self acknowledge the untenability of his reading of reality. The confusion caused by a bewildering reality is acknowledged and, as Gerald Graff observes, is built "into the texture of the work." The split point of view is the narrative correlative of the schizophrenic reality. These transformations of commentary into anti-comments by acts of transcendence—reaching a meta-state—are performed by the book's narrative point of view—the use of the third person vantage point by the first person actee.

Armies is the narrative of a narrativist, and what is narrated should not be confused with what is narratively conceived. The book reflects an agonizingly pressured self under an exacting situation and registers minute by minute the confrontation of that self, bewilderingly divided into an actant and an actee, with the ongoing events. The actant, Mailer the public man, acts to bring about changes in the outside world as the only authentic means of existential cognition. Through deeds, he will achieve an existential coherence which will lead to a vision—a view or a totalization of the reality surrounding him. This is the man who in *Armies* willfully superinduces metaphysical attributes to his experience; develops theories about America, past, present, and future; and conveys his message through elaborate networks of metaphors. Side by side with Mailer the actant, the omniscient interpreter of American experience, exists Mailer the Scribe, who passively records the acts, ideas, and dreams of the performer. The book presents the Mailer who performs and yearns to grasp the overall pattern of the behavior of reality, but it also presents the narrational device which enacts Mailer's complete awareness of the futility of his yearnings and the arbitrariness of his interpretations. The scribe who records the interpretations of the performer is recording Mailer's surrender to the actual and his self-mockery of his ambitions to reach an all-inclusive reading of reality. The existence of the Performer and the Scribe signals a gap between "yearning" and "getting," "wanting" and "achieving." The gap reveals that the most ardent interpreter of American reality over the last two decades is beginning to acknowledge the untenability of superimposing meaning on the emerging reality of an America in which even he finds himself somewhat disoriented. By registering the confrontation between Mailer's will to totalize and the defiant, emerging actualities, *Armies* enacts Mailer's awareness of the futility of reductive super-imposition of grand patterns of meaning on the actual.

In *The Naked and the Dead* (1948), Mailer, like most members of his generation, had a good grasp of the outside reality, and was in command of that segment of it that he was putting into his novels. The world seemed to follow an understandable course, and the narrative techniques he had learned from the Big Brothers such as Dos Passos were quite adequate to depict this reality and its occasional eccentricities. By the time he was writing *An American Dream* (1964), the eccentricities had become the rule rather than the exception, but Mailer refused to accept the obsoleteness of meaning-mongering. Instead he tried to give unruly reality an order by imposing an aesthetic pattern on it in his "novel." One can even argue that the feeling that American reality was no longer available to the fictive novel had dawned on Mailer as far back as the late 1950s, when he was putting together his generically curious book, *Advertisements for Myself* (1959). This book purported to tame American reality by an amalgamation of all literary genres. The very form of the book is a commentary on the impossibility of squeezing American experience into a fictive novel. But Mailer did not take his *Advertisements* very seriously and continued to write fictive novels because, as Richard Gilman suggests, his antiquated conception of the fictive novel prevented him from thinking of any other form of literary art as powerful and as capable of dealing with reality as the novel. "Beginning with a fundamentally bourgeois idea of fiction," Gilman believes, Mailer's "idea has always been of the novelist as someone whose gift of intuition and prophecy enable him to see more deeply than other men into society and human organizations." Carrying the old romantic notion of the novelist within him, Mailer puts that concept to the test in *Armies*. By articulating his divided loyalties in the actant and the actee, he transcends the limitations of his fictive vision, and mocks his own effort to view the actual through his fictive imagination. *Armies*, through its double narrational perspectives, registers both the brute facts of the world outside and the changing perception of Mailer. He abandons both realistic portrayal of an orderly reality and aesthetic ordering of the lawless actualities. In his "commentary," Mailer longs for the old grand pattern of meaning, and by recording that desire through his alter ago, the Scribe, he mocks it, "comments" on it, and transforms it into meta-commentary. "Commentary," he now sees, is an act of will; and throughout the book, Mailer parodies and ridicules his willful, meaning-seeking self. Mailer's posture as "clown" in *Armies* is not as innocent a gesture as most critics would have us believe. The "clown" is the seer who, like another "clown," Ken Kesey at the end of *The Electric Kool-Aid Acid Test*, seeks the meaning of America and admits that he "blew" it.

Mailer's growing awareness of the complexity of reality and the impossibility of rendering it in a conventional, realistic manner can be seen in his earlier writing and comments. In "The Man Who Studied Yoga," Sam has given up writing his novel "temporarily," because he cannot find a form. "He does not want to write a realistic novel because *reality is no longer realistic*" (emphasis added). In a speech given at the Modern Language Association of America and printed in *Commentary*, Mailer again expressed his doubts about the authenticity of the conventions of the fictive novel for dealing with contemporary reality: "The realistic literature had never caught up with the rate of change in American life, indeed it had fallen further and further behind, and the novel gave up any desire to be a creation equal to the phenomenon of the country itself; it settled for being a metaphor." The incorporation of these "ideas" into his writing two years later produces *Armies*, an attempt at "a creation equal to the phenomenon of the country itself."

Armies is an odyssey of a self yearning for a grand pattern of meaning behind its fragmentary experience but aware of the futility of such hungering. This awareness, signaled by a split point of view similar to the strategic use of the split screen in films to represent contradictory impulses, creates in the book a sub-text that effectively undercuts and negates the text. In the text, Mailer clearly commits himself to the metaphysical search; in the sub-text, Mailer the Scribe consciously mocks his commitment. The resulting book is a registration of his "lonely odyssey into the land of the witches." The separation between the Performer, the quester for and projector of meaning, and the Scribe, the receptor of the actual, is so great that Mailer himself is bewildered by his own actions. He acknowledges that it seems to him "as if he were watching himself in a film." The book should be read not in terms of the surface comments and ruminations of the public man, but as the recording of those comments and ruminations by the private Scribe, who observes from the outside and registers the desire for coherence and the frustration of that desire by the engulfing chaos and confusion that befog the consciousness. The witness narrative stance of the book, then, operates at two levels: Mailer the public man witnessing the public events as clues to the meaning of American experience, and Mailer the private Scribe witnessing the public man haunted, like Poe's fictional figure of Arthur Gordon Pym, by the white phantom of meaning. But the phantom is elusive; and coherence, solidity, and meaningfulness are only dim memories of the past (the "voice" is that of the private Scribe):

> He is awakening Friday morning in his room at the Hay-Adams after his night on the stage of the Ambassador and the party thereafter. One may wonder if the Adams in the name of his hotel bore any relation to Henry; we need not be concerned with Hay who was a memorable and accomplished gentleman from the nineteenth century (then Secretary of State to McKinley and Roosevelt) other than to say that the hotel looked like its name, and was indeed the staunchest advocate of that happy if heavy style in Washington architecture which spoke of *a time when men and events were solid, comprehensible, often obedient to a code of values.* . . . [emphasis added]

The witness stance of the private Scribe in relation to the public performer is reflected in the image of the book as a "house of mirrors," as if there are always two persons surprised at each other's vastly different existence. The split self has its counterpart in the split nation—the book is full of references to the schizophrenia of America. The narrative is indeed a literalization of a metaphor—Mailer acting out his interpretations and comments—not a metaphorization of the literal, which is the strategy used in the fictive novel. There is nothing metaphoric in the registration of events.

The events themselves are charged with metaphors. The book is a demonstration in its very narrative apparatus of the untamability of contemporary "reality" which, to use Mailer's own phrasing, is "an intersection between history and the comic book, between legend and television, Biblical archetypes and the movies."

In his reading of *Armies*, Warner Berthoff maintains that the "formal precedent" of the book is Thoreau's *Walden*. But Berthoff's comparison is not supportable. In *Walden*, a voice *directly* records his own actions and responses in a very serious tone. Thoreau presents his own experience as a paradigm of a mode of life he would like to see universalized. No double perspective exists in the book and, consequently, no tension. The reality Thoreau depicts requires no such dual vision; the dual vision, with its implications of crippling doubt, is detrimental to his utopian views. But in Mailer's book a utopian model—the remnant of Mailer's past search persisting into the present—joins a voice which constantly undercuts that search, reminding the reader that the quest, in the face of the enormity of contemporary reality, is being turned into a mock-quest. Thoreau writes as the "future leader," while Mailer is the "future victim."

Armies, significantly enough, open with Mailer looking at himself from the outside—from the point of a *Time* magazine reporter. Such focusing on self from without, through alien eyes, signals the emergence of the private Scribe who will examine Mailer the performer. The mode of what Richard Poirier calls "self-watchfulness" is thus established. The difference between Wolfe's testimonial narrative stance and Mailer's is that while Wolfe witnesses other people's activities, Mailer is a self-witness; his *données* are Brownian motions of his "ego" caused by the bombardment of the actual events. In *Armies*, the counterpointing of the "factual" and the "fictional" is done on various thematic and structural levels: "ego" and "events," "the actor" and "the scribe," and "History as a Novel" and "The Novel as History."

External observation of the self at the opening of the book is an indication of the Performer's awareness of the tension which exists between the ego and actuality: two components of his "image." The private Scribe is quick to note the sensitivity of the performer to his image, which is essentially a carry-over from the past when the performer was searching for the all-embracing concept of the real:

> Mailer had the most developed sense of image; if not, he would
> have been a figure of deficiency, for people had been regarding
> him by his public image since he was twenty-five years old. He
> had in fact learned to live in the sarcophagus of his image—at
> night, in his sleep, he might dart out, and paint improvements on

the sarcophagus. During the day, while he was helpless, newspapermen and other assorted bravos of the media and the literary world would carve ugly pictures on the living tomb of his legend. Of necessity, part of Mailer's remaining funds of sensitivity went right into the war of supporting his image and working for it. Sometimes he thought his relation to his image was not unlike some poor fellow who strains his very testicles to bring in emoluments for his wife yet is never favored with carnal knowledge of her.

The "image" is that of the fictive novelist who, by some mysterious ritual, is aware of the workings of reality and possesses the all-embracing metaphor which leads to a total reading of reality. But Mailer is also aware of the difference between the "image" and the "person." The fictive novelist's squeezing of reality to yield meaning is not unlike the straining of testicles to lead to "carnal knowledge," since the fulfillment, the knowledge of the body of the real, is too complex to be related to a simple act of will. The consciousness of "image" on another level is a consciousness of all the people whom he names and whose bias and prejudice distort his image until the image generator, the real Mailer, cannot recognize it. The substantial difference between the projected image and the received image generates a paranoia about the very core of his identity which at the beginning was the spring and source of his image.

Part of the paranoia is created by the intense life that the Participant lives. To be on the frontiers of contemporary American reality means to live in excitement, confusion, and chaos. *Armies* reports from such outposts of American reality, where the preestablished norms fail to order life and reality. The book is an extended enactment of Keats's concept of "negative capability," the development of the ability to live in organic disorder and to check the desire for imposing a wished-for order on the ambiguous, thus falsifying it. Mailer, more than most contemporary American writers, is cultivating this ability to accept chaos as the norm, because he has been more committed to the search for order. His first commitment was to the recognizable order without, then to the order generated within and projected to the outside world. In *Armies*, he acknowledges the futility, the sheer unviability, and the falsehood of such an anthropomorphic ordering of life.

His journey to the frontiers of reality starts with a border crossing— leaving the familiar Brooklyn and traveling to Washington, a city which makes Mailer feel "small." Washington is the focal point of confrontation between established reality and the new forms of actualities. This urge to seek the edges of experience has earned Mailer, the Participant, such titles as the "whitest Negro," and "the oldest Hippie"; his position on the edge provides him with a vision alien to the insiders. The border crossing is another attempt on Mailer's part to literalize his metaphors—to actualize his outsider's views and to project his views of reality into the actual. His micropolitics is a form of "prank," and he himself operates as a Merry Prankster of neo-politics.

Mailer's odyssey begins at a party given by a liberal couple in a house so "oversecure" as to smell of "the scent of the void which comes off the pages of a Xerox copy." The secure, sheltered, and tamed mode of middle-class life is joltingly followed by the bizarre, Dadaistic sense of the Ambassador Theater, where the political pep-rally before the March is turned into a "happening," in itself a miniature of the surprising concatenations of events in the outside world. Mailer's actions here are rather ambivalent: they are the acts of a man who, like the youths in the audience, has taken up political activism as a clue to understanding the works of the body politic of his country, but, at the same time, by his irreverent behavior is intimating that such undertakings in a post-political, post-humanist society, whose frames of references and values are shaped by a technology-generated reality, are no more than evening amusement for middle-class children. The scene enacts Mailer's transformation of commitment (the search for clues to reality) into a meditation on commitment, and thus exposes the complexity and difficulty of distinguishing "the dancer from the dance," the establishment from the anti-establishment, selfishness from selflessness, and the "actual" from the "fictional." What he does in the Ambassador Theater resembles the projected fiction of the Pranksters; it heightens the unreality of the purported solid reality of the rally. The deliberately fictive scene that Mailer arranges hints at the "bad faith" with which the middle-class youths dull their senses to the "smell of the void" which exudes from their lives in suburban homes. They are:

> the Freud-ridden embers of Marxism, good old American anxiety strata—the urban middle-class with their proliferated monumental adenoidal resentments, their secret slavish love for the oncoming hegemony of the computer and the suburb, yes, they and their children, by the sheer ironies, the sheer ineptitude, the *kinks* of history, were now being compressed into more and more militant stands, their resistance to the war some hopeless melange, somehow firmed, of Pacifism and closet Communism. And their children—on a freak-out from the suburbs to a love-in on the Pentagon wall.

Mailer angers everyone. The leaders of the March "depose" him from his role of Master of Ceremonies. The audience treats him more as an entertainer than an American "provo"—a self in search of an anchor. Nevertheless, the "provo" regards himself as the General of the army about to attack the bastion of capitalism and smash the machinery of technology-land. "The Beast" (one of many epithets the Scribes uses for the Performer) is "in a good mood." Before speaking, he goes to the men's room:

> [He] stepped off into the darkness of the top balcony floor, went through a door into a pitch-black men's room, and was alone with his need. No chance to find the light switch for he had no matches, he did not smoke. It was therefore a matter of locating what's what with the probing of his toes. He found something finally which seemed appropriate, and pleased with the precision of these generally unused senses in his feet, took aim between them and a point twelve inches ahead, and heard in the darkness the sound of his water striking the floor. Some damn mistake had been made, an assault from the side doubtless instead of the front, the bowl was relocated now, and Master of Ceremonies breathed deep of the great reveries of this utterly non-Sisyphian release—at last!!—and thoroughly enjoyed the next forty-five seconds, being left on the aftermath not a note depressed by the condition of the premises. No, he was off on the Romantic's great military dream, which is: seize defeat, convert it to triumph.

The performer's projected image as general of the dissenter army is mimicked by the military images used in describing the scene. He "locates" and "probes" as if in a dark night of assault, and expresses satisfaction with the "precision" of his senses. He takes "aim" and the water "strikes" the floor. Missing the right goal is an errant "assault" so he has to "relocate" the bowl. The duration of the act is exactly "forty-five" seconds, and the tactic for converting "defeat" to "victory" is a "military" dream. The same language is used by the private Scribe to put the image of General Mailer in the total context of his quest. The Performer thinks of the March as a "Civil War"; he develops a theory that every man in a war should dress as he pleases as long as the dress makes him "ready for assault"; he decides the middle-class runaways are "crusaders" going out to "attack" the hard core of technology-land with "less training than armies were once offered by a medieval assembly ground." The overall tone conveys a relentless assault against chaos and confusion. The man in command hopes to put an end to the disarray and discover the pattern of meaning and order.

Mailer's subsequent confession of his washroom adventure to the audience intensifies the fictivity of all the evening's activities. Political rally and vaudeville merge. The reality resists the nice ordering planned by the rally's leaders. Mailer emerges from the "experience" and its retelling as a half-fictional, half over-real person; the performer gradually assumes dimensions larger than life, and the private Scribe registers the growth of the fictive-factual dimension with such precision and clarity that one critic felt "as if the techniques and faculties of fiction were invented for such a penetration of real life." The manner in which the Scribe registers the welling up of fictuality in the scene reminds the reader that he is reading a factual account. In this sense, the split point of view of the book—one part of Mailer looking at his other part—has an alienating effect on the reader. It prevents the reader from losing himself in the "illusion" of reality. The Scribe keeps him aware of the factuality of the situation and forces him to use his critical judgment about the fictive reality of the world he inhabits.

After the Ambassador Theater incident, Mailer goes to another party, drinks more, and eventually ends up in his hotel. He is tired, baffled, and caught in the confusions of his own actions. Pressured by the fictual experience he has gone through, he compares the harsh actuality of registering one's bewilderment in dealing with reality and the fictive novelist's reassuring solutions: "Sometime in the early morning, or not so early, Mailer got to bed at the Hay-Adams and fell asleep to dream no doubt of fancy parties in Georgetown when the Federal period in architecture was young. Of course if this were a novel, Mailer would spend the rest of the night with a lady." But the book is rooted in facts, so Mailer must sleep alone. Indeed his preoccupation with facts is so intense that he, the old fictive novelist, the co-founder of *The Village Voice*, and the sponsor and supporter of many underground newspapers and magazines, at one point finds himself mocking one such underground publication: "Since this interview was printed in the *East Village Other*, one cannot be certain it exists; psychedelic underground papers consider themselves removed from any fetish with factology."

On Friday morning, he wakes up with a hangover. The comment of the Scribe is another undercutting of Mailer's commitments: "Revolutionaries-for-a-weekend should not get hangovers." The day drags on and eventually, after the rallies, demonstrations, draft-card surrenders, and speeches, the March begins, with Mailer "stationed between Lens and Lowell." Being so positioned he feels "the separate halves of his nature well-represented, which gave little pleasure, for no American citizen likes to link arms at once with the two ends of his practical working-day good American schizophrenia." General Mailer, under the scrutiny of a camera crew from the BBC, heads the March with assistance from such other notables as Robert Lowell and Dwight Macdonald. The presence of a camera enhances Mailer's preoccupation with his "image." The camera watches Mailer who also watches Mailer who participates in the March. Reality is filtered through so many reflectors a Chinese-box structure seems to surround the core of the alleged real.

As he marches, the sense of America "divided on this day" suddenly releases in him "an undiscovered patriotism." Contradictory feelings attack him from every sensory direction, and, as he nears the Pentagon, the mystery and incomprehensibility of events increase. The Novelist ponders "what a mysterious country" America is. By now, he is "virtually in love with the helicopters not because the metaphors of his mind had swollen large enough to embrace even them!"—another comment on the nature of his metaphor-searching guest—but "he loved helicopters because they were the nearest manifestation of the enemy." Gradually Mailer finds himself dissolving the harsh and untamable actual into a more controllable private fantasy, a defense strategy he also uses in other episodes recording his encounter with unyielding and stubborn reality. Whenever the real defies his totalizing metaphors, he retreats to the fantastic, over which he has total control:

> . . . Mailer, General Mailer, now had a vision of another battle, the next big battle, and these helicopters, press, television and assorted media helicopters hovering overhead with CIA-FBI-all others of the alphabet in helicopters—and into the swarm of the choppers would come a Rebel Chopper in black, or in Kustom-Kar Red, leave it to the talent of the West Coast to prepare the wild helicopter; it would be loaded with guns to shoot pellets of paint at the enemy helicopters, smearing and daubing, dripping them, dropping cans of paint from overhead to smash on the blades of the chopper like early air combat in World War I, and Fourth of July rockets to fire past their Plexiglas canopies. That was the way, Mailer told himself, that was the way. The media would scream at the violence of those dissenters who attacked innocent helicopters with paint. . . .

The March ends at the Pentagon's North Parking Lot, where Mailer listens to the music of the Fugs. The members of the band are dressed in "orange and yellow and rose colored capes and looked at once like Hindu gurus, French musketeers and Southern cavalry captains." Then the most bizarre act begins: the ritual exorcism of the Pentagon. To the accompanying sounds of an Indian triangle, cymbal, trumpet, finger bells, and drums, the

Marchers engage in the "Holy Ritual of Exorcism" to cast out the evil. Then a solemn voice intones:

> In the name of the amulets of touching, seeing, groping, hearing and loving, we call upon the powers of the cosmos to protect our ceremonies in the name of Zeus, in the name of Anubis, god of the dead, in the name of all those killed because they do not comprehend, in the name of the lives of the soldiers in Vietnam who were killed because of a bad karma, in the name of sea-born Aphrodite, in the name of Magna Mater, in the name of Dionysus, Zagreus, Jesus, Yahweh, the unnamable, the quintessent finality of the Zoroastrian fire, in the name of Hermes, in the name of the Beak of Sok, in the name of scarab, in the name, in the name, in the name of the Tyrone Power Pound Cake Society in the Sky, in the name of Rah, Osiris, Horus, Nepta, Isis, in the name of the flowing living universe, in the name of the mouth of the river, we call upon the spirit . . . to raise the Pentagon from its destiny and preserve it. [ellipses in original]

And the voices join in the climax of incantation:

> "Out, demons, out—back to darkness, ye servants of Satan—out, demons, out! Out, demons, out!"
> Voices from the back cried: "Out! . . . Out! . . . Out! . . . Out!" mournful as the wind of a cave. Now the music went up louder and louder, and voices chanting, "Out, demons, out! Out, demons, out! Out, demons, out!"

The reality is so heightened that a fiction oozes out of it; the two merge. The rite of exorcism, as one critic suggests, echoes the supernatural of traditional epic narratives with the difference, of course, that in *Armies*, which is more a meta-epic, the supernatural is generated by the actual and the natural itself. The supernatural agent is technology, which is the matrix of the entire registered experience.

After the arrest, Mailer and the other demonstrators are taken to a makeshift courthouse in a post office. Hours pass, and Mailer's thoughts move from public issues to his relationship with his wife, and the ultimate unknowability of other people, leading him to think again about the function of the fictive novelist. His wife of four years is still a "stranger"; this outrages the novelist in him. As a fictive novelist, he regards himself as a kind of "seer," a penetrator into the psyches of other people, a reader of minds. Now, confronted with the opacity of today's people—who, exposed to a complex reality, have learned to internalize their sophisticated environment, banish their true feelings, and develop a surface life of social roles in the overcrowded, urbanized culture—Mailer feels that his imagination no longer helps. This is particularly annoying because, like all fictive novelists, "he prided himself on his knowledge of women." Once more he confronts the stubborn, untamable, description-defying reality, this time on the level of family life and marriage. He draws a parallel between his wife and America and implicitly acknowledges the realization that both elude his habitual and learned categories of knowing and connecting. The sense of living in an impenetrable world—on both public and private levels—leaves Mailer the Performer estranged and deeply hurt.

Mailer's release from prison ends the first part of the book, the part narrated from the eyewitness stance. In the second part, Mailer the *histor* tries to retrieve the events he did not personally observe by use of the techniques of the exegetical nonfiction novel. He likes to think of the second book as a kind of "collective novel" which is "scrupulous to the welter of a hundred confusing and opposing facts," as the first book was "scrupulous to fact and therefore a documentary." The March on the Pentagon was an enactment of America's schizophrenia, and he wanted to be an eyewitness to it all. His existential confrontation with the events did not give him a solid sense of the present-day American reality, because, the Scribe whispers, he was looking for what was no longer there. He could not identify with any of his fellow marchers or take more than symbolic interest in his arrest and imprisonment; he showed a kind of world-weariness in facing the events. For the Knight of Meaning, all problems and questions were, if not solved, at least categorized. In Book Two, he wants to investigate what happened when he was not present, and to discover if others have managed to find the America he was seeking. Of course, that America does not exist. This is why Mailer finds himself moving from one source to another like a lost child seeking his parents. He finds all accounts contradictory and confusing and talks about using "the strange lights and intuitive speculation which is the novel" to capture the elusive America. As the heading of the sixth part of Book Two indicates, Mailer is using all his resources, a complete "palette of tactics," to reach the white phantom of meaning. Failing in this, he settles for a metaphor and turns away from embracing the vibrant actuality.

As a quest for the grand informing pattern of meaning behind the facade of chaotic reality, *Armies* is a failure, but as an enactment of the tension between "interpretive" frames of reference and the untamable flow of actualities, it is a great triumph. It does not proclaim the inability of totalizing models to decode current fictuality, but it enacts such inability on a split screen on which we see simultaneously the Old Quest and the New Actuality. Whether one reads the last part of the book, "The Metaphor Delivered," with an alien ear, as does Conor Cruise O'Brien, or an American ear, as does Warner Berthoff, the ending fails to achieve Mailer's conception of the novelist's task: to create something "equal to the phenomenon of the country itself." It is "settling for a metaphor," an evasion rather than a formulation. But that is the essential point: *Armies* is a nonfiction novel of self-exposure. The actual acting out, verbally and actionally, reveals the impossibility of overall formulations. Only by rejecting the antiquated ambitions of the fictive novelist can the writer, confronted with an event like the March on the Pentagon—in Mailer's words, "a paradigm of the disproportions and contradictions of the twentieth century itself"—create something equal to that event by permitting the inner dimension of facts to become visible through techniques of registration and by allowing the complexity of the real to find its resonance in the mythic pattern of the factual. The rhetoric of "The Metaphor Delivered," which is a *coup de theatre* by the fictive novelist, is a warning to questers for grand patterns of the informing meaning of reality. Such questers, the Scribe implies, will be reduced to sermonizing. The tension throughout the book between the seeker and the observer culminates in this finale: the gap between the solipsistic, meaning-imposing self and actualities opens wider, and the metaphor is delivered in this chasm. The actualities elude the metaphor and, uncaught, move on. If "totalitarianese," like "technologese," is a language stripped "of any moral content," then the language of "The Metaphor Delivered" (Mailerese) is tripped of any earthly, secular, and terrestrial substance. Both "technologese" and "Mailerese" fail to grasp the mythic dimension of contemporary experience. "Technologese" imposes a mechanical order on the unruly experience, and "Mailerese" superinduces a rhetorical order; neither is equal to the ambiguous nature of the fictual.

The book, however, uses the rhetoric of the final sermon as a concrete example of the "bad faith" of the fictive novelist's falsifying self-assurance, not as an escape from complexity. *Armies* ends with the sermon, but behind the sermon are silhouettes of:

> . . . naked Quakers on the cold floor of a dark isolation cell in
> D.C. jail, wandering down the hours in the fever of dehydration,
> the cells of the brain contracting to the crystals of their thought,
> essence of one thought so close to the essence of another—all
> separations of water gone—that madness is near, madness can
> now be no more than the acceleration of thought.

The book retains its complexity through the private Scribe, who exposes the impossibility of a fictive patterning of actualities in current America by registering Mailer's will to totalize and, at the same time, the nontotalizable experiences he undergoes.

Like other nonfiction novels, *Armies* is based on a double perspective on reality: the empirical facts of the outside world and the inner fiction released by registration of the apocalyptic facts. The out-referential dimension of the book, the March on the Pentagon, is the external field of reference and the empirical data of the book. Within this larger field of external reference are the mental processes of Mailer's reactions to the outer circle of actualities. The performer immediately brings to the narrative that larger ring of the actual, while the private scribe registers the inner circle of subjective reality. The outer and inner circles continually mingle and provide the basis for a transcendence of interpretation to meta-interpretation.

The out-referential dimension contains the verifiable facts and the core of documentation—references to people, places, events, publications—for authenticating these facts. One of the most challenging problems in the out-referential field is the introduction of actual living people. Here problems of terminology arise. The word "character," as I have suggested before, is quite misleading in discussing living people who appear in a nonfiction novel. In a fictive novel, there are criteria (for example, "flat" and "round"), no matter how arbitrary, for measuring the degree of the writer's success or failure in delineating his characters. By definition, all "persons" in a nonfiction novel are "round" characters. On the jacket of *Armies*, Robert Lowell, a well-known poet, is pictured arm in arm with Mailer, Dr. Benjamin Spock, Noam Chomsky, Dwight Macdonald, and other protesters. While it is true that no two eyewitness accounts of Robert Lowell on the March or at the pre-March party would be identical, the degree of "distortion" in the presentation of his character is limited (if only because of legal considerations). The difficulty added to the problem of "characterization" is that all leading people in the book (Paul Goodman, Macdonald, Lowell) are well-known citizens. All these notables appear in the book both as people whose identity can be verified and as people who have an extrafactual dimension. The tension between the Lowell who has a file with the FBI and who may hold a driver's license, and the person who appears in *Armies* with "languid grandeurs of that slouch" creates both a living human being and an embodiment of something meta-factual. Lowell is both a person and an archetype: "Robert Lowell gave off at times the unwilling haunted saintliness of a man who was repaying the moral debts of ten generations of ancestors." The out-referential dimension tries to bring the solid facts of the outside world into the narrative, but under scrutiny that factual dimension is sooner or later enveloped by the fiction it releases. The barriers, as Alfred Alvarez has observed in his essay on *Armies*, between fact and fiction, life and art, are thus broken down. According to him, Mailer "has written a full-scale imaginative work in which almost every detail can be verified."

The in-referential axis of the narrative facilitates the release of the hidden mythic dimension of the factual and demonstrates what I have called the ultimate "fictuality" of experience. The "Microlanguage" of the book, one of the elements of the in-referential dimension, provides a tight network of military images and battle words, giving General Mailer a context of operation and implying the Civil War–like division of America. The "Microlanguage" of the narrative also releases the mythic undertone of the visible; an example of this is the use of the word "white" in a pre-March episode in the book. Mailer is not the user of the word—he is not playing a linguistic trick here. The meanings of the word are released by the facts themselves. Initially the word has a literal meaning, but gradually it becomes an emblem of not just present American crises but the past as well:

> . . . he [Harris, the Negro leader] now stared out at the listening onlookers, picked up the bread and said, "Anyone like some food? It's . . . uh . . ." he pretended to look at it, "it's . . . uh . . . *white* bread." The sliced loaf half-collapsed in its wax wrapper was the comic embodiment now of a dozen little ideas, of corporation-land which took the taste and crust out of bread and wrapped the remains in wax paper . . . the white bread was the infiltrated enemy who had a grip on them everywhere, forced them to collaborate if only by imbibing the bread (and substance) of that enemy with his food processing, enriched flours, vitamin supplements, added nutrients; finally, and this probably was why Harris chuckled when he said it, the bread was *white* bread, not black bread—a way to remind them all that he was one of the very few Negroes here. Who knew what it might have cost him in wonder about his own allegiances not to be out there somewhere now agitating for Black Power. Here he was instead with White bread—White money, White methods, even White illegalities.

In his analysis of contemporary American narratives, Tony Tanner observes that "a writer seeking to get at American reality might do well to combine the documentary and the demonic modes, to develop a sense of magic without losing the empirical eye, and to admit his own relationship to the material he is handling and the interpretation he is offering." Tanner then labels Mailer's novels "demonized documentary," which, though not a correct description of *Armies*, is certainly a suggestive one. The label points to the complexity of the book and especially its movement between the dark side of the novelist's quest (Tanner's *demonic*) and the pressure of actualities (Tanner's *documentary*). Such a reading could become simplifying outside the context of the testimonial stance described in this chapter. The schizophrenia, which is not just stated in the book but enacted in its very narrative fabric and point of view, is a manifestation of the brute facts of contemporary experience and the agonies of the "isolated self, the multifaceted and complex 'I'" which "rises above the communal, historical and extra-rational events, and assumes mythic proportions of its own," and loudly asserts "I am my own myth."

Such tension between the public reality and the private consciousness—and also the inadequacies of the narrative techniques devised by fictive novelists to map this ever-increasing gap—is surely at the heart of *Armies*. In this book, as one reviewer observes, Mailer "gives the impression of a writer so disoriented from his art that he is perhaps consciously writing the equivalent of Fitzgerald's *Crack-up*; the idea being that if he shows his mind with complete honesty the public will understand why he cannot write the great novel which is expected of him." Norman Mailer himself has summed up the predicament of the contemporary fictionist: "The nature of existence cannot be felt any more. As novelists, we cannot locate our center of values."

A. CARL BREDAHL

An Exploration of Power:
Tom Wolfe's Acid Test

Tom Wolfe's writing is the most vivid instance of the role of the journalist in American literature, a role that has played a major part in the development of twentieth-century prose fiction. Unfortunately, even Wolfe himself, in his introduction to *The New Journalism* (1973), seems content to distinguish his work from that of novelists and to look for influences in "examples of non-fiction written by reporters." He does not but should recognize that the novel is a dynamic form, that in the hands of such journalists as Stephen Crane and Ernest Hemingway the novel has developed in this century just as it did in the eighteenth and nineteenth centuries. In the novel the imagination has always been concerned with particulars of a real world, a concern that has only been intensified in the twentieth century. The journalist, once depicted in literature as a mere observer and thus only a second-rate artist, has begun to emerge as an individual especially well trained to work with particulars. Certainly, all journalists are not suddenly novelists, but in several significant ways New Journalism is actually in the mainstream of the developing American novel. In *Green Hills of Africa* Hemingway speaks of pushing the art of writing prose fiction much further than it has ever gone before, and Wolfe, like Hemingway, is a writer who, instead of reporting facts for the consumption of a mass intelligence, is consuming the physical world as a part of his own nutriment. Like

From *Critique: Studies in Modern Fiction* 23, no. 2 (Winter 1981–82). © 1981 by The Helen Dwight Reid Educational Foundation.

Hemingway eating the kudu's liver, this new journalist is thriving on the materials available to him: Ken Kesey and the Pranksters.

The Electric Kool-Aid Acid Test (1968) is a story of individuals keenly sensitive to the fact that they live in a new world and delighted by the prospect of exploring it. Tom Wolfe's story describes individuals anxious to say "Shazam" and draw new energies into themselves. Ultimately, however, they fail to become Captain Marvel:

> "We blew it!"
> ". . . just when you're beginning to think, 'I'm going to score' . . ."
> "We blew it!"

Henry Adams dreamed of the child of power, but the twentieth-century child has discovered that power is not enough; the excitement of Eugene Gant must be combined with the cool skills of Hemingway. *The Electric Kool-Aid Acid Test* reflects Gant's exuberance in its free use of the medium, the language and syntax; but it is at the same time a carefully structured work. Neither an uncontrolled celebration of drugs nor an ordered documentary on Ken Kesey and the Pranksters, *The Electric Kool-Aid Acid. Test* is an expression of a narrative imagination that sees the possibilities of the twentieth century embodied in the Pranksters. That imagination has discovered the need and ability to integrate both the exuberance and the structure if it is to function in a world characterized by electric energies.

Wolfe's values are evident in the book's opening sequence:

> That's good thinking there, Cool Breeze. Cool Breeze is a kid with three or four days' beard sitting next to me on the stamped metal bottom of the open back part of a pickup truck. Bouncing along. Dipping and rising and rolling on these rotten springs like a boat. Out of the back of the truck the city of San Francisco is bouncing down the hill, all those endless staggers of bay windows, slums with a view, bouncing and streaming down the hill. One after another, electric signs with neon martini glasses lit up on them, the San Francisco symbol of "bar"—thousands of neon-magenta martini glasses bouncing and streaming down the hill, and beneath them hundreds, thousands of people wheeling around to look at this freaking crazed truck we're in, their white faces erupting from their lapels like marshmallows. . . . Kneeling in the truck, facing us, also in plain view, is a half-Ottawa Indian girl named Lois Jennings, with her head thrown back and a

radiant look on her face. Also a blazing silver disk in the middle
of her forehead alternately exploding with light when the sun hits
it or sending off rainbows from the defraction lines on it.

As one of several reporters covering Kesey's story, Wolfe comes to San
Francisco with a pre-arranged idea of what his story will be—"Real-life
Fugitive"—and interviews Kesey with all the usual questions. In spite of these
limitations, Wolfe is moving, fascinated with the Pranksters, and able to
focus on the details of the physical world. That world is one of objects that
explode with an energy all their own. Nothing is static in the opening scene—
faces erupt, lights explode, and the city bounces out of the back of the
heaving, billowing truck. The description is, of course, that of the narrator
Wolfe in contrast to the reporter Wolfe; but even as a reporter, Tom Wolfe
is himself moving West, attracted to Kesey and the Pranksters.

"Stolid" and two years out of date as a result of being from the East,
Wolfe enters a world that stimulates his senses rather than his mind. He has
only a limited amount of information about Kesey, and his rational questions
of what, when, and why are distinctly out of place in the world of day-glo
paint and marshmallow faces—but he sees a great deal: Kesey

> has thick wrists and big forearms, and the way he has them
> folded makes them look gigantic. He looks taller than he really
> is, maybe because of his neck. He has a big neck with a pair of
> sternocleido-mastoid muscles that rise up out of the prison
> workshirt like a couple of dock ropes. His jaw and chin are
> massive.

His first encounter with Kesey takes place in a jail, a sterile, rigid, and
confined environment that contrasts sharply with the physically healthy
individual who responds immediately to Wolfe's interest. That same contrast
is also evident in the "conversation" between Wolfe and Kesey. Tom Wolfe,
like the television reporter who later interviews Kesey but does not get the
answers he is looking for, does not hear what Kesey is saying: "The ten
minutes were up and I was out of there. I had gotten nothing, except my first
brush with a strange phenomenon, that strange up-country charisma, the
Kesey presence." The early relationship between Wolfe and Kesey is imaged
in the telephone they use to speak to each other:

> Then I pick up my telephone and he picks up his—and this is
> truly Modern Times. We are all of twenty-four inches apart, but
> there is a piece of plate glass as thick as a telephone directory

between us. We might as well be in different continents, talking over Videophone. The telephones are very crackly and lo-fi, especially considering that they have a world of two feet to span.

Physically they are close, but imaginatively they are miles apart. Wolfe is a note taker and instigator of talk, and Kesey's responses about moving and creativity lose Wolfe: "I didn't know what in the hell it was all about." Little is *answered*, but Tom Wolfe has been "brushed" by Kesey's energy.

After leaving Kesey, Wolfe continues his journalistic efforts and investigates the environment of the Merry Pranksters: "Somehow my strongest memories of San Francisco are of me in a terrific rented sedan *roaring* up hills or down hills, *sliding* on and off the cable-car tracks. *Slipping* and *sliding* down to North Beach" (italics added). Moving enthusiastically but not with much control, Wolfe discovers that an old world is vanishing: "But it was not just North Beach that was dying. The whole old-style hip life—jazz, coffee houses, civil rights, invite a spade for dinner, Vietnam—it was all suddenly dying." Wolfe's "blue silk blazer and . . . big tie with clowns on it" reflect that hip world, a world that Wolfe understands and enjoys. Now he stands on the edge of a new world and is "starting to get the trend of all this heaving and convulsing"; he is, however, one of the few. The straight world of the cops and the courts thinks in terms of keeping Kesey trapped and forcing him to preach their cause or be denounced by his friends—and the "heads" are unable to understand Kesey's talk about "beyond acid."

While these two groups want to "Stop Kesey," their efforts in essence directed at stopping movement, we get an insight into Kesey's values in the actions of his lawyers who are able to pull off the miracle of his release. They make things happen, in contrast to those who try to stop activity. In the best Ben Franklin sense of the word, Kesey "uses" people. The cops and heads are using Kesey as a tool to keep a structured environment rigid, but Kesey—like Ben—sees a world of continuous possibility in which individuals (and drugs and machines) can be of use to each other in realizing that possibility. The opening situation of the book, Kesey coming out of jail, thus embodies two major impulses in the narrative: the explosive activity of Kesey to make things happen and the efforts of those who fear change and wish to lock him up.

Tom Wolfe is responsive to his new world: "Well, for a start, I begin to see that people like Lois and Stewart and Black Maria are the restrained, reflective wing of the Merry Pranksters." Wolfe is beginning to see actions and a world that glows; he also hears—"From out of the black hole of the garage comes the sound of a record by Bob Dylan and his raunchy harmonica and Ernest Tubb"—and knows what he is hearing. Wolfe has possibilities of doing more than just recording data since he is both responsive and knowledgeable, but he is still unsure as to what is happening: "that was what Kesey had been talking to me about, I guess."

"For two or three days it went like that for me in the garage with the Merry Pranksters waiting for Kesey." Kesey is the unifying and stimulating ingredient; without him the Pranksters do not function. As Wolfe gets further into their life, he sees them as a gathering of individuals who, without Kesey, live amid a piled up "heap of electronic equipment" and talk, however eloquently, about abstractions. Above all else, they wait.

> Through the sheet of sunlight at the doorway and down the incline into the crazy gloom comes a panel truck and in the front seat is Kesey. . . . Instead of saying anything, however, he cocks his head to one side and walks across the garage to the mass of wires, speakers, and microphones over there and makes some minute adjustment. . . . As if now everything is under control and the fine tuning begins.

Kesey enters the gloom of the garage through a doorway of light, and with his fine tuning, Wolfe himself feels the electricity: "despite the skepticism I brought here, *I* am suddenly experiencing *their* feeling."

> "Don't say stop plunging into the forest," Kesey says. "Don't stop being a pioneer and come back here and help these people though the door. If Leary wants to do that, that's good, it's a good thing and somebody should do it. But somebody has to be the pioneer and leave the marks for the others to follow."

Kesey's drive is to keep moving, to explore new energies. He has no question about *whether* possibility exists or *whether* it is demonic; the energy is there, and Kesey wants to use it, go with its characteristics rather than impose his requirements on it. These qualities also characterize Wolfe's art, a skillful exploration of the possibilities of prose fiction. Together, the book and Kesey tremble with energy that can either transform Billy Batson into Captain Marvel or blow a fuse.

With Chapter Four Wolfe begins a flashback which carries through much of the book. We should remain aware, however, that though the focus is on Kesey, we are really seeing Wolfe "evaluate," take the strength from, Kesey and the Pranksters. The flashback is, then, a continuation of the narrative fascination with Kesey, a fascination that leads to Wolfe's own growth. Both Kesey and *The Electric Kool-Aid Acid Test* focus on physical objects that sparkle with life:

That was the big high-school drive-in, with the huge streamlined sculpted pastel display sign with streaming streamlined superslick A-22 italic script, floodlights, clamp-on trays, car-hop girls in floppy blue slacks, hamburgers in some kind of tissuey wax paper steaming with onions pressed down and fried on the grill and mustard and catsup to squirt all over it from out plastic squirt cylinders.

No corresponding attention is paid to the talk *about* life. The Perry Lane sophisticates turn "back to first principles" of Greece, but Kesey is into the modern western hero who is capable of transformation into a being of superhuman energies: "A very Neon Renaissance—And the myths that actually touched you at that time—not Hercules, Orpheus, Ulysses, and Aeneas—but Superman, Plastic Man, The Flash." The power of the verbal "Shazam," like the new drug LSD, sparks an electrical power surge which makes an individual begin "traveling and thinking at the speed of light." Attuned to this new power, Kesey is able to see detail and movement:

The ceiling is moving—not in a crazed swirl but along its own planes of light and shadow and surface not nearly so nice and smooth as plasterer Super Plaster Man intended with infallible carpenter level bubble sliding in dim honey Karo syrup tube not so foolproof as you thought, but, little lumps and ridges up there, bub, and lines, lines like spines on crests of waves of white desert movie sand each one with MGM shadow longshot of the ominous A-rab coming over the next crest for only the sinister Saracen can see the road and you didn't know how many subplots you left up there, Plaster man, trying to smooth it *all* out, *all* of it, with your bubble in a honey tube carpenter's level, to make us all down here look up and see nothing but ceiling, because we all know ceiling, because it has a *name*, ceiling, therefore it is nothing but a ceiling—no room for A-rabs up there in Level Land, eh, Plaster man.

He can also see the muscles in the doctor's face or his pulse as an accurate measure of his life or Chief Broom as the key to his new novel. As his perception is altered, Kesey becomes aware of a potentially frightening world where few people want to go but which is also a place where a moving line can suddenly become a nose, "the very miracle of creation itself."

Kesey's early activities after taking LSD are burstings forth of "vital energy." The move to La Honda, the appearance of the intrepid traveller, and the bus trip are all forms of this eruption. The bus trip "Further," like the flashback technique Wolfe uses in his narrative, is a movement back in preparation for new directions. The bus heads *East* toward the old intellectual world of the Learyites and Europe. The trip carries the Merry Pranksters down through the pressure-cooker heat of the South, something like the first stages of a sauna bath where the body is flushed of internal poisons. The trip back culminates in "the Crypt Trip" where the pressure is of a different kind. The Pranksters expect to be received joyously, but all along the road they encounter a variety of threatening responses. When they visit the Learyites, they discover that the "Pranksters' Ancestral Mansion" is not a home; rather its "sepulchral" atmosphere and "Tibetan Book of the Dead" emphasize that the Pranksters have broken off from the intellectual Eastern world:

> . . . the trouble with Leary and his group is that they have turned *back*. But of course! They have turned back into that old ancient New York intellectual thing, ducked back into the Romantic past, copped out of the American trip. New York intellectuals have always looked for . . . another country, a fatherland of the mind, where it is all better and more philosophic and purer, gadget-free, and simpler and pedigreed.

The Pranksters are a new group, living in a new world. They have no roots and must seek their life in constant discovery. When they emerge from the Crypt, they turn westward, but the bus now takes the cooler, Northern route. The trip ultimately integrates and unifies the Pranksters; they become a special group rather than a collection of idiosyncratic individuals.

Kesey's interest in energy and art have also been developed while on this "risk-all balls-out plunge into the unknown." Simply becoming aware, sensitive to power is not enough:

> Kesey said he wanted them all to do their thing and be Pranksters, but he wanted them to be deadly competent, too. . . . They should always be alert, always alive to the moment, always deep in the whole group thing, and be deadly competent.

Being alive to the moment is integrally related to Kesey's particular understanding of art. For him art is a way of getting totally into the now, a world where one experiences an event at exactly the same time it is occurring: "The whole *other world* that LSD opened your mind to existed only in the moment itself—*Now*—and any attempt to plan, compose, orchestrate, write a script, only locked you out of the moment, back in the world of conditioning and training where the brain was a reducing valve." While Kesey wants to be the artist who can organize such an experience, he also wants an art form that does not determine the experience. Being trapped in the rules of syntax and the referential properties of language, while it allowed him to break through the "all-American crap" earlier, would destroy his present commitment to the now. In pointing to the bus and in creating the miracle in seven days and the acid tests, Kesey imagines an artist who can artificially create conditions but not the experience of the work. Each individual must do that—get on the bus—for himself.

"It could be scary out there in Freedom land. The Pranksters were friendly, but they glowed in the dark." The frightening power of the new electricity is epitomized in the Hell's Angels:

> The Angels brought a lot of things into synch. Outlaws, by definition, were people who had moved off of dead center and were out in some kind of Edge City. The beauty of it was, the Angels had done it like the Pranksters, by choice. They had become outlaws first—to *explore*, muvva—and then got busted for it. The Angels' trip was the motorcycle and the Pranksters' was LSD, but both were in an incredible entry into orgasmic moment, *now*.

As the Angels' motorcycles roar into La Honda, the energy that has been discovered and explored thus far surges forth. It is not just a test of the Pranksters; it is an event which embodies just how far the Pranksters have gone in their exploration of power. No group in America could seem more demonic than the Angels, but their tremendous energies are now being taken into the Pranksters and used by a group of highly skilled individuals. What could have been a "time bomb" becomes instead a vibrating two-day party.

With all the energies of the Angels in their movie, the Pranksters are now able to achieve a "miracle in seven days." This chapter is at the center of the book and culminates the efforts of Kesey to get in tune with his environment, discover the Power that is available, and use that Power through his own art to bring others to see what it is like out on Edge City. What the conference allows Kesey to do is demonstrate that he is able to make his current fantasy work. When it is all over, "it's like all the Pranksters' theories and professed beliefs have been put to a test in the outside world, away from La Honda, and they're working now, and they have . . . Control."

So that creative impulse to burst forth from the all-American crap, an impulse that is the driving force during the first part of the book, culminates in an artistic production that is non-verbal and unprogrammed. The actors and audience become one movie—but something is wrong:

> Kesey also had his court appearances to contend with and more lying, finking, framing, politicking by the constables than a body could believe—he looked like he had aged ten years in three months. He was now some indeterminate age between thirty and forty. He was taking a lot of speed and smoking a lot of grass. He looked haggard, and when he looked haggard, his face seemed lopsided.

The final word of the chapter is "Control," and the last few pages stress "Power," but the lives of the Merry Pranksters are soon to become like a nuclear reactor that has gone beyond critical mass. The image of energy bursting forth, impulsing outward, which dominates the first half of the book, is the same image which dominates the second, but that energy is rapidly getting out of control.

Kesey's efforts have been to discover and release energy; he is beginning to find, however, that that energy may not be easily handled. Two chapters demonstrate what is happening: the one which closes the first part of the book, "The Hell's Angels," and the one which opens the second, "Cloud." In the Hell's Angels chapter the Pranksters welcome tremendous outlaw energies into their movie—"The Merry Pranksters Welcome the Hell's Angels." The situation is the same in "Cloud"—"The Merry Pranksters Welcome the Beatles"—but what had worked in the earlier chapter becomes ugly and dangerous in the second. The Beatles fantasy is an effort to continue moving, but now the vibrations are bad because the value that Kesey has been striving for—Control—is absent:

> It is like the whole thing has snapped, and the whole front section
> of the arena becomes a writhing, seething mass of little girls
> waving their arms in the air . . . and they have utter control over
> them—but they don't know what in the hell to do with it.

Instead of energy working, the Pranksters find themselves in a pen in which "mindless amok energy" threatens to become a cancer, uncontrolled and self-consuming.

The implications of that cancer are developed in the chapters after "Cloud," but one would be mistaken to suggest that the first part of the book does one thing and the second part something different. Rather, the factors that result in the blown fuse are present during the early successful activities of the Pranksters; they have just gone unrecognized by Kesey (but not by Wolfe—since they are part of his narrative). They are integral aspects of some of Kesey's major assumptions. The problem is evident in the opening of "Cloud," the chapter in which the energy becomes cancerous.

> They lie there on the mattresses, with Kesey rapping on and on and Mountain Girl trying to absorb it. Ever since Asilomar, Kesey has been deep in to the religion thing . . . on and on he talks to Mountain Girl out in the backhouse and very deep and far-out stuff it is, too. Mountain Girl tries to concentrate, but the words swim like great waves of. . . . Her mind keeps rolling and spinning over another set of data, always the same, Life—the eternal desperate calculation. In short, Mountain Girl is pregnant.

Kesey has gotten so completely into his current fantasy that he has lost touch with the physical environment he is seeking to touch. Mountain Girl is pregnant, but Kesey is unaware. She is about to bring forth life, but Kesey is sensitive only to ideas.

Evidence of the difficulty appeared in Chapter Eleven when the Merry Pranksters returned from their trip East having discovered a new unity: "What they all saw in . . . a flash was the solution to the basic predicament of being *human*, the personal *I*, *Me*, trapped, mortal and helpless, in a vast impersonal *It*, the world around me." Kesey began with the urge to create from within himself and to involve himself in his world, drives which suggest a need to experience fully what it means to be human. But in Chapter Eleven the implication is that being human has become a "predicament" that needs to be altered. At the same time, however, the movie is demanding some very human skills if it is not to become its own uncontrolled cancer:

> But the Movie was a monster . . . the sheer labor and tedium in editing forty-five hours of film was unbelievable. And besides . . . much of the film was out of focus. . . . But who needs that old Hollywood thing of long shot, medium shot, closeup, and the careful cuts and wipes and pans and dolly in and dolly out, the old bullshit. Still, plunging in on those miles of bouncing, ricocheting, blazing film with a splicer was like entering a jungle where the greeny vines grew faster than you could chop them down in front of you.

The cutting needed in the jungle or in the editing of the movie *requires* a human response that is not just a submersion of the individual into the physical, a submersion that is implied in the statement, "Suddenly!—All-in-one!—flowing together, *I* into *It*, and *It* into *Me*, and in that flow I perceive a power, so near and so clear, that the whole world is blind to." These words have Emersonian overtones, where the individual is in danger of losing his individuality—or where he can lose his ability to see the particular because he has become intellectual.

Chapter Eleven explores the human "predicament" as Kesey understands it, talking of Cassady:

> A person has all sorts of lags built into him, Kesey is saying. One, the most basic, is the sensory lag, the lag between the time your senses receive something and you are able to react. . . . He is a living example of how close you can come, but it can't be done. You can't go any faster than that. You can't through sheer speed overcome the lag. We are all of us doomed to spend our lives watching a movie of our lives. . . . That lag has to be overcome some other way, through some kind of total breakthrough . . . nobody can be creative without overcoming all those lags first.

Kesey's statement that no one can be creative—that the creative impulse cannot burst forth and fully express itself—without overcoming this lag, this humanity, invites a potentially destructive conflict between his beliefs and the physical properties of his environment. Once the lag is ended, the individual will be completely in tune with the pattern: "one could *see* the larger pattern and move with it—Go with the flow!—and accept it and rise above one's immediate environment and even alter it by accepting the larger pattern and grooving with it." However, they are left with "the great morass of a movie, with miles and miles of spiraling spliced-over film and hot splices billowing around them like so many intertwined, synched, but still chaotic and struggling human lives." Such a life is Mountain Girl's and in all the theory and talk, Kesey has missed that individual. The loneliness and pregnancy of Mountain Girl, an individual who is so thoroughly a Prankster, calls attention to the dependency upon Kesey that most, if not all, the Pranksters have developed. "Kesey was essential to Mountain Girl's whole life with the Pranksters" just as he was essential to the success of the party with the Hell's Angels. Kesey's initial urge had been personal, and he sought to extend his own perception while also stimulating others to begin perceiving for themselves. The Pranksters—as well as those drawn into their movie—should be developing that individuality, but their dependency on Kesey's energy has apparently limited their ability to concentrate and explore their own. What was to have stimulated the individual to discover himself has become a social enterprise where the group is dependent on a leader. If such a problem is developing, the removal of that leader ought to bring movement to a halt and perhaps to cause that tightly welded unit to disintegrate. These problems develop in the second part of the book, the section that begins with power out of control at the Beatles' concert and with the power surge in New York that blows all the city's fuses and transformers.

Events in the book, then, have begun to anticipate the breakup of the Merry Pranksters. In "Departures" Kesey prepares to head for Mexico, for the first time responding to the actions of others—the police—rather than initiating action himself, and Mountain Girl goes to New York to try to get herself back together. Sandy also leaves for New York, again the victim of what for him will apparently always be "the demon Speed." As if to emphasize the social thrust of their recent activities, the two chapters preceding Kesey's trip focus on the skills of the Pranksters "to extend the message to all people," with Kesey very prominently at the controls. No longer is each individual Prankster striving to become deadly competent, a functioning individual alive to the moment. Rather each is concentrating entirely on the collective enterprise of conveying their "message"—with all the verbal and social connotations of that word—to a group. Instead of the effort of the individual to go "further," the Pranksters create an authorized, organized Now.

The Mexican chapters parallel in many ways the earlier bus trip, but where the pressure cooker had then been restricted to the heat of the sun, now Kesey and those with him are subjected to disease, filth, and death. What had been an intellectual crypt trip now becomes almost too real. Wolfe's handling of the opening scene in Mexico is both a vivid description of the paranoid state into which Kesey has fallen and a major indicator of the developing difference between Kesey and Wolfe. Earlier, Wolfe had been stimulated by Kesey's skill, but now Wolfe himself is demonstrating that skill. Kesey's helpless mental state is presented with an incredibly sharp eye for detail:

> Kesey sits in this little rickety upper room with his elbow on a table and his forearm standing up perpendicular and in the palm of his hand a little mirror, so that his forearm and the mirror are like a big rear-view mirror stanchion on the side of a truck and thus he can look out the window and see them but they can't see him. . . . Kesey has Cornel Wilde Running Jacket ready hanging on the wall, a jungle-jim corduroy jacket stashed with fishing line, a knife, money, DDT, tablet, ball-points, flashlight, and grass.

Kesey is seeing very little—his mind is alive largely to the details of his latest fantasy—but Wolfe is able both to focus on the reality of Kesey's world and to convey the quality of Kesey's paranoid experience, each second of which lasts no more than a minute and is agonizingly detailed and examined in the best Prankster day-glo color. Wolfe is in control, and in his hands the verbal medium comes alive.

Kesey's energies are also alive but trapped within himself—not the artificial rules of syntax. His tremendous energies are still there, and they continue to pull people back to him: Black Maria and Mountain Girl, now back with the Pranksters and eight months pregnant—as well as some Pranksters left at La Honda—begin to regroup in Mexico. What they find there is the ugly world in which Kesey has been living: "All the vibrations outside were bad. Corpses, chiefly. Scrub cactus, brown dung dust and bloated corpses, dogs, coyotes, armadillos, a cow, all gas-bellied and dead, swollen and dead. . . . This was the flow, and it was a sickening horrible flow." The intensity of the Mexican experience is epitomized in "The Red Tide," "a poison as powerful as aconitine" which is produced by the plankton in the ocean waters and which is death to the fish. That death mirrors the death on the land where the Pranksters are "stranded like flies in this 110-degree mucus of Manzanillo." The red tide and the Mexican disaster are less efforts at journalistic accuracy than metaphors for the Prankster experience at a time when death and stagnation are as much a part of their lives as they are in the filthy pressure-cooker world of the environment. The drugs which were opening doors earlier are now only a means to escape the heat.

Under these same conditions, however, Mountain Girl has her baby, her dyed hair gradually returns to its natural state, and Kesey begins to see what is happening to them: "they have made the trip now, closed the circle, all of them, and they either emerge as Superheros, closing the door behind them and soaring through the hole in the sapling sky, or just lollygag in the loop-the-loop of the lag . . . either make this thing permanent inside of you or forever just climb draggled up into the conning tower every time for one short glimpse of the horizon." The "current fantasy" has become just that, a fantasy; they have lost contact with reality. "Mommy, this movie is no fun any more, it's too *real*, Mommy." That reality—in the form of the Mexican police—reaches out to capture Kesey but succeeds only in spurring him into activity: "It was time to get the Movie going on all projectors. And the bus."

Kesey's return to California is a curious mixture of continuing to live in fantasy and yet wanting to get back in touch with the environment, separate values that mirror Kesey's own state of mind—"Kesey veering wildly from paranoia and hyper-security to extraordinary disregard for his own safety, one state giving way to the other in no fixed order." His commitment is once again to movement, this time beyond acid and beyond the stagnant condition of the tests which have quickly become the in-thing, the sport of college students and New York intellectuals. Kesey is once again probing the "western-most edge of experience," and that scares those who are content to remain where they are. It is the Hell's Angels side of the Kesey adventure that panics the hip world because the Angels are "too freaking real. *Outlaws* . . . the heads of Haight-Ashbury could never stretch their fantasy as far out as the Hell's Angels."

Kesey is also having to work his imagination; at the moment he is theorizing and playing a game of cops-and-robbers with the California authorities:

> It will be a masked ball, this Test. Nobody will know which freak is who. At the midnight hour, Kesey, masked and disguised in a Super-hero costume, on the order of Captain America of the Marvel Comics pantheon, will come up on stage and deliver his vision of the future, of the way "beyond acid." *Who is this apocalyptic*—Then he will rip off his mask—Why—it's Ken Kee-zee!—and as the law rushes for him, he will leap up on a rope hanging down from the roof at center stage and climb, hand over hand, without even using his legs, with his cape flying, straight up, up, up, up through a trap door in the roof, to where Babbs will be waiting with a helicopter, Captain Midnight of the U. S. Marines, and they will ascend into the California ozone.

This seems less movement than fantasizing, less Captain Marvel than a child who is exercising his power to defy authority. Once again Kesey finds that "the current fantasy . . . this movie is too real, Mommy." Appropriately, Kesey's capture is put in terms of a little boy with torn pants.

The last chapter of *The Electric Kool-Aid Acid Test* details the anticlimax of Kesey's efforts to go beyond acid; they blow it. In the final scene, the Pranksters who are striving to move are sitting on the floor of the Warehouse surrounded by too much noise and too many TV cameras. Whatever Kesey has been driving for is imaged as a much publicized stagnation: "It's like a wake." Wolfe has later said that during the abstract expressionist movement of the 1950's,

> The artists themselves didn't seem to have the faintest notion of how primary Theory was becoming. I wonder if the theorists themselves did. All of them, artists and theorists, were talking as if their conscious aim was to create a totally immediate art, lucid,

stripped of all the dreadful baggage of history, an art fully
revealed, honest, as honest as the flat-out integral picture plane.

To a Prankster as well as an abstract expressionist this passage might appear
an irritatingly inaccurate evaluation of their activities, but it indicates much
about Wolfe's own artistic values and does indeed point to the crucial
weakness in the Prankster way of life. The emphasis in the passage is on the
Word in its most sterile form: and it is this that would annoy the Pranksters
because their whole effort is dedicated to going beyond an abstract
verbalization which is the epitome of the distance between the event and the
experiencing of it.

The desire to open oneself up to the world, not unique with the
Pranksters, allows us to see them in the mainstream of American thought and
literature reaching back through Hemingway, Whitehead, Melville,
Thoreau, and Emerson to Franklin and the Puritans. Whitehead's emphasis
on creativity and novelty illustrates the potential vitality of the Pranksters:

> "Creativity" is the principle of *novelty*. An actual occasion is a
> novel entity diverse from any entity in the "many" which it
> unifies. Thus "creativity" introduces novelty into the content of
> the many, which are the universe disjunctively. The "creative
> advance" is the application of this ultimate principle of creativity
> to each novel situation which originates.

The world is continually being "renewed"; there is no stasis, no biblical
Garden of Eden. Kesey's concern with "beyond acid" is absolutely right, for
it indicates continuing novelty; however, when he says that we are "doomed"
to watch our lives and that without overcoming lag "nobody can be creative,"
his stress is not on movement but on goal, one that is disturbingly Edenic. At
such a theoretical point, the world might be moving but the individual would
be carried along with it.

Kesey points to Cassady as someone "going as fast as a human can go,
but even he can't overcome it. He is a living example of how close you can
come, but it can't be done. You can't go any faster than that." Cassady,
however, is an individual who burns himself out, and Kesey's praise of
Cassady should warn us of dangers implicit in Kesey's drives. When Kesey
starts to talk about overcoming rather than opening, his drives become self-
destructive rather than liberating. In addition, the existence of Wolfe's art
indicates that, far from limiting creativity, lag is what makes creativity
possible. Kesey urges the Pranksters to "go with the flow," but the danger, as
any defensive tackle will verify, is always that such movement can result in

being swept along. Kesey's interest is in the ability to perceive and evaluate flow so as to develop not dissolve individuality. Such perception necessitates lag. The discovery and assertion of personal skills—"The most powerful drive in the ascent of man," says Jacob Bronowski, "is the pleasure in his own skill"—is not a goal but a process that demands vision and objectivity. Kesey has all the right impulses, but when he begins to talk about overcoming lag, he is in danger either of becoming self-destructive or of being swept along by the flow.

While Kesey sees goals and ideas, Wolfe sees objects:

> But my mind is wandering. I am having a hard time listening because I am fascinated by a little plastic case with a toothbrush and toothpaste in it that Hassler has tucked under one thumb. . . . Here Hassler outlines a pyramid in the air with his hands and I watch, fascinated, as the plastic toothbrush case shiny shiny slides up one incline of the pyramid.

Ultimately, the difference between Wolfe and the Pranksters is evidenced in Wolfe's ability to keep his narrative eye focused on the physical world of the Pranksters and to unify *The Electric Kool-Aid Acid Test* in contrast to the talk and endless feet of film and electrical wires that the Pranksters can never manage to bring together. Kesey worries that his experience cannot be verbalized: "But these are *words*, man! *And you couldn't put it into words*. The white Smocks liked to put it into words, like *hallucination* and *dissociative phenomena*." Wolfe, however, goes for the vitality rather than the intellectual abstraction, a quality that distinguishes him from the reporters who come to cover the story of redeveloping Perry Lane:

> The papers turned up to write about the last night on Perry Lane, noble old Perry Lane, and had the old cliche at the ready, End of an Era, expecting to find some deep-thinking latter-day Thorstein Veblen intellectuals on hand with sonorous bitter statements about this machine civilization devouring its own past.
> Instead, there were some kinds of *nuts* out there. They were up in a tree lying on a mattress, all high as coons. . . . but they managed to go back with the story they came with, End of an Era, the cliche intact.

These men see with their clean, structured minds; thus the cliches. But Tom Wolfe is able to open his eyes and see the vitality of the Prankster world. His willingness to look rather than to theorize allows him to perceive "shape and pattern" in his verbal exploration of the Pranksters. The result is a functioning narrative voice in an exciting new world: "That's good thinking there, Cool Breeze. Cool Breeze is a kid with three or four days' beard sitting next to me on the stamped metal bottom of the open back part of a pickup truck. Bouncing along. Dipping and rising and rolling on these rotten springs like a boat." Good thinking and movement and concrete objects—these are Tom Wolfe's values.

Kesey and Wolfe share many of the same values, but Wolfe succeeds where Kesey and the Pranksters blow it because Wolfe is able to look at physical laws as something to be used to one's advantage—evaluated—rather than as frustrations to be overcome. *The Electric Kool-Aid Acid Test* is thus a book about art, about the individual's effort to get it all together. Telling one's story and getting one's skills finely tuned are finally the same thing. Kesey has the skills to tune a piece of machinery, but he is also interested in fine tuning himself. Ultimately, he and the Pranksters fail to look at themselves or at each other as individuals (the Who Cares girl) just as they prefer to look at the physical world as metaphor rather than object. Games, roles, metaphors, and abstractions become Prankster values in spite of their talk about opening doors and going further. Tom Wolfe's uniqueness is his recognition that perception and skill must be developed together, that one can only discover his strengths by evaluating his environment.

RICHARD A. KALLAN

Style and the New Journalism:
A Rhetorical Analysis of Tom Wolfe

Few journalists have generated as much critical attention as Tom Wolfe. His message, his style, his school of journalism all have provoked response from a spectrum of sources, including journalism reviews, literary monthlies, and political periodicals. Moreover, there is polarity in the popular criticism expressed: Karl Shapiro, for instance, believes that Wolfe "writes like a master," while Dwight Macdonald sees Wolfe as a demagogic parajournalist.

Despite the abundance of diverse commentary, analyses of Wolfe's writings are usually superficial or incomplete. Unfortunately, few scholarly investigations specifically deal with Tom Wolfe. Apparently no rhetorical scholar, for example, has researched the area. And while essays by Thomas Edwards, Rick Rogoway, and Ronald Weber are occasionally insightful, they are not totally illuminating. A notable figure in American journalism has yet to be systematically studied.

This essay focuses on Wolfe the stylist. The thesis is that Wolfe's message represents an oral, electronic rhetoric expressing itself, paradoxically, via the printed page. Primarily it is Wolfe's stylistic techniques that enable him to achieve this unique posture wherein form triumphs over content and the medium-transcends-message sermon of Marshall McLuhan becomes the speaker's guiding doctrine.

From *Communication Monographs* 46 (March 1979). © 1979 by the National Communication Association.

The style, of course, befits the times. To an electronic, media-bred audience, having learned always to expect, if not crave, excitement, Wolfe is an appealing rhetorical experience. His irreverently dazzling, rapid-flow, non-linear prose seems most akin to television and the television-created mentality. David Culbert, for one, agrees:

> The New Journalism is primarily an attempt to apply the techniques of a visual medium to the printed page. Marshall McLuhan's famous dictum about the medium being the message can also refer to New Journalism's idea of massaging, or engaging the reader's attention, by giving the feel of an event instead of simply reporting what has happened. It is hardly necessary to argue that since television inspired the New Journalism it is therefore better, but it is surprising that so few practitioners of the New Journalism have recognized the obvious source of their inspiration. The ubiquity of television along with ritualistic pronouncements about its pervasiveness in American life have apparently obscured the relation between the new nonfiction and good old television.

Culbert, who proceeds to draw certain parallels New Journalism shares with television news and talk shows, says, "The host is what the New Journalist wants to be." In the end,

> The New Journalist really wants to be seen in print—to be a television celebrity, or at least a visible reporter. Since he cannot be literally seen in print he does the next best thing: he injects part of a carefully-constructed persona into his stories so that the reader is tempted to believe he can see the reporter who has written the story.

The style consciousness of Wolfe, or any New Journalist for that matter, stems from this desire to be a television personality. As in television, a non-linear rhetoric emerges, the hallmarks of which are its *excitement, immediacy*, and *credibility*. Perhaps to the extent that television is popular with the reader, Wolfe's television-similar style is popular.

In pursuing this line of argument, I shall offer (1) an analysis of the four stylistic devices central to New Journalism generally, (2) a survey of those stylistic tokens more peculiar to Wolfe, and finally, (3) some conclusions concerning the future of Wolfe and his new journalist/rhetorical mode. The analysis draws its supporting data in particular from *The Kandy-Kolored*

Tangerine-Flake Streamline Baby, The Electric Kool-Aid Acid Test, The Pump House Gang, and *Radical Chic and Mau-Mauing the Flak Catchers*—four of Wolfe's more popular and better known works. Presented is a consideration of how the stylistic components of Wolfe's symbolic expression coalesce to create an oral, "televisionic" journalism.

I

Wolfe maintains that four stylistic devices are common to all New Journalism writing: third-person point of view, scene-by-scene construction, extensive dialogue, and recording of status-life symbols.

Third-person point of view is the stylistic device most prominently associated with New Journalism. Proffering numerous perspectives—not just the author's, as in most previous nonfiction writing—third-person point of view, says Wolfe, is "the technique of presenting every scene to the reader through the eyes of a particular character, giving the reader the feeling of being inside the character's mind and experiencing the emotional reality of the scene as he experiences it." Third-person as contrasted to first-person point of view, at the very least, possesses the *texture* of objectivity because it portrays the perspectives of all the story's central characters. The author appears as but a disinterested scribe who reports and posits with the reader the whole of any reality. The data buttressing this reality are gathered by careful scrutiny of one's stimulus field, the writer sensitive to even the slightest character nuance that might express viewpoint. Hence the "evidence" from which the reader forms judgments is supplied by the depicted behavior of the story characters. This reliance on primary source materials—the thoughts, words, and actions of the subjects themselves—functions rhetorically to further augment the perceived authenticity of the document.

The rhetorical potential of third-person point of view extends beyond the capacity to establish and maintain story believability. Part of its power approximates that of film and television where, says Edmund Carpenter, "distance and angle constantly shift. The same scene is shown in multiple perspective and focus. The viewer sees it from here, there, then over here; finally he is drawn inexorably into it, becomes part of it. He ceases to be a spectator." Similar to the television experience, the reader of third-person point of view becomes consumed by a fetching panorama of character that engulfs the sensibilities. Ultimately, the reader becomes part of the story, a silent but reactive character for whom critical distancing is suspended.

Scene-by-scene construction is "moving from scene to scene and resorting as little as possible to sheer historical narrative." Scene-by-scene construction perhaps is illustrated best in *EKAT*, the chronicling of novelist Ken Kesey's search for truth through experimentation with hallucinogenic drugs. The reader is joined with Kesey and his following, the Merry Pranksters, as they journey in quest of reality from city to city, adventure to adventure, prank to prank. With rapid-flow immediacy, events unfold; the reader suddenly there, seeing and hearing firsthand, listening to Kesey's vision, interacting with Kesey and the Pranksters, experiencing the soaring heights of their highs. As is true of television, the pervading sense of the present prevails; always there exists the feeling of everything happening *now*. Not surprisingly, Wolfe writes in the present tense; no historical distance, no detached perspective is permitted to evolve.

Usually because any narrator projects a measure of detachment—a voice that distills the actual experience from its interpretation—it becomes all too evident that the event described has been *re*-created. But in scene-by-scene construction no literary liaison severs source and receiver; rather the reader is transported to an action that speaks for itself. The effect corresponds to that of third-person point of view—the reader absorbed in the story's sequential development. One reads, unmindful of any author . . . a story without a storyteller.

Extensive dialogue adds to the realism of New Journalism. It is not especially original to note that dialogue possesses an aura of believability with characters assuming a certain concreteness because their existence is "tangibly" demonstrated. The mere presence of their speech—a normal, human endeavor—is a constant reminder that the characters are plausible and human.

This genuineness of character encourages and fosters audience-character intimacy. "Add more dialogue" frequently reads the advice to beginning writers by experienced editors who have long since recognized dialogue's engrossing appeal. The enveloping power of television derives in part from the simple fact that it presents almost all dialogue. Similarly, the characters about whom Wolfe writes can be "heard," and because they are personified by their own words they are viewed with less suspicion than if they were presented by narrative description. Seemingly, the New Journalist but delivers to his audience the data to judge for themselves.

Recording status-life symbols involves observing all the ways people communicate. It includes noting

> everyday gestures, habits, manners, customs, styles of furniture, clothing, decoration, styles of traveling, eating, keeping house, modes of behaving toward children, servants, superiors, inferiors, peers, plus the various looks, glances, poses, styles of walking and other symbolic details that might exist within a scene.

These status-life symbols, Wolfe believes, render any story more realistic because they are cues to how people live and how they want to live. Even the furnishings of Hugh Hefner's Chicago mansion, for example, are noteworthy because they symbolize Hefner's persona.

The connotative richness of Wolfe's status-life symbols results from the author's descriptive reliance on popular proper nouns, nouns instantly recognized and appreciated: "The grape workers were all in work clothes, Levi's, chinos, Sears balloon-seat twills, K-Mart sports shirts, and so forth." The use of name brands here invokes a wealthier field of associations than is possible by generic description alone. Wrought is a cultural identification, a reader lodged in familiar surroundings.

Television offers a parallel experience. The popular signposts provided its audience—the correlates to the comforting proper noun—are familiar values and accepted ideology. Laden with these consubstantial appeals, television, like popular culture generally, mirrors its audience's preconceptions of reality. The security—one's bearings so to speak— emanates from experiencing the pervasive reflection (and, so consequently reasoned: the validity) of one's world view.

The four stylistic devices thus discussed combine to produce an exciting, immediate, but still credible "televisionic" journalism—the New Journalism. And yet these devices represent only part of Wolfe's rhetorical appeal. Additional stylistic actions afforded by New Journalism but more peculiar to Wolfe need be surveyed.

II
Punctuation and Typography

The desire to secure an audience prompts Wolfe's innovative use of punctuation and typography. Once a feature writer for the New York *Tribune's New York* magazine, Wolfe had encountered the usual problem. "They [Sunday supplements] were brain candy, that was all. Readers felt no guilt whatsoever about laying them aside, throwing them away or not looking at them at all." Wolfe experimented with styles that would excite the audience enough to read on. Fortunately, because "Sunday supplements had no traditions, no pretensions, no promises to live up to, not even any rules to speak of," Wolfe could attempt just about anything. "I never felt the slightest hesitation about trying any device that might conceivably grab the reader a few seconds longer. I tried to yell right in his ear: *Stick around!*"

Apparently they did. Wolfe quickly became a celebrity. By 1965, *Newsweek* concluded that Wolfe was "one of the most stylized, imaginative, discussed, and sought-after magazine writers in the country," adding later that he had made "the biggest impact of any new journalist in years." Again and again, popular critics reacted first to Wolfe's flamboyant style, while budding, would-be Wolfes inundated magazine editors with their stylized imitations. Style, more than any other feature in his writing, became Wolfe's trademark.

Sometimes Wolfe toys with almost *no* punctuation as in his introductory paragraphs of "The Girl of the Year" and "The Noonday Underground":

> Bangs manes bouffants beehives Beatle caps butter faces brush-on lashes decal eyes puffy sweaters French thrust bras flailing leather blue jeans stretch pants stretch jeans honeydew bottoms eclair shanks elf boots ballerinas Knight slippers, hundreds of them, these flaming little buds, bobbing and screaming, rocketing around inside the Academy of Music Theater underneath that vast old mouldering cherub dome up there—aren't they supermarvelous!

> Just keep straight. Keep your desk straight, keep your Biros straight, keep your paper clips straight, keep your Scotch tape straight keep your nose straight keep your eyes straight keep your tie on straight keep your head on straight keep your wife on straight keep your life on straight and that is Leicester Square out there and that is a straight square and this is a straight office, making straight money—hey!—

The eye-catching absence of punctuation in these passages solicits the reader's attention while simultaneously stimulating curiosity. The inability to make complete sense of Wolfe's unpunctuated ramblings forces one to read on to learn what Wolfe means by it all. The absence of punctuation, moreover, sets the appropriate scene and story mood. Run-on adjectives and phrases, for example, indicate a whole that cannot be severed or compartmentalized. "Bangs manes bouffants beehives Beatle caps butter faces brush-on lashes" depict a single, unified impression. Too, the "keep straight" passage speaks to one dominating idea: these office boys/girls are asked to be "straight," cautious and carefully upstanding; everything demanded of them merges into that singular thought. By not parting the passage into several sentences, Wolfe effectively accentuates its unity. Similarly, in describing the acid trips of Ken Kesey and the Merry Pranksters, Wolfe captures the state of hallucinatory stream of consciousness by using a minimum of "stopping" punctuation—leaving, for example, periods off sentences. The style enables the reader to experience the *flow* of hallucination, wherein all stimuli fuse and nothing is discrete, nothing is finite. The sensory awareness and sensory bombardment of the hallucinatory experience thus are rhetorically approximated.

Wolfe sometimes invents his own punctuation. The use of multiple colon (:::::), for instance, serves to emphasize certain words and phrases, as illustrated in Wolfe's description of a Merry Prankster's paranoic hallucination:

> As his insomnia got worse, he started having more fragmented vision and finally . . . he looks at the wild-painted bus and the lurid chaos of the swirls changes into . . . the tunnel! A tunnel they had gone through, a long tunnel, in which he had been possessed by instense claustrophobia and the paranoid certainty that they would never emerge from the tunnel, and now the tunnel appears on the side of the bus in horrifying detail. He turns away . . . there is the cool limelit bower, cathedral in the redwoods, serenity . . . he turns back to the bus slowly ::::::: It is still there! The tunnel! ::::: The bus :::::: Now painted as if by a master, a very Titian :::: An Hieronymus Bosch :::: A Matthias Grünewald :::: With the most horrifying scenes of my life.

Wolfe finds that he can even key words typographically. More importantly, Wolfe sometimes utilizes typography as a symbolic argument to reflect the essence of his thesis. This occurs in Wolfe's essay on McLuhan wherein he fittingly plays with his medium and experiments with linear form.

> What if he's right What . . . if . . . he . . . is . . . right W-h-a-t i-f- h-e i-s r-i-g-h-t
>
> | | R | | |
> |---|---|---|---|
> | W | | I | |
> | H | IF | G | ? |
> | A | HE | H | |
> | T | IS | T | |

Or a slightly different example—Wolfe paraphrasing McLuhan's address before the General Electric Company:

> Light is a self-contained communications system in which the medium is the message. *Just think that over for a moment—I-am-willing-to*-be [patient]—When IBM discovered that it was not in

the business of making office equipment or business machines—

> - - - - - - - but that it was in the business
> of processing
> information,
> then it began
> to navigate
> with
> clear
> vision.
> Yes.

Conventional items—italics, exclamation points, ellipses—help give Wolfe's writings another measure of realism. Wolfe, himself, recognizes their rhetorical value.

> I found that things like exclamation points, italics, and abrupt shifts (dashes) and syncopations (dots) helped to give the illusion not only of a person talking but of a person thinking. I used to enjoy using dots where they would be least expected, not at the end of a sentence but in the middle, creating the effect . . . of a skipped beat. It seemed to me the mind reacted—*first!* . . . in dots, dashes, and exclamation points, then rationalized, drew up a brief, with periods.

Although the punctuation and typography of Wolfe's later articles are more tempered, inventiveness is not forsaken completely. Wolfe still occasionally experiments, employing unique stylistic devices as rhetorical props for securing audience attention, and for suggesting emphasis, mood, and thought.

Language and Syntax

When Wolfe is not experimenting with form or trying to be stylized, his language and syntax are typically light and casual, rarely hinting at self-consciousness. He says that he imagines himself composing a letter to a friend. Often his articles have the characteristics of personal correspondence: simple and spontaneous, much like a stream of consciousness. Note the conversation-like opening paragraph of the piece that christened Wolfe's rhetorical voice:

The first good look I had at customized cars was at an event called a "Teen Fair," held in Burbank, a suburb of Los Angeles beyond Hollywood. This was a wild place to be taking a look at art objects—eventually, I should say, you have to reach the conclusion that these customized cars *are* art objects, at least if you use the standards applied in a civilized society. But I will get to that in a moment. Anyway, about noon you drive up to a place that looks like an outdoor amusement park, and there are three serious-looking kids, like the cafeteria committee in high school, taking tickets, but the scene inside is quite mad. Inside, two things hit you. The first is a huge platform a good seven feet off the ground with a hull-gully band.

Frequently Wolfe ends a sentence with "or something" or "et cetera." Wolfe believes that "because that's the way people talk," such language is appropriate and particularly credible. Indeed, when used in speech, "or something" and "et cetera" may even serve as convenient forms of oral punctuation. But the more rhetorical potential of this open-ended language stems from its ambiguity, an ambiguity that not only heightens the reader's involvement by encouraging participation in constructing the message presented, but which extends the range of summonable symbolic responses. Wolfe can point the reader toward a general thematic direction without limiting the auditor-specific richness of the experience. One completes Wolfe's thought in a way that has maximum *personal meaning*.

Wolfe's use of metaphor further captures the oral style. Well attended because of its novelty, the metaphor draws its sustenance from the arousal of tension. The incongruity presented, I.A. Richards believes, confuses and strains the intellect; hence, "The mind will always try to find connections." This search for resolution, which becomes the gripping power of creative metaphor, is sacrificed somewhat in public address where the inherently transitory nature of speech constrains the quality of metaphor. Denied to the auditor is the luxury of "leisurely interpretation"; the rhetor must aim for an immediate feedback, using "metaphoric stimuli [which] seek to provide a ready, almost automatic, response." The rhetorical experience, thus, demands a simple metaphor.

Yet, because Wolfe writes the way people commonly speak, his metaphors possess many of the qualities found in those of public address. Casual, colloquial, and readily comprehensible, Wolfe's figures loom oral: "She had an incredible drunk smile that spread out soft and gooey like a can of Sherwin-Williams paint covering the world." Neither poetic nor elegant, Wolfe's metaphors speak to a plebeian mentality. And although appearing in a medium allowing for "leisurely interpretation," they are processed swiftly because the receiver, conditioned by Wolfe's oral-sounding prose, responds as a listening audience would. Wolfe's orality enables him to be seen and heard in print—to become nearly as real as the television personality.

The rapid production demands of speech also influence the use of modifying language. Because oral style precludes any serious linguistic deliberation, the oral adjective and adverb often perform a "repair" function: the inexact conversational noun and verb strengthened by after-the-thought modification. This holds true especially for the speaker who wishes to stress an argument or emphasize enthusiasm. The oral, animated Wolfe thus translates into essays that bow to adjectival/adverbial barrage, particularly to what Joseph DeVito calls "pseudo-quantifying" terms, such words as *many, several, very, great.*

> So one morning about eleven o'clock a flamboyant black man in a dashiki turns up at City Hall. . . . He comes marching up the stairs of City Hall and through those golden doors in his Somaliland dashiki, leading the children's army. And these kids are not marching in any kind of formation, either. They are swinging very free, with high spirits and good voices. The Dashiki Chief has distributed among them all the greatest grandest sweetest creamiest runniest and most luscious mess of All-American pop drinks, sweets, and fried food ever brought together in one place. . . .
>
> And it was here that Bill Jackson proved himself to be a brilliant man and a true artist, a rare artist, of the mau-mau. One of the few things that could stir every bureaucrat in City Hall . . . was just what Bill Jackson was doing now. Even an armed attack wouldn't have done so much. . . . [Because bureaucrats] have a secret: each, in his own way, is hooked into The Power. The Government is the Power, and they are the Government, and the symbol of the Government is the golden dome of City Hall, and the greatest glory of City Hall is the gold-and-marble lobby, gleaming and serene, cool and massive. . . . [S]uddenly here are these black ragamuffins! neither timorous nor bewildered! On the contrary—sportive, scornful, berserk, filling the air, the very sanctum, with farflung creamy wavy gravy, with their noise, their insolence, their pagan vulgarity and other shitfire and abuse! And no one can lay a hand on them!

The style, somewhat surprisingly, does more than emulate orality. With adjective and adverb, Wolfe transcends the constraints of his medium and captures what the television picture would portray instantaneously: the texture and tension of the situation, in this case the atmospheric temper of blacks "mau-mauing" (intimidating) whites. Maybe therein lies the function to which adjective and adverb naturally are suited: to suggest emotional setting—the ambience as opposed to the action sequences. The argument rejects conventional wisdom's assumption that adjective and adverb are inferior parts of speech to be used cautiously and with considerable constraint. In his brilliant discussion of "Some Rhetorical Aspects of Grammatical Categories," Richard Weaver refers to the adjective as "a word of secondary status and force," and cautions against the excessive use of adverb. But how valid is the counsel for a writer as highly skilled as Wolfe? Weaver may have conceded the answer when he links the overuse of adjective to "the inexperienced writer," and when he notes that "beginners should use [the adverb] least." Certainly, Wolfe is no beginner. A gifted artist, his work sustains the judgment that modifying language is capable of under-scoring situational "character." That is a significant demonstration and, admonishments to the contrary, should lead us to reconsider the function and status of adjective and adverb.

Organizational Structure

An outline of almost any Wolfe article reveals a rambling, disjointed structure, possessing at best only a faintly distinguishable pattern of organization. Some passages can be excused as elaboration, but others clearly are redundant. Continually, Wolfe retrieves and reamplifies. His style is to develop one idea partially, to move on to another and another; then, suddenly, to come back to the first idea, to reach again for the third, to embellish the second—as if Wolfe forever were plagued by afterthoughts, never quite willing to concede closure. An unstructured casualness dominates the posture, a nonlinearity which constitutes the very core of the oral tradition.

But at times Wolfe's style taxes the reader, particularly in articles involving chronologically arranged sequences. The order of events depicted in *EKAT*, as a prime example, confuses and disorients. Too much digressing and too many quick shifts in time and place deny spatial perspective. The problem, intrinsic to any nonlinear form, seems not to affect Wolfe's intelligibility nor his popularity—further substantiation that a "disorganized" rhetoric may not necessarily produce adverse communication effects.

Some would explain Wolfe's organization as one more example of a "new" art which rejects orderly structure and systematic development—an art wherein a work's total sensory impact, rather than any single element, is what matters. Susan Sontag maintains that the new art, as opposed to the old, intends to be experienced, not interpreted—to stimulate affectively, not cognitively. Wolfe seems to occupy an uncommon ground between new and old art: he experiences his subject first hand, yet he verbally interprets his consciousness; his organization does not conform exactly to standard notions of linearity, but the storyline proceeds deliberately. Perhaps Wolfe's writings represent a "third" art—a rhetoric falling between the new and the old, whose goal is to stimulate *both* affectively and cognitively.

III

Some critics of New Journalism contend that the form is dying, as evidenced by the "diminishing" fervor surrounding New Journalism. True, somewhat less experimentation than previously transpires, but the explanation is mostly a financial one. "In part," says Everette Dennis, "it might be suggested that a sagging national economy ha[s] taken its toll on the expanded newspaper story (with newsprint cutbacks) and on the experimental spirit of the more abundant 60s." Nevertheless, *the techniques* associated with the New Journalism are practiced pervasively, only now accompanied by less fanfare, less controversy. Admittedly, the New Journalism has not "wipe[d] out the novel as literature's main event," as Wolfe maintains, nor is it favored to outdistance the novel over a longer course. Still, the New Journalism represents more than a passing fancy; as a general movement towards greater reportorial freedom, it remains rooted and growing sturdier.

Certainly Wolfe's journalism will not be forgotten. Because of Wolfe and other New Journalists having shown the way, more innovative and imaginative reporting likely will prevail. Already, says James Murphy, "The hopeful signs of such a movement are apparent in some of the better newspaper journalism today. The influence, at least implicit, of the New Journalistic form is evident in an occasional story even in the daily press, the bastion of traditional journalism." Too, the excitement, creativity, and freedom demonstrated to journalism by Wolfe's rhetorical posture provides an enviable model for the young. Not surprisingly, interest in the college journalism major has soared in recent years. One cannot discount, of course, the fresh glamour given journalism by Watergate reporters, Bob Woodward and Carl Bernstein, or the importance of other factors as well; a case, though, surely can be made that Wolfe represents at least one contributing cause in the rising credibility of journalism and the state of the profession.

Finally, Wolfe's style of journalism testifies once more to the pervasiveness of television's potent influence, and its capacity to spawn such emulators as New Journalism—a non-linear, oral-sounding print that possesses the excitement, immediacy, and credibility so characteristic of television. A once staid, uninventive craft suddenly metamorphizes into a dynamic, challenging art. This New Journalism—this hybrid rhetoric—rejects the stylistic dogma of traditional reporting and serves up a new, complete offering. Informative, entertaining, and persuasive, *televisionic journalism* has arrived.

THOMAS L. HARTSHORNE

Tom Wolfe on the 1960's

When Tom Wolfe emerged into literary prominence in the mid-1960's with the publication of his first book, *The Kandy-Kolored Tangerine-Flake Streamline Baby*, he aroused a great deal of comment, pro and con. Almost immediately, he became the acknowledged leader of a movement that came to be known as The New Journalism and aroused even more comment than Wolfe himself. Many were delighted by the freshness of Wolfe's style and approach. Others, while acknowledging that his style was indeed new and unusual, not to say eccentric, took him to task for dealing with subjects they found somewhat trivial in a manner that did little or nothing to explain why he found them significant enough to write about. Dwight MacDonald saw him as a preeminent example of *kitsch*, that cancer rotting the very foundations of Western civilization, which MacDonald at the time had the United States franchise for defending (before John Simon took it over). Wolfe's next two books, *The Pump House Gang* and *The Electric Kool-Aid Acid Test*, published on the same day, aroused exactly the same sort of critical comment. Once again, many found Wolfe's descriptions of modern manners and mores fresh, exciting, and informative, while others found them overwritten and a waste of time. But whether critics liked what Wolfe was doing or not, they saw in his writing a vivid example of something new. They took him as a representative of the switched-on, rebellious, anti-traditional culture of the 1960's.

From *Midwest Quarterly: A Journal of Contemporary Thought* 23, no. 2 (Winter 1982). © 1982 by Pittsburg State University.

Wolfe himself did all he could to foster this impression. For instance, in describing the new journalism as a deliberate and conscious (if unplanned and unconcerted) rebellion on the part of several young journalists against the stuffy, limiting, boring conventions of traditional journalism, he seemed to be issuing a manifesto, a call to the barricades. And there was his choice of subject matter: custom cars, stock car racing, demolition derbies, "the teen-age netherworld," the psychedelic movement, topless night clubs, and so on. What could better express the general exaltation of popular culture and the corresponding contempt for or indifference to the stodginess of traditional culture that was so much a part of the decade? One can see in Tom Wolfe the taste for inwardness and subjectivity that was so important a part of the "new" culture of the 1960's in the attempts of the new journalists to penetrate "objective reality" to get at the deeper truth that might lie hidden behind it, to probe beneath surface appearances to discover and report on the thoughts and emotions of those they were writing about. And one can see evidences of what critics like Richard Poirier and Tony Tanner have pointed to as characteristic features of the modern sensibility in literature: the deliberate intrusion of the author into what he writes, calling attention to his presence, and making his readers aware of his writing as a performance. While Wolfe has said that the new journalism is a substitute for the novel of social realism which contemporary writers have abandoned in favor of myth, fable, and so forth, his own style reminds one more of the performances of the recent fabulists than the sober reportage of the Victorian novel. We may be fairly sure that Wolfe is not simply making it up as he goes along, but he often appears to be doing just that, and there is an improvisational quality to his writing that puts him in tune with the sensibility of the 1960's in its emphasis on the importance of immediate inspiration.

But Wolfe's position as a prophet of the new wave was undermined when he published "Radical Chic," an account of a fund-raising gathering for the Black Panthers held in Leonard Bernstein's New York apartment. Reviewers of left-wing sympathies were outraged, while those of right-wing sympathies were delighted. In fact, *The National Review* found room to praise the book not once, but twice. While neither reviewer went so far as to claim that Wolfe was a conservative, both saying or implying that he was essentially apolitical, approval from such a quarter could hardly fail to compromise his standing as a spokesman for rebellion.

It was compromised still further a few years later when he published *Mauve Gloves and Madmen, Clutter and Vine*. It now became apparent that Wolfe was far more of a traditionalist than his dandyfied pose and his switched-on style had led people to believe. In reviews, Gerard Reedy called him "an old-fashioned moralist," and Chilton Williamson, Jr. compared him

to Mencken because of his "superimposition of 'stylistic radicalism' upon fundamentally conservative opinions." Certainly the attitudes Wolfe displayed in this book were both moralistic and old-fashioned. There can be little doubt that he was contemptuous of the rampant vanity masquerading as self-improvement in "The Me Decade," that he found the left-wing intelligentsia who predicted the iminent triumph of fascism in America as ridiculous and possibly even dangerous, that he believed that many members of the New Left were simply playacting, and that he re- garded the prevalent obsession with obtaining the modern equivalent of salvation through a multitude of guilty-free orgasms as not very edifying if not downright disgusting. Even those unable to penetrate the flashy surface of his prose—and one of the standard criticisms of him throughout his career had been that he never took sides and one never knew where he stood—should have gotten a clue from one of his drawings: a picture of four pigs in mid-orgy captioned "Swingers Ascending to Heaven Through Group Sex." It might not be quite as blunt as *A Modest Proposal*, but it hardly qualifies as a model of subtlety either.

But what became obvious with *Mauve Gloves and Madmen, Clutter and Vine* had not been obvious earlier. Yet "the old-fashioned moralist" of the 1970's had been there all along. Granted that he wrote about subjects in ways no one had used before (outside of comic books). Granted that he expanded and extended the realm of the magazine essay in both subject matter and style. Still, beneath the Day-Glo surface, beneath the wild typography, the bizarre punctuation, and the groovy language one can find a highly traditional value system, even in the books of the 1960's which seemed at the time to be charting a radical new path toward the understanding of radical new phenomena, those books concerned with the "whole crazed obscure uproarious Mammon-faced drug-soaked mau-mau lust-oozing 60's in America. . . ."

Admittedly, it is often difficult to discover Wolfe's attitudes toward the people and events he describes. He almost never informs his readers about them directly; they must be deduced or inferred. And the process of inference is complicated by his habit of adopting points of view different from his own. One must be constantly aware of the possibility that Wolfe might not be speaking for himself at any particular point. Nevertheless, while he does not express his attitudes with absolute clarity, one can discover what they are by following certain rules of interpretation. First, one may be sure that when Wolfe is at his flashiest, when his prose seems to be coming straight from the pages of *Action Comics* and his punctuation from some typesetter's nightmare, that he is speaking for someone else. Conversely, when his style is relatively sober and straightforward, he is most likely to be speaking for himself. Second, one may discover a great deal by noting what Wolfe chooses to talk about and what to omit. His message comes as much from his choice of subject and scene as from anything he actually says.

Toward the end of his "Introduction" to *The Pump House Gang*, Wolfe first put down in print a story he was to repeat later, concerning his participation in a symposium with Gunter Grass, Allen Ginsberg, Gregory Markopoulos, and Paul Krassner in which the discussion centered on repression in America and the imminence of fascism. At one point he said, incredulous, "What are you talking about? We're in the midst of a . . . Happiness Explosion." According to this account, his remark was simply dismissed, although in a later account of the same incident he implies that Grass agreed with him in part and that some of the students in the audience were honestly puzzled by what they were hearing because, while they believed it when such eminent people told them that America was a repressive, depressing society, they had not come into contact with that feature of American life. One student wondered out loud when he, too, was going to grow up and awaken to a consciousness of how terrible things really were here. It is easy and perhaps natural to interpret this to mean that Wolfe was highly impatient with those who saw the impending triumph of fascism— as he was—and also that he was the defender of all those taking part in the Happiness Explosion—which he was not, at least not completely.

Throughout his career, Wolfe's central concern has been status, how it is defined, established, differentiated, and enforced, how people react to status clashes and anxieties, and how various subcultures erect alternative status systems to those prevailing in the dominant culture or in other subcultures. Jack Newfield has said that Wolfe's "basic interest is the flow of fashion, in the tics and trinkets of the rich," but Wolfe is perhaps even more interested in those lower-class subcultures that have emerged since the end of World War II, whose members have become prosperous enough to indulge their fantasies, express their desires, and build and live in a subculture of their own choice and design, in the process achieving enough visibility to worry, shock, and even outrage representatives of the dominant culture. Often Wolfe describes the outrage of the arteriosclerotic, black-shoed, workadaddy defenders of convention (to say nothing of their physical appearance) with such glee that he seems to be on the side of those causing it. But Wolfe is not always favorably disposed toward this popular assault. The new status systems that are at the heart of the Happiness Explosion often prove to be as rigid, as ridiculous, and as cruel as the older ones. Further, the proliferation of such systems results in social chaos, and this, in turn, produces uncertainty and anguish. "People are now reaching the top without quite knowing what on earth they have reached the top of. They don't know whether they have reached *The* Top or whether they have just had a wonderful fast ride up the service elevator." Thus, Wolfe is not necessarily defending the emergence of "prole" culture as an alternative to the stodgy conventions of the dominant culture. Rather, he is attacking all those who attempt to dictate taste and value for others, those who become slaves to status patterns created by others in the hope of establishing their own status thereby, and social climbers who know the ropes and are trying to heave themselves up by them however they can manage it. And he finds these things distasteful whether they occur among the rich, middle class, or the proles.

Thus, in his piece on Hugh Hefner, he describes the pre-eminent example of a man who has succeeded in creating his own status sphere. From Wolfe's account, it is obvious that Hefner is very, very pleased with himself and what he has accomplished. In his own terms, he definitely has it made. But how about Wolfe's terms? At one point, Wolfe compares Hefner to Jay Gatsby, but it is glaringly apparent that Hefner has none of Gatsby's tragic grandeur. Instead, he is a shallow kid, inordinately pleased with the array of gadgets he uses to insulate himself from the world outside his mansion. While he, unlike Gatsby, has succeeded in his quest, one might well ask the same question one asks about Gatsby: Is the prize really worth having? In addition, having dropped out of the conventional status race so that he does not have to try to live up to rules dictated by someone else, Hefner has himself become a powerful dictator of status rules through his magazine. Having achieved a successful rebellion, he has become the source of a new status establishment.

And who, if not Hefner, has a better claim to be called the High Priest of the Happiness Explosion? And if it is indeed Hefner, or someone like him, who presides over this elaboration of status spheres and this proliferation of life styles, is it really accurate to say that the Happiness Explosion leads to happiness? I do not think Wolfe believes that it does. Consider, for example, his various descriptions of the largest group to have established its own status rules during the prosperous years since 1945: the young. As the putative prophet of what is new and Happening Now, one would expect Wolfe to be a partisan of the young and their life styles. But he is not. In his portrait of "The Pump House Gang," he depicts the surfer culture of southern California as characterized by callous irresponsibility and a deliberately cultivated inability to see beyond the immediate moment. "The Noonday Underground" is the British equivalent of The Pump House Gang, not quite as callous, perhaps, but equally hung up on small nuances of status, equally empty and irresponsible, equally devoid of any sense of or concern for the future, and equally meaningless and desperate. And in "The Life and Hard Times of a Teenage London Society Girl," Wolfe combines several of his favorite themes: the ridiculousness and cruelty of the status system of fashionable society, the mindless conformity of teenage culture, and the shallowness of the people caught up in that culture. Finally, in "Putting Daddy On," he confronts the cultural and generational gap of the 1960's directly. In many ways, the protagonist, Parker, is one of Wolfe's typical targets, a New York City advertising man, deeply involved in the status games that go with such an occupation. On the other hand, he is sincerely concerned about his son, Ben, who has dropped out of Columbia University and gone to live the hippie life on the Lower East Side. Deeply disturbed by the way he sees Ben living, Parker is unable to communicate with him effectively. And Ben thwarts whatever efforts Parker does make in what seems to be a deliberate fashion. If Parker's understanding of Ben is limited, Ben apparently has none at all for his father. In fact, he comes off as an inarticulate, unfeeling clod who does nothing to stop his friends from cruelly putting his father on and adding to his obvious distress. Parker, wrong though he may be in some ways, cares about his son in a way his son quite obviously does not care about him. In this confrontation between the generations, the older looks much better than the younger, showing concern and compassion totally lacking in the young.

If the young themselves do not always come off very well in Wolfe's descriptions, neither do the various hangers-on of what he calls the teenage netherworld. The disc jockey, Murray the K., seems to be an amoral con man with a genius for self-promotion based at least partly on the constant public repetition of hip jargon in a meaningless cascade of words. Phil Spector, the song-writer and record producer, is introduced to us in the throes of a childish, neurotic panic about flying, and we subsequently learn that he is a whole bundle of neuroses, paranoid, depressive, aggressive, obsessive about his status. His redeeming qualities are that he genuinely likes the music he is involved with (he is not cynically exploiting a fad for money), he is genuinely good at writing and/or producing hit records, and the people arrayed against him in the record business or in their dislike for rock and roll are often less palatable human beings than he is. And we first see the wealthy young New York socialite, Baby Jane Holzer, at a Rolling Stones' concert where she seems to be desperately concerned with demonstrating to everyone in the audience that she knows the Rolling Stones personally. She is completely a creation of the press in its attempt to keep up with the latest trends, fads, fashions, and fancies, with no discernible talent except for being a celebrity. (She is a perfect example of Daniel Boorstin's definition of a celebrity as someone who is well-known for his well-knownness.) And to cap it all she is deadly serious about being a celebrity and seems to regard it as somehow vitally important.

Another of the groups toward which Wolfe is often supposed to be favorably disposed in his contempt for conventional society and those pathetic denizens of the middle class who are striving desperately to be accepted into it, are those "raw, vital proles" who, like the young, have suddenly acquired money and the capacity to pursue happiness on their own terms in the general prosperity of the post-World War II era. But here, as with the teen netherworld, the results are not always happy. Wolfe notes in "The Big League Complex" that ". . . New York is the status capital of the United States, if not the whole hulking world. . . ." and that this fact ". . . has curious effects on everyone who lives here. And by that I mean everyone, even people who are not in the game." He proceeds to detail instances of deliberate and unnecessary cruelty perpetrated by such raw, vital prole types as men's room attendants, door men, and cab drivers in their effort to establish that they are indeed part of a big league town. In "O Rotten Gotham—Sliding Down into the Behavioral Sink," he extends this description of what a terrible place New York can be, how it produces anti-social behavior, and how much of this behavior is, again, perpetrated by proles. In "Clean Fun at Riverhead," he compares demolition derbies to gladiatorial combats, describes the spectators as a bloodthirsty mob and the drivers as inarticulate louts who enter the "races" not for money or even fame but simply for the sheer aggressive joy of bashing someone else's car. His description of an accident at a motorcycle race in *The Pump House Gang* ought to convince anyone that he has reservations about motor racing and especially about the sort of people who go to such races, craving destruction and the privilege of being witnesses to it. The capital of prole culture in the United States is Las Vegas, built by and for ". . . the first uneducated, prole-petty-burgher Americans to have enough money to build a monument to their style of life." And, of course, Las Vegas is pure nightmare, not only producing psychosis, but constituting a form of psychosis in itself.

Many of Wolfe's attitudes toward the cultural changes of the 1960's come together in *The Electric Kool-Aid Acid Test*, his account of the career of the novelist Ken Kesey and his band of Merry Pranksters and their role in the creation of the psychedelic movement and the counter culture. The book seems to be an allegory of the 1960's, an account of promise gone sour, of power failing, of fantasy coming into conflict with and being crushed by reality, of the dominant culture's stubborn, unimaginative, but ultimately effective resistance to change. The Kesey that emerges from Wolfe's pages is a figure of enormous charisma, but charisma alone proves to be an inadequate foundation for the movement he hopes to build, and his message becomes distorted and perverted so that the drug experience is transformed from a kind of sacrament, an intrepid experiment with the limits of self and perception, into a simple means of escape, the flower childrens' equivalent of the older generation's booze. In the end, the Prankster saga fades away into anti-climax, and the moral of the story is contained in the phrase "We blew it," repeated over and over and over again. *The Electric Kool-Aid Acid Test* is unmistakably a chronicle of failure and of the transient nature of the fads and leaders of the 1960's. It seems designed to show precisely that the search for new, alternative life styles which has been stimulated by the Happiness Explosion can and does lead to unforeseen and often unpleasant consequences.

Thus, Wolfe has reservations about the Happiness Explosion and is less than favorably disposed toward those people who allow a concern for status to control or even substantially influence their behavior. What does he admire? He takes obvious delight in those who rebel against conventional status patterns. He also respects people who are skilled at their chosen craft. Most of all, he admires those who are good at what they do precisely because they are so thoroughly wrapped up in it that they are totally indifferent to status and cannot be bothered to worry about what other people might think. At one point, Wolfe compares modern society with the society Louis XIV created at Versailles noting that in both one can often find a separation between real power and what he calls "grandeur." In much of what he writes, especially in writing about Society (with a capital "S"), Wolfe's subjects are those people concerned with grandeur. But sometimes he concerns himself with those who, on whatever level of society, actually do things besides trying to present their most fashionable face to the world. And it is the people who do the work, whatever it is, that he respects.

We find a specific example of this in his piece on the art collectors, Robert and Ethel Scull. In many ways the Sculls fit squarely into the Society art world Wolfe described devastatingly in *The Painted Word* and in other pieces like "The Saturday Route" and "The New Art Gallery Society," that world in which gallery-going "bears approximately the same relation to Art as churchgoing currently bears to the Church." They also fit the textbook definitions of social climbers, a type Wolfe generally despises. At the same time, however, Wolfe describes them as having retained a sense of where they came from despite their meteoric climb up the social ladder. And it is significant that, of all the Society figures Wolfe has dealt with, Bob Scull is one of the few he has actually shown at work, running his business, which, according to Wolfe, he does very well. Still, for all their good qualities, they are only partially redeemed, for they are deeply involved in the status game, and, in the end, pay the price for it, being stranded at 2:30 in the morning without transportation miles from nowhere, after a party they had given, deserted by both the *haute monde* and the artists.

One can also see a glimmer of respect in Wolfe's treatment of Huntington Hartford. He is not a successful self-made business man like Robert Scull, but rather the super-wealthy heir of hard-driving nineteenth century businessmen who has devoted his life and a large part of his enormous fortune to his twin obsessions of art and religion. He emerges from Wolfe's portrayal as a typical wealthy eccentric, naive and with all sorts of crotchets. But Wolfe treats him rather gently, laughing not at him so much as at the people who laugh at him because of his crusading temperament. For all his eccentricity, Hartford is redeemed by having the courage of his convictions; he is resolutely bucking the establishment in the pursuit of what he believes regardless of how the fashionable world my be reviling him or laughing at him.

Wolfe is charmed by Marshall McLuhan's academic unworldliness, and the consternation he spreads, unknowingly, through the business and literary worlds. Wolfe makes it eminently clear that all the conditions were ripe for McLuhan to become a celebrity. But he remains an ivory-tower innocent, thoroughly wrapped up in his theories, ignoring, not even aware of, the very real possibilities for money and fame. To be sure, Wolfe seems to have some large reservations about McLuhan's ideas. While he does compare McLuhan to Freud, the basis of the comparison is simply that both men provoked vigorous and indignant opposition among their contemporaries. Wolfe points out that McLuhan's oracular manner is often unnecessarily cryptic and even descends on occasion into simple unintelligibility. But for all his doubts about the worth of McLuhan's ideas, Wolfe still admires his character.

Much the same may be said of his attitude toward the men who design and build the fabulous signs that are the trademark of Las Vegas. Despite what one may suspect are some reservations about the quality of what these men produce—the signs, after all, are the most potent visual symbols of the culture Las Vegas represents—Wolfe clearly admires their lack of pretense and phoniness and the fact that they have not succumbed to the posing and posturing that often occurs in the traditional world of art.

The clearest example of Wolfe's admiration for the craftsman absorbed in his work is his essay on the custom car makers. When he pays tribute to George Barris and Ed Roth as artists his tongue is in his cheek, but only part way. For, again, while the product of the customizer's work is not a work of art in any traditional sense, the process they go through in creating the produce and, most importantly, their attitude toward their work are those traditionally ascribed to genuine artists: a devotion to the process of creation, close attention to the details of the task and the demands of craftsmanship, and contempt for or disinterest in monetary reward, commercial success and ordinary public opinion. Ed Roth does indeed play a public role, and in one sense thus caters to public opinion, but Wolfe tends to excuse him because he does it with flair and a sense of humor, making his pose into an obvious public put-on. George Barris, on the other hand, emerges from Wolfe's account as perfectly serious and completely dedicated, the perfect type of the committed artist concentrating on his work to the exclusion of everything else.

Combined with this respect for work, for what one might almost call the old Calvinist idea of a calling, one finds throughout Wolfe's work repeated expressions of respect for the traditional values associated with nature and with the family. Consider the following quotation. "The husband and wife who sacrifice their own ambitions and their material assets in order to provide a 'better future' for their children . . . the soldier who risks his life, or perhaps consciously sacrifices it, in battle . . . the man who devotes his life to some struggle for 'his people' that cannot possibly be won in his lifetime . . . people (or most of them) who buy insurance or leave wills . . . are people who conceive of themselves, however unconsciously, as part of a great biological stream. Just as something of their ancestors lives on in them, so will something of them live on in their children . . . or in their people, their race, their community—childless people, too, conduct their lives and try to arrange their postmortem affairs with concern for how the great stream is going to flow on. Most people . . . have seen themselves as inseparable from the great tide of chromosomes of which they are created and which they pass on. The mere fact that you were only going to be here a short time and would soon be dead did not give you the license to try to climb out of the stream and change the natural order of things." Here one can see some of the positive values Wolfe believes in: a sense of historical and natural continuity, a sense of being part of a larger group, family, community, or nation, the willingness to sacrifice for that group, a sense, in short, of belonging to something that goes beyond self and is worth striving to preserve.

Again, one can find hints of these attitudes in his early writing. In "Peppermint Lounge Revisited," for example, he writes about Marlene Klaire, one of the dancers at the nightclub, who first came there as one of the crowd of New Jersey teenagers "who had their transistors plugged into their skulls and were taking orders, simultaneously, from somebody like the Ring-leader Deejay." Marlene, however, becomes more than just another conformity-ridden teenager. Like many of Wolfe's other heroes, she is genuinely interested in and good at what she does. What especially redeems her in Wolfe's eyes is her dream of opening her own dance school, in her own home, so that she will be able to teach others the same way she was first taught. And she wants to move away from New York. "I don't like living here," Wolfe quotes her as saying. "There aren't any trees."

Marlene's respect for her craft and for nature stand in contrast to another dancer Wolfe writes about, Carol Doda, she of the silicone-inflated breasts. He is basically gentle with her, presenting her as a fundamentally nice girl who has gotten into something she cannot quite understand or control. He is somewhat harder on the topless culture she represents and hardest of all on the fad for silicone injections and the women who want them in order to "improve" themselves. "Why do people talk about 'the natural order'? Such an old European idea—one means, well, the *wheel* violated the natural order for God's sake; hot and cold running water violated it; wall ovens, spice bars, Reddi-Tap keg beer and Diz-Poz-Alls fracture the natural order—what are a few cubic centimeters of silicone?" To Wolfe, those few cubic centimeters of silicone, in addition to the fact that they may be carcinogenic, *do* fracture the natural order with considerably less justification than the wheel, hot and cold running water, or perhaps even Diz-Poz-Alls. Carol Doda finally emerges from Wolfe's account of her as a nice enough girl, perhaps, but one who falsified herself in order to succeed and is now justly paying a price for it.

Of all Wolfe's heroes, the one who succeeds in embodying most of the traits Wolfe admires is Junior Johnson, the stock-car racer. Once again, one may suspect that Wolfe is not especially impressed with what Johnson does, but there can be no doubt that he is very impressed with the way he does it, and with the sort of man that Johnson is. There is more to it than respect for physical courage and skill at one's job. For the test pilots and astronauts he describes in *The Right Stuff* also possess these qualities in abundance. But they are conspicuously lacking in modesty. Instead, they use their courage and their skills as counters in an elaborate status game. It is not sufficient simply to have the "right stuff." One must also contrive to make public demonstrations of the fact and win public acknowledgement of it. Of course, Johnson puts his courage on constant public display on the stock car circuit, but he does it simply to win races, not to enhance his status. While he is highly competitive, he seems blandly indifferent to most of the claims of fame and untouched and unruffled by commercial hype from the car manufacturers or the worshipful frenzy of his fans.

In addition, Johnson is a maverick, a representative of the rebellion of the proles against established status patterns. As we have seen, while Wolfe is often critical of anti-establishment rebels when they become prey to their thirst for status in their own sphere, he does admire those who have the guts, the gall, and the effrontery to buck the establishment. And Johnson certainly did that. He is a representative of a subculture looked at askance even in his native South; he is a rebel even against the establishment in his chosen field, NASCAR; and, as a long-time participant in the whisky business, he is a rebel against the law.

But there is more to it even than this. Contrast Johnson with another of Wolfe's protagonists, Ken Kesey. Kesey is a rebel, too, and a man of impressive psychic force. Wolfe clearly enjoys the consternation he and the Merry Pranksters caused in the "straight" world. At the same time, however, Wolfe portrays Kesey as a failure, and he locates at least some of the reasons for the failure in Kesey's own personality. For all his talk of freedom and equality, Kesey was definitely the leader, and he did not take kindly to challenges to his authority. Moreover, he is not, according to Wolfe's account, a particularly good husband and certainly not a faithful one. If he is a father in any but the purely biological sense we are never told of it. On the other hand, Johnson's devotion to the traditional ties of family and community are strong. He is engaged to his childhood sweetheart and is building a home for them on land he owns in the community where he was born. He became entangled with the law because of family loyalty, being caught by Treasury officers in a raid on his father's still where Junior, who had been out of the business of running illegal whisky for some time, was simply trying to help out with some of the heavy labor. At the end of his piece, Wolfe describes Johnson setting a new qualifying record for the Atlanta Dixie 400 in between visiting his father at the Atlanta Federal penitentiary and returning home to North Carolina to tend to some of his business responsibilities. The final paragraph, which Dwight MacDonald has referred to as Wolfe's "Pindaric ode" to Johnson, in which Johnson is portrayed as a mythological hero in a yellow Ford instead of on a white horse, is not really Wolfe's ode to Johnson at all, but a representation of the sort of hero worship Johnson receives from his fans. Indeed, to Wolfe it is a large part of Johnson's heroic statue that he has not succumbed to this high-pressure hero-worship but has remained a simple man, devoted to family and business responsibilities, regardless of the strong currents of mythology that swirl around him.

Throughout his career, Wolfe has lived and written mainly in New York City. Much of what he has written has been about New York City. And he has certainly done his very best to play the role of the sophisticated New Yorker. Yet behind the sophistication and the flashy clothes and the flashy language there is a southern boy from Richmond, Virginia. Wolfe's southern origins are important to an understanding of his work. It goes beyond respect for Junior Johnson, another southerner, to a respect for the values which Johnson, and presumably the South, embody. Southerners often feel outside of the mainstream of American life somehow, self-conscious about their origins, feeling that they must be lived up to or lived down. (How much of Lyndon Johnson's presidency, for example, might be explained in terms of his self-conscious southernness?) This makes them, perhaps, more than usually sensitive to questions of status. Having been on the receiving end of what appears to many southerners to be a collective sectional snubbing carried out over a long period of time, they tend to be rebellious, to feel themselves the victims of established status patterns and eager to strike out against them. Hence Wolfe's preoccupation with status and his respect for mavericks. But if there is rebellion, it is a rebellion based upon traditional values: respect for manliness in the most conventional sense, physical courage, skill at one's chosen craft, devotion to the task at hand, devotion to family ties and respect for family loyalties, concern with and respect for nature, respect for country and community. All of these one can find in Wolfe's writing. To be sure, he is often, perhaps even usually glib, sophisticated, and flashy. But sometimes, too, his style becomes sober, straightforward, thoughtful. It is precisely at those times when Wolfe is speaking most clearly for himself rather than articulating someone else's point of view. And it is at those points that one can see and understand most clearly precisely what it is that he values and respects most.

BARBARA LOUNSBERRY.

Tom Wolfe's Negative Vision

I t takes a great deal of elevation in thought to produce a very little elevation of life," Emerson observed in his journals. His wry comment acutely defines the dilemma of nonfiction writers seeking to endow their nonfiction subjects with universal import and appeal: how to transform the particular into the universal, the temporal into the eternal. Traditionally, writers have essayed a variety of techniques, from symbolism to historical and mythological analogy and allusion, to whole rhetorics of suggestive elevated diction, to achieve this end. James Agee, for example, employs Biblical allusion and religious and poetic diction to transform three Alabama tenant families into symbols of failed yet valiant humanity in *Let Us Now Praise Famous Men*. Truman Capote employs sequential narration and black and white imagery to transform his Kansas murder story into an archetypal confrontation between the dark and light sides of the American dream in *In Cold Blood*. Norman Mailer, through extended metaphors, historical allusion, and religious rhetoric makes his own rite of passage during the 1967 march on the Pentagon a model for the passage of the nation as a whole in *The Armies of the Night*.

The formula would seem simple: to increase the significance of a finite historical moment merely elevate the diction and imply, through analogy, allusion, imagery or structural counterpoint, the wider implication. Tom Wolfe, certainly an ambitious nonfiction writer in the tradition of Agee,

From *South Dakota Review* 20, no. 2 (Summer 1982). © 1982 by Barbara Lounsberry.

Capote, and Mailer, has used this formula with partial success. His brilliant coinage "radical chic," used to describe a specific 1970 Leonard Bernstein cocktail party to raise money for the Black Panthers, is now evoked to deflate any effort by the "haves" to assuage guilt by "slumming" with the "proles." Similarly, his characterization of Las Vegas as "the American Versailles" places that desert city in a new and elevated context.

Yet Wolfe adds a twist to his narrative technique eschewed by most of his predecessors and contemporaries. Not content to merely elevate his nonfiction subjects, he frequently undercuts them as well. As a result, readers are often confused as to his ultimate vision regarding his subjects: positive, negative, or somewhere on the edge in between? Such elaborate counterbalancings have indeed caused many readers to believe that Wolfe has no personal or social vision at all, that he is merely an apt imitator of any social rage—or outrage.

Wolfe's personal vision, however, can be defined. Readers simply have to explore the implications of a highly sophisticated narrative technique which bounces back and forth between elevation and damnation. Wolfe's most highly praised work, the 1968 *Electric Kool-Aid Acid Test*, offers a broad canvas for such exploration. *The Electric Kool-Aid Acid Test* is a chronicle of the new psychedelic wave's effort to capture the American consciousness in the mid-1960s. Readers should first note how Wolfe elevates his material, how he extends the basic history of Ken Kesey's life and hard times to one of broader historical implication, and then how he simultaneously wavers on the edge and undercuts his own vision.

Wolfe elevates the story of Kesey and the Merry Pranksters primarily by repeatedly equating it with the major movements in religious history. In Chapter III, after Kesey has just accused Gleason of having "no faith," Wolfe writes in his own voice:

> Faith! Further! And it is an exceedingly strange feeling to be sitting here in the Day-Glo, on poor abscessed Harriet Street, and realize suddenly that in this improbably ex-pie factory Warehouse garage I am in the midst of Tsong-Isha-pa and the sangha communion, Mani and the wan persecuted at The Gate, Zoroaster, Maidhyoimaongha and the five faithful before Vishtapu, Mohammed and Abu Bekr and the disciples amid the pharisaical Koreish of Mecca, Gautama and the brethren in the wilderness leaving the blood-and-kin families of their pasts for the one true family of the sangha inner circle—in short, true mystic brotherhood—only in poor old Formica polyethylene 1960s America without a grain of desert sand or a shred of palm

leaf or a morsel of manna wilderness breadfruit overhead, picking up vibrations from Ampex tapes and a juggled Williams Lok-Hed sledge hammer, hooking down mathematical lab drugs, LSD-25, IT-290, DMT, instead of soma water.

In later passages, the diction itself underscores the process of elevation. In Chapter XIV, titled significantly, "A Miracle in Seven Days," Wolfe states: "the Pranksters [. . . .] all had religion, all right. It was . . . like the whole Prankster thing was now building up some kind of conclusion, some . . . *ascension* [emphasis added]."

Many readers have noted this religious equation, but no one as yet has documented how carefully it is implanted in the text. Indeed the whole volume becomes a Christian typology with Kesey as Christ, Faye as Mary, Mountain Girl as Mary Magdalen, the Pranksters as the disciples, and Sandy (and Wolfe, as I will attempt to illustrate) as Judas.

While Kesey is depicted variously throughout the volume as Esau, when he has sold his birthright and is living in Mexico, as Moses, when he leads his "people" out of the Cow Palace before the "snap," and even as St. Paul, in his religious fit on the sands in Mexico, he is most frequently presented as a Christ figure. Wolfe increases Kesey's stature from the beginning by delaying his entrance until Chapter III, thus making him, like Christ, long awaited and greatly anticipated. Kesey looks "serene" upon his arrival and explains to Wolfe, "I think my value has been to help create the next step." Kesey then proceeds to speak in diction immediately suggestive of Christ's. "If you don't realize that I've been helping you with every fiber in my body," Kesey says, but "in a soft, far-off voice, with his eyes in the distance." "If you don't realize that everything I've done, everything I've gone through . . ." he says, breaking off, as if he were Jesus trying to make his disciples understand his mission. As the story continues, Wolfe explains that "Kesey took great pains not to make his role explicit. He wasn't the authority, somebody else was," and his teachings are all "cryptic, metaphorical: parables, aphorisms." At La Honda the Pranksters take all dissension to him, "all of them forever waiting for Kesey, circling around him," and at a moment of crisis, "Kesey materializes at the critical moment" and "delivers a line—usually something cryptic, allegorical, or merely descriptive, never a pronouncement or a judgment. [. . .] and just as suddenly he's gone." Indeed like Jesus, Kesey is the leader, provider, and protector of his "flock."

As Wolfe unfolds the Kesey saga, his diction continues the Christian typology. Kesey is taken as a prophet by the Unitarians and others. He absents himself in the desert and returns with a new "gospel." While he is absent, Wolfe quotes Hesse to the effect that: "Hardly had [he] left us, when faith and concord amongst us was at an end; it was as if the life-blood of our group flowed away from an invisible wound. [. . .] From that time, certainty and unity no longer existed in our community, although the great idea still kept us together." While in the desert, Wolfe asserts, "Sooner or later Kesey would reunite with the Pranksters," and when he does it is with the ultimate goal of presenting himself "in the flesh," delivering the "vision of the future," and then vanishing, ascending "into the California ozone." In the climactic scene in the garage, Kesey looks distraught when people can't get near him as they circle around him "through the darkness toward the cone of light lighting up [his] head and back."

If Kesey is thus Christ, Wolfe offers Faye to us as Mary. She is "Faye the eternal," "Faye, the eternal beatific pioneer wife," "one of the prettiest, most beatific-looking women I ever saw. [. . .] radiant, saintly," "practically a madonna of the hill country." Mountain Girl is also clearly Mary Magdalen. Wolfe avers that only Kesey "truly understood Mountain Girl [. . . .] it never occurred to anybody that a whole side of her was hidden. Except for Kesey." The Pranksters, of course, become the disciples, with Babbs the favored disciple, but others, like Hassler, preaching and offering "vesper service lecture[s]." The kool-aid LSD becomes the modern equivalent of the sacramental wine, and even the police are given a part in Wolfe's Biblical "movie." It is the role of Pontias Pilate of the Acid Tests: "Christ, man! It's too much for us even! We wash our hands of the ::::: Atrocity."

Wolfe thus elevates his story through religious analogy. He does it a second way by using a subtle rhetorical technique—that of repeatedly emphasizing the *inability* of words to communicate the significance of the experience. This technique has the effect of encouraging readers to indulge their most vivid imaginings. Wolfe uses this technique again and again in his effort to create in the reader some sense of the LSD experience. When Kesey first takes the drug in the California clinical experiments, and he can see *into* people, Wolfe writes, "how could you tell anybody about this?" Indeed earlier, back in Kesey's high school drive-in days there had been "The Life . . . but how could you tell anyone about it?" When Sandy takes LSD, Wolfe writes, "There is no way to describe how beautiful this discovery is," and when Claire speaks of the Watts test she says: "This closeness is impossible to describe. . . . There is no way to talk about that without sounding goopy." Ultimately it becomes for Wolfe "The Unspoken Thing," a spiritual religious phenomenon beyond words. There is "no metaphor, no conceit, that can be concocted in the English language that is enormous enough."

The meaning of the LSD experience is for Wolfe beyond the specific historical or journalistic plane. It is of higher, and more universal religious significance, and it can be seen, paradoxically, that one of the best ways to suggest this higher plane is to deny your ability to get there. Or as Wolfe says, "*If you label it* this, *then it can't be* that. . . . To put it into so many words, to define it, was to limit it.*" One can sense here Wolfe's own identification with the Prankster's difficulty in communicating an intensified sensory experience. This is his own dilemma as a writer: "how to tell it! How to get it across to the multitudes who have never had this experience themselves? *You couldn't put it into words*. You had to create conditions in which they would feel an approximation of *that feeling*."

Wolfe creates those "conditions" in three ways in his volume. The first is through his highly visual and energetic use of punctuation—dots, exclamation points, and imaginative stylistics of all kinds (:::::) to stimulate the experience. The second is through frequent use of substitutionary narration to describe the "Unspoken Thing" through the drug taker's persona. Wolfe achieves some remarkable effects through these two widely remarked techniques, and indeed it may be for this ability to imaginatively simulate others' consciousnesses that he will be remembered.

But Wolfe also creates conditions by which the inexperienced "multitude" (and reader) can "feel" the new LSD experience by employing metaphors which *bridge* the two perceptual states. These metaphors are electricity and transportation, and together they unite the disparate segments of the volume. Wolfe's basic point in *Acid Test* is that the LSD experience does not represent an entirely new element in American society. The turned-on, wired-up, electrified Superhero lifestyle of Kesey and the Pranksters is merely an *intensification* of what is already present, that is, of the "multitudes'" (the reader's) own lifestyle. This point is made from the opening paragraph in which Wolfe reports seeing "one after another, electric signs with neon martini glasses lit up on them, [. . .] thousands of neon-magenta martini glasses bouncing and streaming down the hill, and beneath them hundreds, thousands of people wheeling around to look at this freaking truck we're in." In short, neon signs and liquor stimulants are staples of postwar American life, as are energy-powered vehicles. They are the status quo. Kesey's father had been part of the "incredible postwar American electro-pastel surge into the suburbs!" and Kesey had grown up among the "soaring 35-foot Federal Sign and Signal Company electric supersculptures." He had seen drivers in Oregon running off the road, "chasing street lights! [. . .] cruising into neon glories of the new American night," and indeed his own developing religion had been influenced by these sights. A radio tower with the blinking red light of station KORE is located right behind Kesey's Oregon home: and at night he used to get down on his knees to say his prayers and there would be the sky and the light blinking—and he always kind of thought he was praying to that red light." The status quo, Wolfe thus provocatively reminds us, is

> a fantasy world *already*, this electro-pastel world of Mom&Dad&Buddy&Sis in the suburbs . . . *you're already there, in Fantasyland*, so why no move off your snug-harbor quilty-bed dead center and cut loose—go ahead and say it—Shazam!—juice it up to what it's already aching to be: 327,000 horsepower, [. . .] Edge City, and ultimate fantasies, current and future . . .

Wolfe's point is that the only thing Kesey and the Pranksters are "guilty" of, if that word applies, is of taking the neon horsepower world about them and *internalizing* it, of literally consuming the "rusky-dusky neon dust" (LSD) and then vibrating themselves, of making electric guitar extensions of their own bodies, and of being "on the bus" all the time. Babbs is described by Wolfe as having "American lightbulb eyeballs," and the Pranksters, "Babbs and Gretch and Page and others, take to the bandstand, all electrified, and [. . .] start beaming out." That there is something natural in this movement is suggested in Wolfe's parallels with electricity in nature. Kesey, describing his Paul-like conversion to the beyond acid philosophy, says:

> we had reached the end of something, we weren't going anywhere any longer, it was time for a new direction—and I went outside and there was an electrical storm, and there was lightning everywhere and I pointed to the sky and lightning flashed and all of a sudden I had a second skin, of lightning, electricity, like a suit of electricity, and I knew it was in us to be superheroes and that we could be superheroes or nothing.

Ultimately, in Wolfe's view, the Haight-Ashbury LSD lifestyle is simply "picking up on anything that works and moves, every hot wire, every tube, ray, volt, decibel, beam, floodlight and combustion of American flag-flying neon Day-Glo and winding it up to some mystical extreme carrying to the western-most edge of experience."

Electricity thus becomes a basic structural metaphor for Wolfe. Speaking from the Pranksters' viewpoint, he writes: "It's like we're strands of wire intertwined in a great cable that runs through a slot, the Pranksters, the Beatles, the Vietnam Day Committee." Similarly these are the "strands" of Wolfe's story which he is intertwining. But unlike the religious metaphors used solely in reference to Kesey and the Pranksters to elevate their story, electricity is a metaphor which both the Pranksters and the "multitudes," to differing degrees, share. It becomes, then, a metaphor which Wolfe can use to "flow" from one of his perceptual poles to the other. As in that remarkable opening paragraph, he can be, *almost simultaneously*, the Pranksters looking down at the bouncing martini-glassed-multitudes, or the multitudes looking back at the bouncing truck.

Wolfe makes his transportation metaphors work in the same way. Everyone in *Acid Test* is on some kind of literal or figurative "trip," and their means of transportation, like their shoes, are for Wolfe highly revelatory of their positions. As with electricity, the Pranksters' wired-up bus represents only a "Further" intensification of the current American status quo signified by "Mom&Dad&Buddy&Sis in their Ocelot Rabies 400 hardtop sedans" out on Route 84, or by "the family car, a white Pontiac Bonneville sedan—*the family car!*—a huge crazy god-awful-powerful fantasy creature to begin with." This is "America's tailfin civilization," "cruising in the neon glories of the new American night." Such vehicles are admirable neither to the Pranksters nor Wolfe. Similarly when the Vietnam protest rally is abandoned to a "*bunch of fraternity men in their Mustangs!*", Wolfe stresses that "there is no more scathing epithet imaginable." And when TV talk show host Frankie Randall looks "as if any moment he is going to tell a long story about something that happened to his El Dorado convertible in a parking lot in L.A.," we know what kind of "trip" *he's* on.

The position of the Hell's Angels as "outlaws of America," then, is revealed clearly in their deviant motorcycle transportation. It is perhaps for this reason alone that Kesey embraced them; they too were trying something new. As Wolfe states: "The Angels brought a lot of things into synch. Outlaws, by definition, were people who had moved off of dead center and were out in some kind of Edge City. [. . .] The Angels' trip was the motorcycle and the Pranksters' was LSD, but both were in an incredible entry into an orgasmic moment." For ultimately in Wolfe, no matter how many different kinds of transportation (motorcycles and Mustangs, panel trucks and buses), it is always reducible to a conflict between two forces: the new and the status quo, the bus and the American tailfin civilization, the cops and those trying to "cop" urinations, and the Pranksters "sticking one vast vibrating Day-Glo palm out at the straight world floating by comatose." The lines are always drawn, as Wolfe makes clear through another transportation metaphor, when Bill Graham reneges on Winterland, saying to Cassady, "I got off the subway in 1955, but you're still on it. We're in two different worlds. You're a hippie and I'm a square."

To continue the transportation metaphor, what Wolfe finds admirable in Kesey and the Pranksters is that, unlike the Hell's Angels with their private

cult or those similarly retreating into Eastern philosophies, they choose to
challenge the status quo on its own turf on its own terms:

> somehow they're going to try it right down the main highway,
> eight lanes wide, heron-neck arc lamps rising up as far as the eye
> can see, and they will broadcast on all frequencies, waving
> American flags, turning up the Day-Glo and the neon of 1960s
> electro-pastel America, wired up and amplified, 327,000
> horsepower, a fantasy bus in a science-fiction movie, welcoming
> all on board, no matter how unbelievably Truck Stop Low Rent
> or raunchy.

Indeed the Pranksters begin to feel their trip is a kind of crusade, a crusade
for which they are not unprepared. Bob Stone, for example, is the "Intrepid
Traveler," and Page Browning has a "thick Shellube pit voice." Furthermore
they have the "Gestalt driving" of that veteran "revved up" *On the Road*
traveler, Neil Cassady.

Most of all, in Wolfe's version of the story, Ken Kesey has a fitting
history to become "Superhighway Cosmo hero" and leader of the crusade.
His early life in Oregon poignantly foreshadows both the role he will play
in the saga and his ultimate catastrophe in respect to that highly ambivalent
symbol—the bus. Kesey's altruistic character is revealed from his youth
when he and his father would go out to see if they could help drivers
"draggle [themselves] out of the muck" after they'd "run off the bend." In
a work in which the road represents the course of America, this tableau is
significant. Kesey from the beginning seeks to help, to right things with the
American vision. This is underscored further in the high school incident at
Gregg's drive-in—itself certainly an emblematic site. Here, in what once
again becomes an allegory of the later LSD-status quo confrontation, Kesey
confronts a driver going "the wrong way, so nobody could move." In
Wolfe's narration of the incident, Kesey takes this as a "test," and sticks a
potato up the fellow's exhaust pipe causing his motor to conk out and Kesey
to face a judge. This, of course, is what Kesey later does to the stalled,
comatose, and inappropriately acting society. He "tootles" the multitudes,
or deflates the Vietnam rally. He ultimately wants to change the course of
the whole LSD movement, and ends up before the judge many times in the
process.

Kesey's major literal and figurative tool in his confrontation with
society is the bus, the rich and strangely ambivalent central symbol of the
volume. As the major transportation symbol, it is depicted by Wolfe in terms
which suggest its relationship to both the status quo and the Pranksters.

Through the Pranksters' sophisticated sound engineering, the wire-up bus becomes a receiving set and reflector for the American status quo:

> all the sounds of the true American that are screened out everywhere else, it all came amplified back inside the bus, while Hagen's camera picked up the faces, the faces in Phoenix, the cops, the service-station owners, the stragglers and the strugglers of America, all laboring in their movie, and it was all captured and kept, piling up, inside the bus.

Thus on one hand the bus broadcasts the American status quo to its fullest, and on the other, it becomes the literal embodiment of the new "wave" seeking to overcome the status quo.

The literal bus trip across America becomes a symbol of the coming of LSD to the nation. Wolfe's diction underscores this repeatedly. The bus (LSD), he writes, "was great for stirring up consternation and vague befuddling resentment among the citizens." "They were all over town on the bus [read "on LSD"], befuddling the communal brain." Thus Kesey's elliptical "You're either on the bus or off the bus" has literal as well as religio-mystical meaning: you're either on LSD or you're not; you're either part of "the experience" or you're not. And the boy in Boise who tries to run and jump on the bus becomes "like a preview—allegory of life!—of the multitudes who very shortly will want to get on the bus . . . themselves," for Kesey and the Pranksters have considerable success in their crusade. They move the Pump House gang from the beach to the parking lot and bring the Hell's Angels "on the bus." The Unitarian youths, representing the "student rebels in an age of mediocrity," are drawn around the bus, and several of their ministers, the "Young Turks," get "on the bus for good." Indeed at Paul Sawyer's Unitarian Church

> hundreds were swept up in *an experience*, which builds up like a dream typhoon, peace on the smooth liquid centrifugal whirling edge. In short, everybody in *The Movie*, on the bus, and it was beautiful . . . They were like . . . *on!* the Pranksters—now primed to draw the hundreds, the thousands, the millions into *the new experience*, and in the days ahead they came rushing in :::::

The bus is thus carefully elevated through Wolfe's diction from a literal 1939 International Harvester bus to the major metaphor and symbol for the whole psychedelic odyssey. What is surprising about Wolfe, however, as I have noted, is that he refuses to leave it there. It is as if Wolfe doesn't quite believe his own analogy of the Prankster saga to the great religious movements of history, and that despite his admiration for Ken Kesey, he still harbors doubts "out front" in passages of reflection, or as part of being light. Instead, however, of discussing his ambivalence or his doubts "out front" in passages of reflection, of as part of being the author in the middle of the action like Agee or Mailer, Wolfe instead plants all sorts of reservations regarding his religious figures and his major symbols *in the text*, with the result that he is simultaneously building up and undercutting his own chronicle.

This same magical bus, for example, has no brakes and frequently breaks down. Furthermore, conditions "on the bus" are not always euphoric. Jane Burton, for example, is nauseated practically the whole time, and she and Sandy have to get "off the bus" to get a square meal. Sleep, too, is "almost impossible" on the bus, and indeed Wolfe characterizes the bus as a "pressure cooker" and a "crucible."

Perhaps as a result, Wolfe's twentieth century new psychedelic religious journey is tarnished by "bad trips" and subtly planted reservations from start to finish. Some of the Hell's Angels, Wolfe tells us, "had terrible bummers—bummer was the Angels' term for a bad trip on LSD." A young Unitarian girl freaks out on her first LSD capsule and "starts wailing away," but fortunately the Pranksters are able to redeem her. Her "wails," however, foreshadow those of the "Who Cares Girl" who is not restored. In fact, Clair's rather positive account of the Watts "trip" is substantially undercut by the episode involving the "Who Cares Girl," and also by the minor detail that seven people were committed following this first big "test." Even, in fact, the manufacturers of LSD, the "Mad Chemist" and Owsley, undergo "bad trips" in the course of the volume—the Mad Chemist becoming "loose in the head, [. . .] his brains all run[ning] together like goo," and Owlsey, perhaps symbolically, ending up in a car wreck. Indeed the accident and mortality rate is high in *The Electric Kool-Aid Acid Test* with injuries to Julius and Mike Hagen, paralysis for Norman Hartweg, death at age thirty-two for Ron Boise, and, most ominously of all, for the "Gestalt driver," Neal Cassady, whose body is found, again symbolically, beside a railroad track.

These accumulating "bum trips" function as ominous counterpoint undercutting Wolfe's religious analogy, for he does not extend his analogy to depict the catastrophic sides (or side effects) of Christianity, Buddhism, or Taoism. In fact, Wolfe seems to harbor special reservations about LSD in respect to women and children. In three distinct but related moments in the saga, the validity of the LSD odyssey is called into question by reminders of women and their relationships with children. The first and most dramatic incident occurs on the symbolic bus trip when only Stark Naked, with somebody else's little boy in her arms is bouncing and vibrating.

And there, amid the peaceful Houston elms on Quenby Road, it dawned on them all that this woman—which one of us even knows her?—had completed her trip. She had gone with the flow. She had gone stark raving mad.

This harrowing mother and child portrait casts a pall over the whole "trip" for many readers, and it is picked up and subtly amplified in a later moment between Kesey and Mountain Girl. Here, in Wolfe' depiction, Mountain Girl's pregnancy takes precedence over her LSD involvements:

> Ever since Asilomar, Kesey has been deep into the religion thing. [. . .] on and on he talks to Mountain Girl out in the backhouse and very deep and far-out stuff it is too. Mountain Girl tries to concentrate, but the words swim like great waves of . . . The words swim by and she hears the sound but it is like her cerebral cortex is tuned out to the content of it. Her mind keeps rolling and spinning over another set of data, always the same. Like—the eternal desperate calculation. In short, Mountain Girl is pregnant.

Finally, at the "beyond acid" graduation, it is a child's crying in the midst of the "synch" and a woman's voice asking that something be done for it, that keep the final "synch" from materializing. Wolfe here appears to be subtly, perhaps even unconsciously, introducing personal doubts regarding the biological effect of LSD use upon future generations.

His reservations regarding the LSD movement are also conveyed through his extensive development of Sandy Lehman-Haupt's perspective. The most compelling conflict in this segmented volume is that between Kesey and Sandy, the only Prankster "on the bus" who ever extensively doubts or challenges Kesey. To return to the Christian typology, Sandy indeed represents Judas. He betrays Kesey by stealing the Ampex, "the guts of the Acid test," and through religious diction, Wolfe carefully places this theft in religious context:

> to the Pranksters there was not the slightest doubt in the world that the equipment was the Pranksters'. Not Prankster Sandy Lehmann-Haupt's but the Pranksters'. The Prankster family, the Prankster order, superseded all straight-world ties, contracts and chattel laws and who is my mother or my brethren? And he

looked round about on them which sat about him, and said,
Behold my mother and my brethren! For whosoever shall do the
will of God, the same is my brother, and my sister, and my
mother.

Sandy views the Ampex as the "Prankster salvation machine," and Kesey, like
Christ, has a foreboding of his betrayal.

Wolfe gives a great deal of attention and sympathy to Sandy's
perspective—his "bad trip on the bus" and his reservations regarding Kesey—
and this serves to create doubts in the reader's mind about Kesey's vision.
Indeed Wolfe's intensive identification with Sandy is relevant in respect to
the lack of development of his own narrative persona in *Acid Test*. Wolfe
seems to have elected Sandy to speak for him. Sandy's role in *The Electric
Kool-Aid Acid Test* is that of ambivalent straddler of the "sheerly Diluvial
divide." He is by turns "on the bus" and "off the bus," just as Wolfe is as he
switches through his substitutionary narration from pro-Kesey/LSD
perspective to anti. But ultimately Sandy has "an unspecific urge to *get off the
bus*," and this too can be said of Wolfe. Sandy's name is Dismount in the
story, his role is that of Judas, and again, in examining the whole motif of
"bum trips" and reservations which permeate *Acid Test*, one might posit that
in trying to continuously straddle his two perceptual modes, LSD and the
status quo, Wolfe is ultimately Dismount too. He betrays Kesey as a religious
prophet at the same time he is proferring him as such. For to stay at the
"divide," he must continuously undercut his elevated subject, just as Sandy
suggestively does when "he stares at the bus and . . . *unpaints it*. He strips one
whole side down to its original sunny school-bus yellow. The whole
Prankster overlay is gone."

In a 1980 interview, Wolfe asserted that *The Electric Kool-Aid Acid Test*
"was not a sendup, was not mockery or satire." Yet despite this claim, and
despite the exuberance of his style and the elevation of half of his diction,
there is a preponderance of negativity in Wolfe's vision. Tom Wolfe indeed
is the writer of the American "bum trip," whether it be that of Lenny and the
Black Panthers, the mau-mauers and the flak-catchers, the bohos versus the
art buyers (*The Painted Word*), the astronauts and the public (*The Right
Stuff*), or Kesey and the tailfin civilization. Wolfe is never swept away by the
New Age phenomenon he is chronicling. Dangerous excesses or failures of
vision are mercilessly rendered in Wolfe's texts. At the end of the Kesey saga,
for example, the superhero falls victim to the same fate as those he had
helped in his childhood. He is run off the highway. And even though, as
Wolfe makes clear, he is on the farthest "edge"—Hassler sitting on the edge
of the highway on the edge of the bay, while Kesey runs through the "last

blasted edge of land you can build houses on before they just sink into the ooze and compost"—Wolfe also suggests that Kesey has been lulled into the American mainstream and thus into failure. This is apparent through the diction of hypnotism used in this final sequence. Kesey is caught in the Bayshore freeway during rush hour:

> shiny black-shoe multitudes are out in their 300-horsepower fantasy cars heading into the rush hour, out the freeway, toward the waiting breezeway slots. It's actually peaceful, this rush hour [. . . .] It's relaxing, the rush hour is, and hypnotic, it drones [. . .] and [Kesey] takes off his disguise [. . . .] The cops keep floating abreast grimacing and flapping, and drifting back and pulling even again [. . . .] The great swarm of cars with hard-candy tails keeps sailing past, hypnotically.

Kesey and his new religious vision ultimately are not powerful enough to overcome the droning hypnotism of the American status quo.

Yet while Wolfe records the failings of most new wave phenomena, he is even more negative about the American status quo. As John Hellman has perceptively noted: "[Wolfe's] insistent choices of hyperbolic, kinetic, or baroque words and phrases make his descriptions as much an assault as a representation. . . . These stylistic traits work like those of the cubists to break up the reader's usual modes of perception." Practically *any* new mode of perception, *any* sensory flourish, to Wolfe is preferable to the status quo, and thus in both style and subject matter he explores new modes of perception.

Thus Wolfe's criticisms of Kesey and other new wave phenomena should be understood in the context of his larger criticism of the status quo. That Wolfe feels the tragedy of Kesey's failed experiment is suggested in the emblematic story of the "kid with the boiling teeth":

> A dead towhee and a rumpled road and lying in the dust, a *mistake . . . a mistake*, but it's not important . . . Making a mistake is not *important* it's the context in which the mistake is made. . . .
> A rumpled road and a dead towhee [i.e., the psychedelic movement] and four gasoline stations, white and sterile, refueling tailfins in mid-air for fat men in sunglasses who do not see the rumpled road and the dead towhee . . .

The psychedelic movement may have been in some ways a "mistake," but Wolfe is emphasizing the context in which it was made, that of a comatose sterile neon tailfin civilization. And here readers should see the positive side to Wolfe's place in American letters as bum trip chronicler. In seeking out and chronicling each new wave's, each new fad's, each new group's collision with the American status quo—bum trips though they all may be—Wolfe is simultaneously affirming, as he writes in *Acid Test*, that "there is no limit to the American trip." Surely there is something positive, even Saroyanesque, in that, and thus at the end, the best way that ambivalent bus should be taken is as only a symbol of potential. Kesey and the psychedelic world may indeed have "blown it," but the final vision Wolfe gives us is not of Kesey's defeat, or of Neal Cassady's ominous death—although they are close by—but of the spring, and the return of the faithful, and most of all of Further the bus parked beside the house, like Wolfe, ready to go once again.

ED COHEN

Tom Wolfe and the Truth Monitors: A Historical Fable

> The story of the ambiguous relationship between language and historical research runs through our tradition like a negative ground, an anti-story which is as important to the survival of that tradition as its more publicized truth claims.

> . . . the possibility exists for fiction to function in truth, for a fictional discourse to induce efforts of truth, and for bringing it about that a true discourse engenders or "manufactures" something that does not as yet exist, that is, "fictions" it. One "fictions" history on the basis of a political reality that makes it true, one fictions a politics not yet in existence on the basis of a historical truth.

Far from simply being an "academic" issue, the relation between what we call "history" and what we call "fiction" profoundly structures our understanding of the world. Indeed, the oppositional connotations that these two terms have taken on since the nineteenth century mark out two of our culture's primary interpretive axes. As "history" has sought to imbue itself with the "objectivity" of "scientific" methodologies and thereby attain the legitimacy accorded to such authoritative forms of knowledge over the last two hundred years, "fiction" (whether graphic or filmic) has become

From *CLIO: A Journal of Literature, History and the Philosophy of History* 16, no. 1 (Fall 1986). © 1987 by Ed Cohen.

increasingly contaminated by an affective contagion communicated by undifferentiated "subjectivity." Thus, while "objective" historical information reputedly empowers us to "know" the "real," "subjective" fictional experience is seen as merely obscuring the "facts."

It is not my intention here to rehearse the polemics of "positivism contra relativism" which have consumed so much paper in the past century. Rather, by focusing on one particular instance of this contestation played out twenty years ago in the pages of what were arguably America's most popular "literary" publications (i.e., the *New Yorker* and the *New York Review of Books*), I hope to illustrate the enduring power of these polemics to delimit the interpretation of contemporary textual practices. For, when Tom Wolfe took on the *New Yorker* in his inimitable, acerbic style, he provoked a series of counter-charges disseminated by the *New York Review of Books* aimed at reasserting the hegemony of these (and all) "Literary" institutions. Not surprisingly, the major articulation of this pro-Literature-with-a-capital-"L" position was based on a strict opposition between "fact" and "fiction." Since, as Derrida points out, "in a classical philosophical opposition we are not dealing with a peaceful coexistence of a *via-à-vis*, but rather with a violent hierarchy," the reassertion of one term of this couplet (fact) over its "antithesis" (fiction) signals a larger struggle aimed at preserving the ground of literary "authority."

However, lest I become unwittingly implicated in this logic of "either/or" and thereby doom myself to repeat ad infinitum the swing from one pole to the other, let me conclude my introduction by calling your attention to the subtitle of this essay: "A Historical Fable." In this (perhaps oxymoronic) phrase, I play the "fictionality" of the genre against the "facticity" of its modifier in order, self-consciously, to call the status of my own writing into question. While leaving the displays of this uncertainty to your own "subjective" interpretation, I cite one "objective" reference which has left its trace: in troping upon Voltaire's observation "that Fable is the elder sister of History," Linda Orr produces what could be understood as both this text's credo and caveat: "Fable is always the double or other of History."

Once upon a time, a long, long time ago (Sunday, 11 April 1965, to be precise), *New York* magazine—the Sunday supplement of the now defunct *Herald Tribune*—featured the first of two vituperative attacks on the *New Yorker* by self-proclaimed cultural-gadfly Tom Wolfe. Attempting to infest the living corpse/corpus of this quasi-official literary standard-bearer, Wolfe did not hesitate to draw blood. The next morning New York's literary community awoke shaking, and quickly dragged out its most potent critical-

pest-control. It seemed Wolfe had stung the very heart of the institution and the aging lion was not about to go down without a roar.

Occasioned by the *New Yorker*'s fortieth anniversary, Wolfe's articles purported to provide the story behind the story of the magazine that, perhaps more than any other, has provided an institutional context for American *belles lettres*. Wolfe focused on the history of this literary kingmaker because he detected behind it a lurking explanation for what he perceived as the lack of innovation in American fiction during the 1950s and 1960s. Unfortunately, Wolfe's notion of history was limited to personal (and perhaps libelous) biography so that his pieces on the *New Yorker* constituted a rather vicious *ad hominem* attack on the then-general editor, William Shawn. In Wolfe's narrative, Shawn assumed power upon the retirement of the journal's first general editor, Harold Ross, and proceeded to retrench behind an editorial policy set down in the early part of this century. "New authors, new ideas, the *New Yorker* wants none of you"—Wolfe made his message clear in the title he gave to the first article: "Tiny Mummies! The True Story of 43rd Street's Land of the Walking Dead!" [*"True Story?" The New York literati shrieked in reply. "You call this trash truth?"*]

While many have contested the judiciousness of Wolfe's verbal assault, to question the "truth" of his claims or the "justice" which they afford their subject will hardly sustain our interest in this now (hopefully) long-forgotten incident of cultural infighting. Rather what provokes a (re)consideration of these textual skirmishes are the larger meanings which we can cull from the barrage of condemnations that were evoked. From almost every quarter, the *New Yorker*'s supporters simultaneously fired upon Wolfe. He was decried as "unintelligible," "nightmarish," "brutal," "delinquent," "contemptuous," "savage," "subcollegiate," and "McCarthy-ite." He was denounced by the likes of E. B. White, J. D. Salinger, William Styron, Edward McCabe, Muriel Spark, and Walter Matthau (Walter Matthau?). But even more engaging than this immediate volley of replies was the slower, more calculated, response launched by the literary establishment itself on the front pages of the *New York Review of Books*. "PARAJOURNALISM" the title read and the title stuck. "Parajournalism" was an article—the first of two—written by "high culture" apologist Dwight MacDonald who here admirably performed his role as the duty-bound champion of Literature (with a capital "L"). Attempting not only to return Wolfe's agonizing sting but more significantly to negate his very utterance, the establishment spoke through MacDonald's words and the message was clear: it wasn't just Wolfe's writing that was at issue—it was his very <u>authority</u> to write. For, it seemed that the only way the institution would recover from this challenge to its monolithic/monologic power was to destroy the offender's voice <u>retroactively</u>. Thus, it was MacDonald's task to rewrite history, and he revelled in the undertaking.

As a master tactician, MacDonald's strategy was to undermine the "legitimacy" of Wolfe's writings by rearticulating certain fundamental assumptions upon which American literary practices (reading, writing, teaching, and publishing) rest. Specifically, he invoked the necessity of respecting a monologic foundation for generic classification (what Derrida calls "the Law of Genre") as the ground for literary intelligibility. The tactic was clever.

> It ["parajournalism" or as it is now better known, "New Journalism"] is a bastard form, having it both ways, exploiting the factual authority of journalism and the atmospheric license of fiction. Entertainment rather than information is the aim of its producers, and the hope of its consumers.

Fact vs. Fiction. Entertainment vs. Information. New Journalism is contradictory and therefore "bastard." It simply isn't "legitimate." But what constitutes "legitimacy?"

According to MacDonald's institutional voice, legitimacy derives from tradition. It is an inheritance. Literary forms have "authority" because they have proven themselves in the past and because their bloodlines have withstood the test of time. If Wolfe's enterprise was to be thrown into radical doubt, then the best way to begin was by attacking its family tree. Hence, MacDonald continues:

> Parajournalism has an ancestry, from Daniel Defoe, one of the fathers of modern journalism, whose *Journal of the Plague Year* was a hoax so convincingly circumstantial that it was long taken for a historical record, to the gossip columnists, sob sisters, fashion writers, and Hollywood reporters of this century. What is new is the pretension of our current parajournalists to be writing not hoaxes or publicity chit-chat but the real thing: and the willingness of the public to accept this pretense. We convert everything into entertainment.

The implications of this genealogy are clear: New Journalism is a literary descendant of Defoe's parody and a lateral cousin of "gossip columnists, sob sisters, fashion writers, and Hollywood reporters" whose genetic defects it willingly embodies. It's a "hoax," not the "real thing." It's "entertainment," not "history." Therefore, as the prefix "para-" suggests, it is a faulty and abnormal mutation. An uncanny double. What Baudrillard might, less condemningly, call a "simulation."

But what do these "defects" mean? And why did they seem so threatening to the literary community? The answer to these questions lies, in part, in the way particular discursive practices support the <u>authority</u> of literary institutions. That is to say, the way in which they reinscribe the positions from which one obtains—in Foucault's words—"the privileged or exclusive right to speak of a particular subject." What is at stake, then, in the struggle between Tom Wolfe and the Truthmonitors is who gets the "real thing," and hence who gets to say what "true history" is. Not a negligible right to be sure.

In defense of this privilege, MacDonald looks at New Journalism as if it were simultaneously fiction and non-fiction, journalism and non-journalism. For him, it is a double contradiction. A conundrum. It "doesn't stand up as fiction," yet it's certainly not "fact." It oscillates. It is never entirely itself, and therefore can never possibly begin to say anything "true." And this is MacDonald's point. If New Journalism can hold two "opposing" generic categories (fact/fiction, history/entertainment, etc.) in tension without resolving them, then it must be some malignant mutation of both. In the second part of his article, MacDonald defends himself against (unvoiced) charges that he is overreacting by stressing precisely this point.

> Some interpret the whole thing as a spoof—the author [Wolfe] when pressed on humdrum matters of fact edges in this direction—but there the theory breaks down because there are distinct traces of research. A parodist is licensed to invent and Tom Wolfe is not the man to turn down any poetic licentiousness that is going. He takes the middle course, shifting gears between fact and fantasy, spoof and reportage, until nobody knows which end is, at the moment, up.

Here MacDonald tropes mundanely: genres permit "license" but this "license" conversely necessitates obeying the rules of the road which demand that we pursue a single "end." Or, in Derrida's more abstract formulation: "as soon as genre announces itself, one must respect a norm, one must not cross a line of demarcation, one must not risk impurity, anomaly or monstrosity." Since genres define themselves by establishing exclusionary criteria through which they constitute themselves as "a set of identifiable or codifiable traits," those elements which impugn their boundaries necessarily threaten the entire classificatory system. By violating the <u>non-contradictory</u> logic which makes such determinations of "genre" coherent, New Journalism gives rise to a fear that must be exterminated before it spreads confusion throughout all social distinctions. At all costs, MacDonald's argument implies, these underlying categories must be saved.

In attempting to do just this, MacDonald retreats to the epistemological ground of positivist "objectivity." Since Wolfe makes "fictional" statements about "factual" events, he submerges the "objective" in the "subjective" and thereby excludes himself from the realm of "natural" (or "rational") understanding. Here MacDonald waxes eloquent.

> The specific *kitsch* device here is intimacy. Intimacy with the subject not in the old fashioned sense of research, but an intimacy of style. The parajournalist cozies up, merges into the subject so completely that the view point is wholly from inside, like family gossip. . . . There is no space between writer and topic, no "distancing" to allow even the most rudimentary objective judgment, such as for factual accuracy. Inside and outside are one. It might be called topological journalism after those experiments with folding and cutting a piece of paper until it only has one side.

The tenor of this metaphor resounds: Wolfe's writing, like a mobius strip, is a mind game that confounds the obviousness of "real" distinctions—even one as obvious as between inside and outside. By folding back upon itself, New Journalism denies its boundaries, thereby excluding and including everything all at once. Hence, like its topological analogue, it is an anomaly, a quirk. It collapses the "space between writer and topic" and doesn't even "allow for the most rudimentary objective judgment, such as for factual accuracy." From this perspective, "objective facts" must stand at several removes from the observer; thus, "reality," the locus of "objectivity," removes itself beyond the observer's experience which undiscerningly "merges into the subject so completely that the viewpoint is wholly from inside, like family gossip." The implication of this position relegates the status of a speaker/writer who "identifies" with his or her subject to that of a "gossip," calling the truth status of such a speaker/writer's utterance into question as less than legitimate.

This characterization of New Journalism as "gossip" becomes even more invidious in MacDonald's dismissal of the subject matter of Wolfe's texts. According to MacDonald's taxonomy, New Journalism deals primarily with two types of stories: those about "celebs" and those about "the Little Man (or Woman) who gets in trouble with the law, or who is interestingly poor or old or ill or best, all three." In all cases, the technique involved in telling these tales reveals these individuals as "characters"—it concentrates on their daily lives and "indulges in idle speculation" about them. For MacDonald, it is clearly not interested in communicating <u>facts</u> and instead revels in merely "entertaining."

> While the reader knows a great deal, too much, about [the subjects of New Journalism] . . . this is not real knowledge because they are, in their public aspect, not real. They are not persons but *personae* ("artificial characters in a play or novel"—or a parajournalistic reportage) which have been manufactured for public consumption with their enthusiastic cooperation. Notions of truth or accuracy are irrelevant in such a context of collusive fabrication on both sides; all that matters to anybody—subject, writer, reader—is that it be a good story.

MacDonald's problem with entertainment, it seems, is not merely that it makes truth "irrelevant" to its forms but that it also encourages its audience to think that "notions of truth or accuracy are irrelevant." Hence, it creates a (con)text of "collusive fabrication" in which the quality of the "story" impedes the precedence of "true" history. What is at issue, then, is not just who gets to tell the stories, but also who gets to listen to them and who decides how they are to be understood. Entertainment allows the entertained to forget to prioritize informational content over affective experience, thereby rendering the knowledge obtained from New Journalism suspect—i.e., it confuses "fact" with "fiction." MacDonald finds proof of this confusion in what he determines to be the profound ignorance of the New Journalist's audience. As he says: "The first resource of a parajournalist is that his audience know less than he does." But his ignorance is not just a lack of knowledge, it is primarily a lack of "culture." MacDonald continues: "The post-war 'culture boom' has greatly increased the number of Americans who are educated, in the formal sense that they have gone through college, without increasing proportionately the number who know or care much about culture."

This association of (capital "T") <u>T</u>ruth with (capital "C") Culture is an association that is crucial to the establishment of cultural hegemony. If we consider the role which Michel Foucault ascribed to the "will to truth" as a means of structuring power/knowledge, we see that those discursive practices which define the opposition between "true" and "false" within a particular sociohistorical context also determine (in a very material sense) what kinds of knowledge count as social knowledge. Or, in other words, the strategies which establish the boundary between the "true" and the "false" in a culture also establish what kinds of utterances <u>legitimately</u> serve as the basis for making social decisions or instituting social change. To the extent that New Journalism seems to blur the distinctions between these essential logical categories that literary institutions (as institutional supports of larger social relations) seek to establish, it threatens the ability of Culture to (re)produce its hegemony. New Journalism calls into play a different kind of knowledge—an affective knowledge of people's lives—and this knowledge undermines the epistemological ground of the dominant social relations. For what would happen if people suddenly began to use their own experience as a gauge of "truth?" How could we maintain social values? What would happen to morality?

These questions, and others like them, illuminate the strategies by which access to positions of power is regulated in our society. So long as social practices mask themselves as "natural" they appear invulnerable to change. This perception applies not only to Marx's analysis of the bourgeois economists' appeal to "natural economic laws" but also to such other "natural" systems as those of sex/gender identification, youth/age distinctions, racial differences, etc. If these categories were open to interpretation by an individual's everyday experience, then we might need to begin to explain some of the contradictions between ideology and personal experience that could call the entire structure of our society into question. (For example, if American capitalism is constructed within an ideology which insures the right to "life, liberty, and the pursuit of happiness," then why does such a large percentage of our population live hungry, homeless, inadequately educated, underemployed, and underpaid?) However, if "true" reality is located somewhere beyond the here and now, then the "truth" of social relations cannot be assailed by such unfortunate aberrations. Social problems seem illusory in comparison with the deeper problems of keeping the system intact.

Since New Journalism concerns itself primarily with such individual experience—both the author's and the subjects'—it must be represented as the enemy. Aligned by MacDonald with both Hitler and Senator Joseph McCarthy, Tom Wolfe appears as a cultural viper sucking at the very breast of American existence. And, perhaps in his own way, he does threaten the American way of life by seeking to undermine the received conditions of possibility for producing "true" statements about it. In MacDonald's view, then:

> The difference between Tom Wolfe and such types [as Hitler and McCarthy] is that he doesn't tell lies, big or small, since lying is a conscious process, recognizing the distinction between what is

and what would be convenient to assume is. He seems to be honestly unaware of the distinction between fact and fabrication. You might call him a sincere demagogue.

Admittedly it is very hard to present Wolfe's work as a paradigm for social discourse (indeed, it's a bit like being an A.C.L.U. lawyer assigned to defend Larry Flynt's first amendment rights); yet, somehow he doesn't seem in quite the same league as Hitler and Joseph McCarthy. What Wolfe does is to redefine the locus of literary activity. After Wolfe, fiction can no longer be defined simply as "internally referential" nor history defined solely as "externally referential" since these categories can no longer be seen as mutually exclusive. By blurring the opposition between fact and fiction, Wolfe's work resituates the individual within the context of his or her own experience and suggests a new way of interpreting that reality: the life of the individual becomes the primary text from which one can "read off" the meanings that structure social relations. This occurs because New Journalism redeploys the conventions used to identify "fictions" within the context of other social discourses, thereby extending the transparency of language that underlies literary "realism" a step further, making reality transparent to discourse. If we read our lives as "fictions," as constructions, this does not mean that they are any less "real." Rather, it simply introduces a new way of interpreting that reality and generates a new knowledge of experience by invoking a different interpretive frame. And it is the right to make this kind of reinterpretation that is at stake in this verbal battle over New Journalism.

Since I began by calling this piece a "historical fable," I feel obliged to provide some sort of moral. So here it is:

Institutions are not unassailable monoliths that determine human practices but rather are arrangements of practices that are both determining of and determined by the social activities of our culture. These institutions, which are themselves comprised of interlocking and often contradictory activities, are in turn tactically organized into sites over which power is systematically organized—here, I invoke Gramsci's conception of hegemony. What this means is that institutions do in a very material way structure the ideas and actions of people in their everyday lives but simultaneously and as a consequence these structures are vulnerable to being changed by these same ideas and actions.

In looking at one very specific set of institutional practices (or "discourses")—those that circumscribe New Journalism within our social category Literature—I have tried to uncover some of the strategies which institutions use to establish "authority" within a specific sociohistorical locus of power. If we accept Michel Foucault's notion of the "will to truth" as one of the organizational tactics through which institutional practices are made concrete, then we can see how vital it is to the self-perpetuation of these institutions that the categories of truth and fallacy, of fact and fiction, remain mutually exclusive. For it is only by distinguishing "fact" from "fancy" that our society can determine which kinds of knowledge will be used to make social decisions. For example, if women's history or black history or chicano history or gay history is not "true" history then it is perfectly <u>logical</u> to deny them a place in the great bastion of our culture, the academy—or even more importantly to ignore the *fact* of people's continuing daily oppression.

What the conflict between Tom Wolfe and the Truthmonitors exposes, then, are the mechanisms by which institutions consolidate their power over the course of specific human lives. In this sense, Tom Wolfe might be seen as challenging the monolithic structure of literary culture—insofar as his writing confronted the "either/or" logic of late American capitalism with its calculus of "true and false"—even if ultimately his work has been recorded and remarketed within the literary mainstream. To the extent that Wolfe's essays blur the distinctions between the "real" and the fantastic, they redefine the "original" text as the everydayness of human life and, what is more, they are entertaining. All of these factors contribute to the <u>interruption</u> of the totalizing claims of American literary discourses because they raise the possibility of an ironic reading of "natural" (ideological) uses of language as defined by the norms of realism. Wolfe's work, then, should not be analyzed only in terms of its genealogy (from Defoe to Rona Barrett) but also in terms of the sociohistorical milieu from which it arises. By situating New Journalism within this context of literary practice, we can begin to expose some of the strategies that institutions use to marginalize voices which resist—in Foucault's terms—their "regime of power" and at the same time we can begin to conceive of ways to interrupt this particular configuration of cultural hegemony.

JAMES N. STULL

The Cultural Gamesmanship of Tom Wolfe

The examination of arcane worlds and societies is one of the central appeals of the new journalism and a fundamental part of Tom Wolfe's writing. While Wolfe ostensibly makes overtures to explain subcultures on their own terms, he in fact describes and understands them all with a strikingly similar method of cultural analysis. Wolfe believes, as he explained in an interview with Tony Schwartz, that "the fundamental unit in analyzing behavior is not the individual, but some sort of status group or status structure." Wolfe privileges an omniscient authorial self and attends to the nuances of status and power within the construction of his carefully controlled literary and social worlds. He is the master gamesman in the white suit whose journalistic performance is predicated upon his ability to establish the rules of the social game and lead the reader to believe that they (the rules) are actually part of the reality they signify.

In *The Electric Kool-Aid Acid Test* Wolfe suggests that there is a game-like interaction between the Merry Pranksters and certain members of mainstream culture. Kesey and the Pranksters' interaction with the police, for example, is identified as the "cops-and-robbers" game. The Pranksters themselves, Ken Kesey in particular, are aware that their identities are determined by socially prescribed (or proscribed) rules and roles of the social game. Their acquired appellations—Neal Cassady is known as "Speed

From *Journal of American Culture* 14, no. 3 (Fall 1991). © 1992 by Ray B. Browne.

Limit," for example, and Kesey is "Chief"—are ironically chosen to illustrate how one's individuality is subsumed by a name that is determined either by a social role or a single, usually superficial, trait. In "Mau-Mauing the Flak Catchers" Wolfe maintains that white civil servants "sat back and waited for you to come rolling in with your certified angry militants, your frustrated ghetto youth." Then the flak catchers knew—"if you were outrageous enough, if you could shake up the bureaucrats so bad"—which groups "to give the poverty grants and community organizing jobs to." In both these works, Wolfe employs a method for interpreting social phenomena, the game metaphor, that is congruent with his subjects' alleged understanding of their own experience. Wolfe all but states that there is a goal-directedness on the part of the social players when he interprets their interaction as a dramatized (or staged) confrontation; the social players— civil servants and "certified angry militants"—knew the "rules" of the game, acted accordingly, and anticipated the expected rewards at the conclusion of the encounter. Ethnic and minority groups received poverty grants while civil servants were assured they had made the right choice in distributing those grants. While a number of cultural critics and historians interpreted the interaction between mainstream culture and various adversarial groups in more "serious" terms—as a symbolic and often real clash of value structures—Wolfe astutely recognized the calculated, even playful interaction between groups whose members presumably understood the tacit, if not overt, rules of the social game.

Generally, however, Wolfe is less successful in explaining in "Mau-Mauing the Flak Catchers" and other works how social players come to understand the rules governing their behavior. While a minority leader named Chaser seems to be cognizant of the "game" he is playing—"he had everything planned out on his side, right down to the last detail," Wolfe tells us—Wolfe is more equivocal when he remarks that "there were people in the Western Addition who practically gave classes in mau-mauing." While the usefulness of the game model does not depend on the awareness of the social actors, Wolfe himself is at times unsure of how the game and its rules originated. He often relies, as the following passage suggests, on a teleological interpretation of social interaction: "The strange thing was that the confrontation ritual was built into the poverty program from the beginning. The poverty bureaucrats depended on the confrontations in order to know what to do." But how did the poverty bureaucrats *know* they had to depend on the confrontations to know what to do? While Wolfe suggests that his interpretation of cultural is based on the observation of, and the interaction between, social players, the frame of sociological analysis is employed to explain, I believe, the ostensible goal-directedness of the principal actors. Wolfe discerns a pattern in a number of social situations and then proposes that it was consciously conceived or recognized by the social players. This allows Wolfe to disguise his method of social analysis by suggesting it is an inherent part of social life and a prerequisite for making sense of it.

Wolfe's authority as journalist and master gamesman is founded, in fact, largely on his ability to reveal what others—press members or social players—are not able to recognize or articulate. This is principally determined by the management of information. Wolfe selectively controls the flow of information and lets readers believe they are privy to esoteric knowledge which is withheld from, or unknown to, social others. In *The Right Stuff*, for instance, Wolfe says, in discussing "the right stuff," that "none of this was to be mentioned, and yet it was acted out in a way that a young man could not fail to understand." In another example, Wolfe asks why members of the press, and seemingly every other human being, were so emotionally moved that they created instant heroes of the seven Mercury astronauts. He explains that

> This was a question that not James Reston or the pilots themselves or anyone of NASA could have answered at the time, because the very language of the proposition had long since been abandoned and forgotten. The forgotten term, left behind in the superstitious past, was *single combat*.

The Right Stuff is filled with similar comments: "The message seemed to be"; "No one spoke the phrase"; "No one knew its name"; and "that was probably unconscious on Al's part." While many of Wolfe's "characters," particularly in *The Right Stuff*, act without being cognizant of what governs their behavior, Wolfe, who is able to articulate the unnameable ("single combat") and make the "unconscious" recognizable or transparent, penetrates the insular and reticent world of the fighter jock and claims, implicitly at least, to speak for uninformed social others. He establishes himself as the only player—and usually omniscient narrator—who has full knowledge of the social game.

This helps to establish, of course, Wolfe's authority as a cultural critic. Wolfe also suggests, however, that it is the epistemological authority of the *New Journalism* which allows him to understand what other press members cannot. Like many other literary nonfiction writers, Thompson and Mailer among them, Wolfe criticizes mainstream journalists for their inability to act autonomously. In *The Right Stuff* Wolfe repeatedly refers to the press as either "the Genteel Beast" or "the Victorian Gent," "a great colonial animal

. . . made up of countless clustered organisms responding to a single nervous system." Wolfe explains that "the animal seemed determined that in all matters of national importance the *proper emotion*, the *seemly sentiment*, the *fitting moral tone* should be established and should prevail." Wolfe does not fully explain what conditions foster this phenomenon, commonly known as "pack" or "herd" journalism. Yet, he criticizes reporters for a behavioral and institutional conformity in which they allegedly have no control over, while he nominally articulates an imperial journalistic self which defies, or escapes from, the tyrannizing rules governing all social membership.

While it is common for many new journalists to rely on first-hand experience, gathering material from witnessed events, Wolfe's two most successful works, *The Electric Kool-Aid Acid Test* and *The Right Stuff*, are based largely on information taken from secondary sources: interviews, public documents, letters, and so on. In part, I believe, Wolfe relies greatly on this material because he is unwilling to participate in events or get too intimate with subjects he later writes about; he refuses to relinquish personal control by stepping out of his role as detached observer (and cultural critic) and confronting—as Hunter S. Thompson does, for example,—the "raw experience" of life. Wolfe seems to feel more comfortable as a journalist and person when he can orchestrate the dynamics of social encounters and tacitly claim an implied power associated with his allegedly neutral journalistic perspective.

The success of Wolfe's journalistic and interpretive performance is largely based, in fact, on his scholarly training, on his ability to wed historical and esoteric ideas and insights to contemporary incidents and ordinary events. In *The Electric Kool-Aid Acid Test*, for example, Wolfe illuminates the religious dimension of The Merry Pranksters' experience by comparing it to other historical religious movements: Christianity, Buddhism, Judaism, and so on. Similarly, in "Radical Chic" Wolfe interprets the courting of Black Panthers by wealthy New York liberals as a recent manifestation of the historically established practice of "slumming": cultivating "low-rent" styles and mixing with people of a lower social class. While Wolfe tries to demystify alien cultural experiences and make them intelligible to his educated, middle-class readers, he relies on conventional and historically established information and frames of reference derived from mainstream culture. Wolfe establishes journalistic authority by defining his role as a cultural interpreter—a disembodied voice—who gives historical depth to events that are ostensibly peculiar to the moment. At some expense, of course. As David Eason points out, Wolfe yokes all idiosyncratic view of reality to "a well-ordered, non-threatening past that promises to extend into the future." In this respect, Wolfe minimizes—and at times depoliticizes—

contemporary experience by encoding it in familiar terms and past social contexts. Within a specific text (context)—for instance, "Radical Chic"— Wolfe may position himself as objective observer who is principally interested in chronicling the political dialogue between two disparate social groups: Black Panthers and New York liberals. Instead of fully recognizing the polyvocality of this social moment, however, all discordant voices are subverted, as they are throughout much of Wolfe's writing, by the monophonic and ideological authority of the transcendent observer. While Wolfe's work nominally represents a democratic mode of expression, it implicitly reveals—as does most literary journalism—both a tacit literary and social elitism and a traditional and conservative interpretation of contemporary experience. According to David Eason, the "ethnographic realism" of Wolfe and other literary journalists "constitutes the subculture as an object of display, and the reporter and the reader, whose values are assumed and not explored, are cojoined in the act of observing." Eason adds that the "effect of this strategy is to reinvent textually the consensus which cultural fragmentation had called into question." Wolfe naturalizes discrepant realities by suggesting that the method used is the most commonsensical way, if not the only way, of making sense of such contemporary experience. Though Wolfe criticizes other conventional journalists for their institutional allegiances, his journalism authority and method of cultural analysis arise from his scholarly training at Yale, from his class position within a hierarchical institutional and academic order.

The social "game" is thematically and formally understood, as I noted, on personal and ideologically conservative terms. Wolfe's exploration of subcultural experience, for example, might be superficially interpreted as a celebration of cultural diversity and American pluralism. Wolfe explains that the proliferation of subcultures and status systems was due primarily, if not solely, to the post-World War II economic boom. Behind the cataloguing of (exotic) status symbols, in other words, is an underlining economic interpretation of subcultural experience which links it to the ideological (material) superstructure of mainstream culture. Wolfe refuses to acknowledge, however, that the emergence of a succession of youth cultural styles might constitute a form of symbolic opposition which reflects a more general dissatisfaction with American life. Instead, Wolfe minimizes ideological and political dissent by focusing on style and interpreting conflict in "dramatic" (literary) and rhetorical terms.

In part, Wolfe achieves this dramatic tension by bifurcating the world into a rigid we-they polarity. In *The Electric Kool-Aid Acid Test*, for example, Wolfe notes "that the world is sheerly divided into those who have had *the experience* and those who have not—those who have been through the door—" (that is, taken LSD). Throughout *The Right Stuff* we are repeatedly reminded that there are those who have it—"the right stuff"—and there are those who do not. Wolfe expresses, of course, the collective sentiment shared by members of each respective status group, Merry Pranksters and test pilots, and successfully dramatizes and exposes status competition, both between and within status structures. In *The Right Stuff* there is, to name a few, the rivalry between fighter pilots and astronauts, astronauts and engineers, and between the astronauts themselves. Overshadowing these conflicts is the race between the U.S. and the Soviet Union to control the heavens. Though the race to conquer space had a political and ideological base, Wolfe's journalistic treatment is principally literary and polemical; he is most interested in the drama, tension, and hysteria behind space flights and the disparity between Soviet successes and U.S. failures. The race into space is reduced almost to an Olympic competition between countries with a familiar protagonist hero (the U.S.) vying against an equally familiar evil antagonist (Russia).

As compelling as Wolfe's writing is in this case, he often over-emphasizes status competition and competitive social interaction and inadequately accounts for the cooperation that occurs between social players. In "Radical Chic," for example, Wolfe is so intent on exposing status incongruities, he does not acknowledge that the "radical chic" evening might be conceived as a bona fide attempt, however superficial or ineffectual, to meliorate social differences and promote racial harmony. Wolfe's insistent preoccupation with status and status differences, in fact, might be interpreted as perverting, or at least undermining, the implied rules of any social game. Theoretically speaking, a game can only be played if participants subordinate themselves to the rules of the gathering. Power, status, wealth, beauty, strength, knowledge—all relevant in many other social contexts—are extrinsic to game interactions. Wolfe's preoccupation with status details, in other words, is irrelevant to how these social players—Bernstein (and friends) and the Black Panthers—participate in this particular encounter. In fact, in order for the game to succeed it is necessary that members from both status groups minimize their social differences and recognize that they both can benefit, as social antagonists do in "Mau-Mauing the Flak Catchers," by abiding by the acknowledged and tacit rules of the social interaction.

Wolfe would have us believe, however, that cooperation between status groups is almost impossible. In both *The Painted Word* and *From Bauhaus to Our House*, Wolfe repeatedly indicates that the artist (painter and architect) is tyrannized by the desire to separate himself (or herself) from the "hated" middle-class—"to cut himself forever free from the bonds of the greedy and hypocritical bourgeoisie." Similarly, Wolfe maintains that "composers, artists, or architects in a compound began to have the instincts of the medieval clergy, much of whose activity was devoted exclusively to separating itself from the mob. For mob, substitute bourgeoisie." While Wolfe clearly reveals that status competition figures more prominently in the world of art than people believe, he frames this discussion in the form of an argument replete with historical generalizations and identifies, I believe, a personal metaphor of self—a preoccupation with status and class—by implicitly revealing a symbolic and perhaps real desire to separate himself as an artist (new journalist) and person from the "hated" bourgeoisie (conventional journalists). Though status competition explains much, it cannot begin to explain why an artist, let alone a great number of artists, produces a particular work of art. The homogenizing nature of consensus history (and social criticism), however, provides a tidy and reassuring picture of how the world works and helps certify the conceptual and explanatory powers of the author. Generalizations and encompassing statements—"every artist knew," for example, and "every soul here"—underscore Wolfe's facile ability to sum up a particular world and make it intelligible. In "Radical Chic," Wolfe punctuates the narrative with his use of "everyone," as in "everyone in here loves the *sees* and the *you knows*." A claimed concensus and Wolfe's implied omniscience—the ability to know what others are thinking and feeling—buttress his authority and objectify his personal interpretations. This is one way in which Wolfe implicates readers and benignly coerces them into seeing the world on his personal and metaphorical terms.

Wolfe's writing, like all written works, addresses a particular audience and establishes communication between a specific sender (author) and a more general receiver (reader). While Wolfe's manner of address may be more indirect than, for example, Joan Didion's, he establishes, nonetheless, an implicit pact in which the reader is privy to the author's knowledge and superior insights. Just as Wolfe divides the world into us/them polarities, so Wolfe and his readers share insights and knowledge about the social and artistic worlds unknown to others. Wolfe establishes a closed interpretive frame and defines the reader as a cooperating participant in the communication exchange. This entente among insiders is established in part by disclosing privileged information to educated readers, but also by the manner of Wolfe's rhetorical address. In "Radical Chic," for example, Wolfe's repeated use of "deny it if you want to" (or "deny it if you wish to") challenges and implicates the reader and, finally, dictates only one response: "But, of course," the reader is supposed to say. "That's how it really is."

In describing the social game and distinguishing one statusphere from another, Wolfe generally relies, of course, on careful observation and documentation of symbolic details—clothes, speech, hair styles. As the following passage reveals, Wolfe is adept as other social observers in identifying status incongruities and conflicts between status structures:

> the grape workers were all in work clothes, Levi's, chinos, Sears balloon-seat twills, K-Mart sports shirts, and so forth. The socialites, meanwhile, arrived at the height of the 1969 summer season of bell-bottom silk pants suits, Pucci clings, Dunhill blazers, and Turnbull & Asser neckerchiefs.

Because Wolfe focuses so relentlessly on status minutiae, however, the personal and psychological dimensions of his subjects are largely ignored. For example, while Wolfe nominally portrays the test pilots and astronauts in *The Right Stuff* as individuals—in some cases as individualists—we are given only a few superficial details of each person and one general characteristic to define them all: that is, of course, "the right stuff." Wolfe suggests that association with a status group is the primary way in which identity is determined. The personal (or core) self is usurped by a socially constructed public identity based on status group membership and, in this case, gender. As Chris Anderson notes, "the pilots and the astronauts are models of the stereotypical American strong-silent male." By not challenging or exploring this stereotype, Wolfe reaffirms his belief in the sanctity of a private self and all but states that emotions and personal idiosyncrasies are of little consequence in understanding or illuminating human nature. Morris Dickstein maintains that Wolfe's subjects are, finally, merely "manikins of chic, butts of social satire"; that even when he writes from inside his characters their "subjective reality remains stubbornly uninteresting or inaccessible." Wolfe ultimately homogenizes "his characters into one inner voice, a single mentality, a collective embodiment of a social attitude." Wolfe is more interested in portraying a static idea—a status distinction, conflict, or incongruity—than with dramatizing diverse interactions of psychologically individuated selves. Wolfe's rendering of characters and his understanding of human nature also reveal, I believe, a characteristic unwillingness of a number of male literary journalists to fully explore the psychological and emotional relationship between self and other, or journalist and subject.

Wolfe, of course, often relies on caricature, and he is capable as any social critic at characterizing and satirizing types. There is the garrulous and cloyingly friendly Texan in *The Right Stuff*, referred to as Herb Snout:

> Hi, there little Lady! Just *damned* glad to see you, too! And then he'd give a huge horrible wink that would practically

implode his eye, and he'd say, We've heard a lot of good things about you gals, a *lot* of good things—all with that eye-wrenching wink.

In *The Electric Kool-Aid Acid Test* and *The Right Stuff*, Doctors (and scientists), referred to as white smocks, are summarily portrayed as impersonal and unfriendly. In *The Right Stuff*, this depiction of doctors allegedly illustrates the typical test pilot or astronaut's feeling about members from this status group. While Wolfe successfully uses stereotypes and caricature to convey animosity between these status structures, his satirical portraits can be unflattering, narrow, snobbishly prejudiced, to some even sexist, racist, and brutal. In "*A* Wolfe *in* Chic Clothing," Christopher Hitchens questions Wolfe's frequent use of racial and minority stereotypes. In "Mau-Mauing the Flak Catchers," for example, Wolfe describes Samoans in the following way:

> Everything about them is gigantic, even their heads. They'll have a skull the size of a watermelon, with a couple of little squinty eyes and a little mouth and a couple of nose holes stuck in, and no neck at all. From the ears down, the big yoyos are just one solid welded hulk, the size of an oil burner . . . They have big wide faces and smooth features. They're a dark brown, with a smooth cast.

Wolfe talks about Chinese, Mexicans, and blacks in a similar sophomoric manner. Hitchens comes to the conclusion that while Wolfe depends heavily on racial caricature, it is a "sign of laziness rather than prejudice." In "Radical Chic," however, Hitchens maintains that "Wolfe is striking much harder than a [responsible] satirist would. His intention was really to do harm, and he succeeded brilliantly."

Of all the status structures and groups Wolfe describes and satirizes, women are portrayed, more often than not, in the most unflattering terms. In "Radical Chic," for example, Wolfe makes at least three references to an allegedly naive but "beautiful ash-blond girl." On one occasion, Wolfe reports that she wants to know what she can personally do, without money or political power, to help the Black Panthers. "Well, baby, if you really"—Wolfe begins, then adds—but [Don] Cox tells her that one of the big problems is finding churches in the black community that will help the Panthers in their breakfast program for ghetto children, and maybe people like her could help the Panthers approach the churches." Wolfe's initial comment—"Well, baby, if you really"—suggests that she can, if nothing else, donate her liberal body to the cause. Clearly, Wolfe is taking liberties by inventing and attributing thoughts to one of his characters, Don Cox, at the young woman's expense.

Throughout Wolfe's writing, women are constructed in a similar fashion. In *The Electric Kool-Aid Acid Test* he notes that the "West Coast" was "always full of . . . long-haired little Wasp and Jewish buds balling spade cats." Wolfe may be suggesting, of course, that such coupling is merely a more intimate yet equally fashionable form of consorting with "raw-vital, Low Rent primitives," but because similar comments appear through much of his work it raises questions about Wolfe's depiction of women. At the Southern stock car races, Wolfe notes, you always see "those beautiful little buds in short shorts . . . spread-eagle out on the top of the car roofs, pressing down on good hard automobile sheet metal, their little cupcake bottom aimed up at the sun." In *The Right Stuff* Wolfe similarly explains that

> The most marvelous lively young cookies were materializing. . . .
> They were just *there* waiting beside the motel pool, when one
> arrived, young juicy girls with stand-up jugs and full sprung
> thighs and conformations so taut and silky that the very sight of
> them practically pulled a man into the delta of priapic delirium.

Wolfe's writing may not be intentionally sexist, but his portrayal of women and his use of stereotypes and satire raise questions about his moral and social responsibility to his subjects, even if they figure only marginally into his work. Because Wolfe depicts women unsympathetically, he tacitly conspires with his subjects in constructing a masculine world based in part on the exploitation of women. In a 1983 interview Wolfe candidly admitted that the gang bang described in *The Electric Kool-Aid Acid Test* was a "horrible scene." Yet, Wolfe's almost comedic treatment of the event—he describes the woman as "some blonde from out of town . . . just one nice soft honey hormone squash"—raises questions about his ability to deal authoritatively and sensitively with women's experience. For a journalist who claims to be a chronicler of contemporary society, much like Balzac was in his day, it is quite surprising that Wolfe—and for that matter, other male literary journalists—almost entirely ignored two of the most important subjects of the 1960s and early 1970s, the "sexual revolution" and the women's movement.

Wolfe's depiction of women, his satirical portraits, as well as his stereotypes and status group generalizations, reveal the political affiliation and social class biases of an educated and fairly well-off white male. His chosen journalistic role of detached observer and the use of the third person, omniscient narrator reflect the social space that separates him from, and perhaps elevates him above, many of his subjects. Wolfe's use of satire and his preoccupation with status details, furthermore, allow him to maintain unimpeded control of the re-imagined social game. If his characters were more dramatically rounded and more psychologically complex, they would acquire identities resistant to stereotyping, satiric snobbery, and status group identification. As it is, Wolfe's social players possess no such voice or identity of their own; them remain participants in a game defined, played, and interpreted by the master gamesman in the white suit, Thomas Kennerly Wolfe, Jr.

JAMES F. SMITH

Tom Wolfe's Bonfire of the Vanities: A Dreiser Novel for the 1980s

> In a word, we must operate on characters, passions, human and social events, as the chemist and physician operate on brute matter, as the physiologist operates on living beings.
> —Emile Zola

> I think of the novel as almost naturalistic.
> —Tom Wolfe

> If you have it in you to be great you must come to New York.
> —Theodore Dreiser

In 1896, prior to the publication of his first novel, Theodore Dreiser wrote in "Reflections":

> The desire to attend and be part of the great current of city life is one that seldom bases itself upon well mastered reasons. . . . Men do not ask themselves whether once in the great city its wonders will profit them any . . . . If they did it would appall them and make them cautious of the magnetic charm that draws them on.

From *Journal of American Culture* 14, no. 3 (Fall 1991). © 1992 by Ray B. Browne.

In 1987, following the publication of his first novel, Tom Wolfe told an interviewer:

> I still get a big kick out of New York. . . . This is the kind of town where if you're not working on something that leads upward, you feel out of it, you feel as if you don't belong in conversations. It's not a place for drones. It's Ambition City right now. You have to have that kind of energy or else the bus fumes and street crime would be intolerable.

Both writers were themselves attracted by the magnet of city life, and both wrote first novels which, among other issues, explore the pleasures and perils of the American Dream set against the backdrop of their respective contemporary urban scenes. *Sister Carrie* (1900) and *The Bonfire of the Vanities* (1987) share a similar vision of urban America, the nature of contemporary society, and the place of an individual within that society. Further, the two works have a strikingly similar relationship to the naturalism that characterized late nineteenth-century literature. Both Dreiser and Wolfe see beneath the conventions of the day, though each seems genuinely intrigued and captivated by them, to the emptiness beneath surface details, leading these two journalists-turned-novelists to question the quality of American life and the American dream itself.

In many ways the 1890s and the 1980s, the respective eras chronicled by Dreiser and Wolfe, share similar characteristics. Chief among these similarities is a popular focus on urban life, corresponding to population shifts toward centers of opportunity in the commercial world. In Chicago and New York, one finds ample evidence of the material abundance and technological progress characteristic of the authors' times, but the glittering surface fades as one recognizes the poverty and social instability upon which the grandeur uneasily rests. Nevertheless, for many casual observers, a kind of self-preserving sentimentality prevents the unpleasant realities from intruding on a more exciting and appealing image of making it to the top. After all, if the apartment is luxurious and on the right block, if the carriage or limousine is rich, and if the companions are enchanting, one can create a safe cocoon of one's own, a sphere of influence where one can at least pretend to be a "Master of the Universe." This kind of contrast between appearance and reality is a well-worn device which allows characters to progress from innocence to experience, dramatizes the cynicism of those who refuse to see beneath the surface, and reveals the hopelessness of whose trapped by circumstance.

In "The Me Decade and the Third Great Awakening," Wolfe comments on the American economy since World War II. "It has pumped money into every class of the population on a scale without parallel in any other country in history. True, nothing has solved the plight of those at the very bottom, the chronically unemployed of the slums." Moreover, as F.O. Matthiessen observes in an essay on Dreiser, "Being poor . . . can be particularly savage in a country where the *mores* of individualism consider it a disgrace, and where the official attitude is, therefore, tempted to pretend that poverty does not exist." This attitude was characteristic of the sentimentality that the naturalistic writers of Dreiser's day offended, and it persists in the present despite the efforts of contemporary muckrakers who use the media to force the public to recognize social problems.

New York City is the setting for nearly half of *Sister Carrie* and for *Bonfire*. In each case, the authors rely on the audience's popular understanding of the fascination this city possesses. In a passage from *Newspaper Days* (1931), Dreiser writes what could be an epigraph for *Bonfire*: "New York . . . had the feeling of gross and blissful and parading self-indulgence . . . Here . . . were huge dreams and lusts and vanities being gratified hourly. I wanted to know the worst and the best." For his own part, Wolfe observes, "My feeling was wonderment—this amazing carnival was spread out before me. I really love New York. It attracts ambitious people, not just at the top. . . . New York is the city of ambition."

The dreams and ambition noted by the authors comprise a central theme of both novels. Insatiable desire is the primary motivating force for the characters. As Carrie Meeber journeys to Chicago, Dreiser notes:

> Since infancy her ears had been full of its fame . . . it was vast. There were lights and sounds and a roar of things. People were rich . . . [Self-interest] was . . . her guiding principle . . . [S]he . . . was quick to understand the keener pleasures of life, ambitious to gain in material things. A half-equipped little knight she was, venturing to reconnoitre the mysterious city and dreaming wild dreams of some vague, far-off supremacy. . . .

When Carrie succumbs to Drouet's seduction only a few weeks after her arrival in the city, she is not captured by the drummer's charms so much as by her own wants. As Sheldon Grebstein observes, "It is made amply clear that her seducer is also modern life, as symbolized in the big city, with its glamour and appeal."

Sherman McCoy's dreams of supremacy have a more specific form as he sees himself as a Master of the Universe:

> [O]ne fine day, in a fit of euphoria, after he had picked up the telephone and taken an order for zero-coupon bonds that had brought him a $50,000 commission, *just like that*, this very phrase had bubbled up into his brain. On Wall Street, he and a few others . . . had become precisely that . . . Masters of the Universe. There was . . . no limit whatsoever!

With money comes the power that McCoy savors. He can purchase his magnificent co-op with a personal loan, he can indulge his wife's penchant for decoration, he can send his daughter to the proper school, he can dally with his mistress, but his most intense excitement comes at the office:

> By five o-clock Sherman was soaring on adrenaline. He was part of the pulverizing might of Pierce & Pierce. Masters of the Universe. The audacity of it all was breathtaking. To risk $6 billion in one afternoon to make *two ticks*—six and a quarter cents per one hundred dollars—and then to make four ticks. . . . Was there any more exciting power on the face of the earth? . . . The audacity of it flowed through Sherman's limbs and lymph channels and loins. Pierce & Pierce was the power, and he was wired into the power, and the power hummed and surged in his very innards.

In the face of such ecstasy, it is no surprise that Wolfe describes the time of *Bonfire* as "the decade of money fever" and remarks that "It's almost impossible for people to be free of the burning itch for money." A corollary to the itch is an increasing consciousness of money when its supply is threatened. The morning after his *faux pas* at the pay phone, Sherman considers the magnitude of his debt, confidently assumed in the go-go eighties, compared to his father's traditional conservate approach to spending: "Two million six hundred thousand dollars, with $1,800,000 of it borrowed . . . $21,000 a month in principal and interest with a million-dollar balloon payment due in two years." Later, plagued by guilt and fear, Sherman is reduced to counting vastly different sums of money as he and Judy return from a dinner party in a hired car, "the six block ride, costing $123.25, which is to say, one half of $246.50, with Mayfair Town Car Inc.'s white-haired driver at the wheel." On a very different level, Dreiser uses the lure of $10,000 in Hannah & Hogg's unlocked safe to tempt George

Hurstwood, who, like Sherman, had come to see his unhappy household "hemorrhaging money." But it is in Dreiser's restaurant scene between Carrie and Drouet where "two soft, green, handsome ten-dollar bills" are seen not only as an opportunity to have better things but as something intrinsically desirable.

> [S]he could not hold the money in hand without feeling some relief. Even after all her depressing conclusions she could sweep away thought about the matter and then the twenty dollars seemed a wonderful and delightful thing. Ah, money, money, money. What a thing it was to have. How plenty of it would clear away all these troubles.

Clearly, then, when Kenneth Lynn writes that "not even Scott Fitzgerald ever talked about money the way Dreiser does," we can easily draw the same conclusion about Tom Wolfe.

"Status isn't only to do with the rich," Wolfe claims. "Status is fundamental, an inescapable part of human life. Whether status is defined by Drouet's flashy jewelry, Roland Auburn's snow-white Reeboks, or Hurstwood's and McCoy's respective social positions, the quest for higher status is critical for characters in both *Sister Carrie* and *Bonfire*. In each novel, we see examples of unfulfilled characters longing for something better, and in each case, the longings take on definite material dimensions.

Consider the disappointment Carrie experiences when she trades her simple background in Columbia City and her dreams of life in Chicago for the dreary round of underpaid toil in a shoe factory and life in a flat shared with her sister Minnie:

> She felt the drag of a lean and narrow life. The walls of the rooms were discordantly papered. The floors were covered with matting and the hall laid with a thin rag carpet. One could see that furniture was that of poor, hurriedly patched-together quality which was then being sold by the installment houses. Too ignorant to understand anything about the theory of harmony, Carrie felt the lack of it. Something about the place irritated her, she did not know what. She only knew that these things, to her, were dull and commonplace.

Similarly, Larry Kramer, the assistant district attorney who ruefully rides the subway from Manhattan to his office in the Bronx where court reporters routinely made nearly twice as much as he, finds his apartment oppressive:

The gloom was right. The presence of the baby nurse had made him and Rhoda acutely aware of what a dump they lived in. This entire apartment, known as a 3 1/2-room in New York real estate parlance, had been created out of what had once been a pleasant but by no means huge bedroom on the third floor of a town house, with three windows overlooking the street. The so-called room he now stood in was really nothing more than a slot that had been created by inserting a plasterboard wall. The slot had one of the windows. What was left of the original room was now called a living room, and it had the other two windows. Back by the door to the hallway were two more slots, one for a kitchen two people couldn't pass each other in, and the other for a bathroom. Neither had a window. . . . The bathroom was pure Tenament Life. There was laundry hanging all along the shower curtain rod. There was more hanging on a line that ran diagonally across the room.

The status gulf between these characters and their betters is carefully drawn by contrasting images. As Carrie rides in a carriage along North Shore Drive, she drinks in the opulence she comes to crave.

Across the broad lawns, now first freshening into green, she saw lamps faintly glowing upon rich interiors. Now it was a chair, now a table, now an ornate corner which met her eye. . . . Such childish fancies as she had had of fairy palaces and kingly quarters now came back. She imagined that across these richly carved entranceways where the globed and crystalled lamps shone upon paneled doors, set with stained and designed panes of glass, was neither care nor unsatisfied desire. She was perfectly certain that here was happiness.

Against the backdrop of Kramer's crowded flat, we are given the picture of Sherman McCoy emerging from his co-op, walking his daughter to the school bus stop.

Misty days . . . created a peculiar ashy-blue light on Park Avenue. But once they stepped out from under the awning over the entrance . . . such radiance! The median strip on Park was a swath of yellow tulips. There were thousands of them, thanks to the dues apartment owners like Sherman paid to the Park Avenue

> Association. . . . There was something heavenly about the yellow
> glow of all the tulips. That was appropriate . . . he felt himself a
> part of God's grace. A sublime state, it was, and it didn't cost much.

The irony, of course, is that in neither instance does the image correspond
to reality. The discontented George Hurstwood and his grasping family live
in just such a house as Carrie admires, and McCoy drinks in his sublime state
even as his world is beginning to unravel.

In the case of both Carrie Meeber and Larry Kramer, the "drag" of
their prosaic lives causes these characters to feel out of place and to envy
those apparent peers who seem to be more fortunate. Visiting a department
store, Carrie recognizes the differences between herself and the women
around her:

> the fine ladies who elbowed and ignored her, brushing past in
> utter disregard of her presence, themselves eagerly enlisted in
> the materials which the store contained. Carrie was not familiar
> with the appearance of her more fortunate sisters of the city.
> Neither had she before known the nature and appearance of the
> shop girls, with whom she now compared poorly. . . . A flame of
> envy lighted in her heart. She realized in a dim way how much
> the city held—wealth, fashion, ease—every adornment for
> women, and she longed for dress and beauty with a whole and
> fulsome heart.

Likewise, on his way to the subway, Kramer encounters Andy Heller, a law
school classmate toward whom he had always felt superior. Heller, who had
joined a downtown law firm, is well groomed, dressed in expensive clothes,
and carrying a $500 attache as he walks toward a waiting chauffeur-driven
Audi. Instead of greeting his old friend, Kramer hangs back. He knows that
if they were to talk, Heller would immediately recognize his lowly status as
a civil servant and the paltry $36,000 per year he was making.

> That was common knowledge. All the while Andy Heller would
> be scanning his dirty raincoat, his old gray suit, which was too
> short in the pants, his Nike sneakers, his A & P shopping bag.
> . . . He turned around just in time to catch a nice fluffy little
> cloud of German-luxury-sedan fumes in the face as Andy Heller
> departed from his office. Kramer didn't even want to think about
> what the goddamned place probably looked like.

Such encounters serve to underscore the attention both Dreiser and Wolfe pay to "status details" as they create their scenes. As Wolfe remarks, "Details are of no use unless they lead you to an understanding of the heart. It's no mystery; it has to do with the whole subject of status." Both Dreiser and Wolfe have an obvious fascination with clothing—both in their own fastidious attention to personal wardrobes and in the careful descriptions of their characters' attire and grooming. Matthiessen observes of Dreiser:

> The symbol he makes most of . . . is that of clothes, which Veblen was singling out at the same time, in *The Theory of the Leisure Class*, as giving a peculiarly representative expression of "pecuniary culture." Clothes in Dreiser are the chief means of display, of lifting a character above where he was, and by that fact above someone else. They lure—but they also separate.

As Carrie, who has become Drouet's mistress, considers her "fallen" state, she is soothed by the fact that she has gained materially from the relationship and that she is somehow "connected" to the fashionable world—at least in outward appearances.

> "I have nice clothes," she would hum to herself in spirit, drowning the urgent voice. "They make me look so nice. I am safe. The world is not so bad now. It is not so dreadful. . . ."
> "Oh, my nice clothes," the senses were saying. "Oh, the cold streets. Was that the wind whistling I heard? I have a fine cloak. I have gloves. It would be a machine again to do without these things."

An even more dramatic way in which clothes "separate" is found in the scene where Drouet has introduced Carrie to George Hurstwood, a man of palpably higher status than the salesman:

> [Hurstwood's] clothes were particularly new and rich in appearance. The coat lapels stood out with that medium stiffness which excellent cloth possesses. . . . His cravat was a shiny combination of silken threads, not loud, nor inconspicuous. What he wore did not strike the eye so forcibly as that which Drouet had on, but Carrie could see the elegance of the material. Hurstwood's shoes were of soft black calf, polished only to a dull shine, while Drouet wore patent leathers, but Carrie could not

help feeling that there was a distinction in favor of the soft leather, where all else was so rich.

Wolfe is equally concerned with clothes as symbol in *Bonfire*. Indeed, the very first glimpse we have of Sherman McCoy wrestling with his reluctant dachshund is couched in specific observation of his L.L. Bean style casual clothes (plaid shirt, khaki trousers, and boat shoes). A contrast is close at hand, for when Sherman finally escapes his co-op on the pretext of walking Marshall so that he can telephone his mistress, he wears a raincoat befitting a Master of the Universe making a self-consciously casual fashion statement: "It was a worn but formidable rubberized British riding mac, full of flaps, straps, and buckles. He had bought it at Knoud on Madison Avenue. Once, he had considered its aged look as just the thing, after the fashion of the Boston Cracked Shoe look. Now he wondered." His doubt is immediately justified when he rides the elevator to street level with his neighbor, Pollard Browning, president of the co-op board, an old schoolmate, and perhaps the only man to make McCoy feel inferior. This feeling is heightened when Sherman notes this "true Knickerbocker's" appearance: "He was only forty but looked fifty for the past twenty years. His hair was combed back smoothly over his round skull. He wore an immaculate navy suit, a white shirt, a shepherd's check necktie, and no raincoat. He faced the elevator door, took another look at Sherman, said nothing, and turned back."

McCoy's attention to his appearance and that of others is consistent throughout the novel, and it is ironic that when he is most fearful, he cannot help but be concerned that he make the right impression. As he prepares to meet the detectives investigating the hit-and-run accident, he agonizes:

> How should he look? Should he put his jacket and tie back on? He had on a white shirt, the pants of a gray nailhead worsted suit and a pair of black cap-toed shoes. With the tie and jacket on, he would look terribly Wall Street, terribly conservative. They might resent that. . . . He put on the tie and pulled it up into a tight knot. . . . He put on the jacket and buttoned it. He lifted his chin and squared his shoulders. Wall Street. He went into the bathroom and brushed his hair back. He lifted his chin again. Be strong. A Master of the Universe.

When he meets the two detectives, he cannot help but note that Goldberg looks "like a great slab of meat with clothes on. His suit jacket sat out from his wrestler's gut like cardboard" and Martin is "wearing a sport jacket and the sort of brown pants a wife might choose to go with it." Neither is at home in his Park Avenue co-op, and he sees that Martin takes in "Judy's tens of thousands of hemorrhaging dollars' worth of perfect little details" like a tourist.

"Clothing, then, makes show-offs of us all; it is one of the few forms of conspicuous display that everyone must practice" (Brooks). Or, as Tom Wolfe himself maintains, "Clothing is a wonderful doorway that most easily leads you to the heart of an individual; it's the way they reveal themselves."

Both *Bonfire* and *Sister Carrie* use the rich documentation of status details to delineate the various strata of the urban world they create. Individual characters, in fact, become subordinate to this world; in some instances, they are "connected" to a particular milieu—in which case they function successfully—or, as happens with George Hurstwood and Sherman McCoy, they become isolated from their world. In the latter instance, the strength of the individual is put to the test. True to the naturalistic writer's perspective, the force directing the action in both novels is a combination of the individual character's desire (a lust for the possibilities that life can offer) and circumstance (the apparent drift of events in the urban maelstrom).

In his Chicago "resort," if not in his contentious North Side residence, Hurstwood can be seen as a man completely in tune with his surroundings. The trusted manager of Hannah and Hogg's lavish saloon, Hurstwood was

> shrewd and clever in many little things and capable of creating a good impression.
>
> . . . For the most part he lounged about, dressed in excellent, tailored suits of imported goods, several rings upon his fingers, a fine blue diamond in his necktie, a striking vest of some new pattern and a watch chain of solid gold. . . . He knew by name and could greet personally with a "Well, old fellow," hundreds of actors, merchants, politicians, and the general run of successful characters about town. . . . He had a finely graduated scale of informality and friendship . . . and was altogether a very acceptable individual of our great American upper class—the first grade below the luxuriously rich.

However, once he is transplanted to New York by virtue of his theft of money and "elopement" with Carrie, he becomes "a common fish" in a tempestuous sea "full of whales." Unable to succeed in establishing a new business, he becomes restive living off Carrie's income as an actress. In a precipitous decline, which some critics find less than convincing, he leaves his flat, eats cast away food, and finally presents a dramatic contrast to his earlier state.

> He was beginning to find, in his wretched clothing and meagre state of body, that people took him for a chronic type of bum and beggar. Police hustled him along, restaurant and lodging-house keepers turned him out promptly the moment he had his due, pedestrians waved him off. He found it more and more difficult to get anything from anybody.

In his isolation and despair, turning on the gas in a lonely room, shrouded by the kindness which is night, is the only dignity he has left.

McCoy's progress is different. Once Pierce & Pierce's number-one bond salesman, Yale educated son of the "Lion of Dunning Sponget," and established member of the New York smart set Sherman becomes paralyzed by guilt over his disintegrating marriage and fear of the police connecting him with a hit-and-run accident. On the same evening he is first interrogated by Martin and Goldberg, he is to dine with his wife at the Bavardages. Entering the "dazzling, effervescent" foyer, McCoy senses a pattern: "All the men and women in this hall were arranged in clusters, conversational bouquets, so to speak. There were no solitary figures, no strays." Because of his own inner turmoil, he is unable to engage the idle social whirl, either at cocktails or at dinner, that under other circumstances would be second nature to him.

> He was stranded again . . . He was facing social death once more. He was a man sitting utterly alone at a dinner table. The hive buzzed all around him. Everyone else was in a state of social bliss. . . . Only he was a wallflower with no conversational mate, a social light with no wattage whatsoever in the Bavardage Celebrity Zoo. . . . *My life is coming apart!*—and yet through everything else in his overloaded central nervous system burned the shame—the shame!—of social incompetence.

His self-flagellation is only a bit more pathetic than his wife's chiding him on the way home for being so inept. Later, in a deliberately parallel dinner party at the DiDuccis after his personal and legal problems have become tabloid headlines and, no doubt, the prime gossip of his social circle, McCoy finds himself welcomed back to the hive, at least as a somewhat scandalous survivor of the criminal justice system. Finding the company enthralled at his embellished tales of incarceration and interrogation, Sherman seems to revel in celebrity:

> Eagerly they stared at him, the entire bouquet—*his* bouquet. . . .
> Their expressions were so rapt, so deliriously expectant! . . . .

During much of the dinner all six of these men and women were tuned in solely to Mr. Sherman McCoy. Crime. Economics. God. Freedom. Immorality—whatever McCoy of the McCoy Case cared to talk about, the table listened.

However, it is important to understand that *this* Sherman McCoy is well on his way to becoming the outcast-rebel of a climactic courthouse melee. There may be enough of Tommy Killian's "Irish" in him (and enough of Scott Fitzgerald's "spoiled priest" in Tom Wolfe) to see the buzzing hive in all its shallowness, even as he savors it.

The nature of the hive—and, in fact, of society itself—is a preoccupation shared by both Dreiser and Wolfe. "In fiction of bygone days what [Wolfe] most admires is the novelists' ambition to create a sweeping, accurate portrait of their whole society. . . ." Wolfe acknowledges his debt to Zola's naturalism and notes the change in post World War II fiction in this way: "It's the idea of the novelist putting the individual in the setting of society at large and realizing the pressure society exerts on the individual. This is something that has been lost over the past 40 years in the American novel."

Wolfe, like Dreiser, began writing fiction after already establishing himself as a journalist; and in spite of the fact that Wolfe is regarded as one of the founders of "the new journalism," he shares many of the characteristics that Dreiser displays in his articles. In *Rolling Stone* (where *Bonfire* appeared in serial form before the publication of the novel) Wolfe delineates the four steps of composition that he sees central to new journalism:

> The first is scene-by-scene construction. In other words, telling the entire story through a sequence of scenes rather than simple historical narrative. Second is the use of real dialogue—the more the better. The third, which is the least understood of the techniques, is the use of status details. That is, noting articles of clothing, manners, the way people treat children, the way they treat servants. . . . The fourth is the use of point of view, which is depicting scenes through a particular pair of eyes.

Scene-by-scene construction, a keen sense of the spoken vernacular, the careful (even overwhelming) use of details, and specific (not necessarily objective) points of view are characteristics shared by *Bonfire* and *Sister Carrie*. These shared characteristics have led reviewers to see both novels, in turn, as "fictionalized reportage" rather than fiction. *Time*'s review of *Bonfire* notes that "The ingeniously rigged plot is clearly fiction, but the details of New York City life, high and low, leap from the legman's notebook" (Sheppard). Against the critics in his day who claimed that *Sister Carrie* was both graceless and immoral (therefore non-literary), Dreiser maintains, "Here is a book that is close to life. It is not intended as a piece of literary craftsmanship, but as a picture of conditions." The vision of American urban society that is presented in these novels may be found in a series of vivid scenes. Readers of *Sister Carrie* are struck by the neighborhoods, dwellings, department stores, restaurants, theatres, Broadway, and the Bowery. Similarly Wolfe offers Park Avenue, the Bronx, precinct houses, court rooms, offices, restaurants, and apartments. The ordering of scenes may sometimes appear to be almost haphazard, indicating the role that circumstance or chance has in the course of human events. Oftentimes, however, scenes are set in obvious contrast. The descriptions of Minnie's Van Buren Place flat and the houses of North Shore Drive in *Carrie* as well as those of McCoy's and Kramer's apartments in *Bonfire* are noteworthy because they offer insight into the characters themselves at the same time they present "a picture of conditions."

Dreiser's novel is filled with images of the sea: Carrie is described as "a lone figure in a tossing, thoughtless sea," "an anchorless, storm beaten little craft"; Hurstwood is "like a vessel, powerful and dangerous, but rolling and floundering without sail." People are described as drifting at the mercy of the inscrutable forces which make up society and life itself. We find "a society in which there are no real equals, no equilibrium, but only people moving up and down" (Matthiessen). The same is true of *Bonfire*. However, Wolfe's late-twentieth-century conscience will not allow the forces which toss people from one status to another to remain anonymous. While Carrie is driven by vague longings for "happiness" and Drouet by his easygoing but undefined animal instincts, characters such as McCoy, Kramer, Reverend Bacon, and even Peter Fallow are driven by specifically defined power goals: mastery of the "universes" of high finance and high society; legal authority as idealistic self-affirmation and sexual magnet; "steam control" as a means of massing a financial and political empire; or the ability to tell his boss to go to hell from the pulpit of Pulitzer-Prize celebrity. But the instability of a society characterized by status seeking, ethnic chauvinism, political manipulation, and racial hostility either thwarts or rewards these power quests at random and, in so doing, call into question some of the most cherished myths of the American dream.

The world according to Wolfe—and to Dreiser and Dickens and Balzac and Thackeray before him—is vast and anonymous except for the vividly typed characters. They appear to emerge from the crowd, only to be skewered by a satirist's pen. We find youthful Lemon Tarts, starved Social X-Rays, "pimp-rolling" Reebok-shod blacks, ruthless politicians, greedy lawyers, and assorted pompous fools. However, to view Wolfe's treatment of people such as McCoy, Kramer, and Fallow only as stereotyped "audio-visual aids" to illustrate a lecture of sociology, as Richard Vigilante suggests is to miss a great deal of *Bonfire*'s depth. For instance, it can be argued persuasively that McCoy is a dynamic character who comes to recognize the limits of his and modern America's narcissism. Wolfe claims that "My intention, my hope, was always to get inside of these people, inside their central nervous systems, and present their experience in print from the inside. That can come out something like satire in some cases where people are leading wacky enough lives." Such people may be ridiculous—as we all can be at times—but we come to understand them and, through their eyes, come to an understanding of their world and our own.

Dreiser's approach to character is similar, as he once declared, "I am Carrie. I am Hurstwood. I am Drouet." Both authors display a genuine understanding, sympathy, and even affection toward their characters at the same time they paint them with a satiric brush. Moreover, these writers emerge as "characters" in their own novels through Dreiser's "looming presence" in insights beyond his heroine's capacity and his self-conscious philosophizing and through Wolfe's delighted satire of language and accents and his enthusiastic exclamation-asides reminiscent of his most noteworthy feature articles.

Bonfire, along with much of Dreiser's work, especially *Carrie*, draws heavily from the tradition of naturalism. Haskell Block argues that naturalistic novels

> depend to a considerable extent on the accurate and literal observation of reality; [they] purport to present human experience honestly and convincingly; and [they] reflect a deterministic view of events that is derived from the natural sciences and represented in the operation of biological and social forces.

Dreiser and Wolfe create works that live up to these expectations to a great extent. The fiction created does depend on the novelists' documentation of individual characters and their milieu. However, neither author seems willing to commit entirely to the naturalistic thesis, for they are caught in the tension that Donald Pizer describes between characters who should be controlled exclusively by "environment, heredity, instinct, or chance," but whose fates are ultimately more complex. "[T]he imagination refuses to accept this formula as the total meaning of life, and so seeks a new basis for man's sense of his own dignity and importance." Perhaps one could even find a twentieth-century existentialist-urge in Sherman McCoy's symbolic death at the hands of the criminal justice system and subsequent rebirth as rebel-hero. Whether we define a character's dignity as Carrie's continuing sense of wonder and longing for something beyond material luxury, Hurstwood's calm repose as he ends his life, or McCoy's continued defiance of a system of social order he had come to understand in a new light and to reject, both Wolfe and Dreiser transcend simple formulas in their novels. It is true of *The Bonfire of the Vanities* that "There are echoes throughout of the classic American twentieth-century novels about the snatching away of worldly success" (Lehman). Tom Wolfe has earned a place among those writers, such as Dreiser and Fitzgerald, who have chronicled the American dream in the twentieth century. The complexity and popularity of *Bonfire* attest to the novel's worth. Wolfe's language is metaphorical and his use of the status details make them repositories of symbolic value. Zola argues that "A great novelist, in our time, is one who has the sense of the real and who expresses nature with originality, by making it live with its own life." Tom Wolfe, if grudgingly, has assured the continued presence of "the social-realist novel" in American literature even as he has established his own reputation as a master of the fiction writer's art.

TOM WOLFE

Stalking the Billion-Footed Beast:
A Literary Manifesto for the New Social Novel

May I be forgiven if I take as my text the sixth page of the fourth chapter of *The Bonfire of the Vanities*? The novel's main character, Sherman McCoy, is driving over the Triborough Bridge in New York City in his Mercedes roadster with his twenty-six-year-old girlfriend, not his forty-year-old wife, in the tan leather bucket seat beside him, and he glances triumphantly off to his left toward the island of Manhattan. "The towers were jammed together so tightly, he could feel the mass and stupendous weight. Just think of the millions, from all over the globe, who yearned to be on that island, in those towers, in those narrow streets! There it was, the Rome, the Paris, the London of the twentieth century, the city of ambition, the dense magnetic rock, the irresistible destination of all those who insist on being *where things are happening—*"

To me the idea of writing a novel about this astonishing metropolis, a big novel, cramming as much of New York City between covers as you could, was the most tempting, the most challenging, and the most obvious idea an American writer could possibly have. I had first vowed to try it in 1968, except that what I had in mind then was a nonfiction novel, to use a much-discussed term from the period. I had just written one, *The Electric Kool-Aid Acid Test*, about the psychedelic, or hippie, movement, and I had begun to indulge in some brave speculations about nonfiction as an art form. These were eventually recorded in a book called *The New Journalism*. Off the

From *Harper's* 279, no. 1674 (November 1989). © 1989 by *Harper's Magazine*.

record, however, alone in my little apartment on East Fifty-eighth Street, I was worried that somebody out there was writing a big realistic fictional novel about the hippie experience that would blow *The Electric Kool-Aid Acid Test* out of the water. Somebody? There might be droves of them. After all, among the hippies were many well-educated and presumably, not to mention avowedly, creative people. But one, two, three, four years went by, and to my relief, and then my bafflement, those novels never appeared. (And to this day they remain unwritten.)

Meantime, I turned to the proposed nonfiction novel about New York. As I saw it, such a book should be a novel *of the city*, in the sense that Balzac and Zola had written novels *of Paris* and Dickens and Thackeray had written novels *of London*, with the city always in the foreground, exerting its relentless pressure on the souls of its inhabitants. My immediate model was Thackeray's *Vanity Fair*. Thackeray and Dickens had lived in the first great era of the metropolis. Now, a century later, in the 1960s, certain powerful forces had converged to create a second one. The economic boom that had begun in the middle of the Second World War surged through the decade of the Sixties without even a mild recession. The flush times created a sense of immunity, and standards that had been in place for millennia were swept aside with a merry, rut-boar abandon. One result was the so-called sexual revolution, which I always thought was a rather prim term for the lurid carnival that actually took place.

Indirectly, the boom also triggered something else: overt racial conflict. Bad feelings had been rumbling on low boil in the cities ever since the great migrations from the rural South had begun in the 1920s. But in 1965 a series of race riots erupted, starting with the Harlem riot in 1964 and the Watts riot in Los Angeles in 1965, moving to Detroit in 1967, and peaking in Washington and Chicago in 1968. These were riots that only the Sixties could have produced. In the Sixties, the federal government had created the War on Poverty, at the heart of which were not alms for the poor but setups called CAPs: Community Action Programs. CAPs were something new in the history of political science. They were official invitations from the government to people in the slums to improve their lot by rising up and rebelling against the establishment, including the government itself. The government would provide the money, the headquarters, and the advisers. So people in the slums obliged. The riots were merely the most sensational form the strategy took, however. The more customary form was the confrontation. *Confrontation* was a Sixties term. It was not by mere coincidence that the most violent of the Sixties confrontational groups, the Black Panther Party of America, drew up its ten-point program in the North Oakland poverty center. That was what the poverty center was there for.

Such was the backdrop one day in January of 1970 when I decided to attend a party that Leonard Bernstein and his wife, Felicia, were giving for the Black Panthers in their apartment at Park Avenue and Seventy-ninth Street. I figured that here might be some material for a chapter in my non-fiction *Vanity Fair* about New York. I didn't know the half of it. It was at this party that a Black Panther field marshal rose up beside the north piano—there was also a south piano—in Leonard Bernstein's living room and outlined the Panthers' ten-point program to a roomful of socialites and celebrities, who, giddy with *nostalgie de la boue*, entertained a vision of the future in which, after the revolution, there would no longer be any such thing as a two-story, thirteen-room apartment on Park Avenue, with twin grand pianos in the living room, for one family.

All I was after was material for a chapter in a nonfiction novel, as I say. But the party was such a perfect set piece that I couldn't hold back. I wrote an account of the evening for *New York* magazine entitled "Radical Chic" and, as a companion piece, an article about the confrontations the War on Poverty had spawned in San Francisco, "Mau-mauing the Flak Catchers." The two were published as a book in the fall of 1970. Once again I braced and waited for the big realistic novels that were sure to be written about this phenomenon that had played such a major part in American life in the late 1960s and early 1970s: racial strife in the cities. Once again the years began to roll by, and these novels never appeared.

This time, however, my relief was not very profound. I still had not written my would-be big book about New York. I had merely put off the at-tempt. In 1972 I put it off a little further. I went to Cape Canaveral to cover the launch of *Apollo 17*, the last mission to the moon, for *Rolling Stone*. I ended up writing a four-part series on the astronauts, then decided to spend the next five or six months expanding the material into a book. The five or six months stretched into a year, eighteen months, two years, and I began to look over my shoulder. Truman Capote, for one, had let it be known that he was working on a big novel about New York entitled *Answered Prayers*. No doubt there were others as well. The material was rich beyond belief and getting richer every day.

Another year slipped by . . . and, miraculously, no such book appeared.

Now I paused and looked about and tried to figure out what was, in fact, going on in the world of American fiction. I wasn't alone, as it turned out. Half the publishers along Madison Avenue—at that time, publishing houses could still afford Madison Avenue—had their noses pressed against their thermopane glass walls scanning the billion-footed city for the approach of the young novelists who, surely, would bring them the big novels of the racial clashes, the hippie movement, the New Left, the Wall Street boom, the sexual revolution, the war in Vietnam. But such creatures, it seemed, no longer existed.

The strange fact of the matter was that young people with serious literary ambitions were no longer interested in the metropolis or any other big, rich slices of contemporary life. Over the preceding fifteen years, while I had been immersed in journalism, one of the most curious chapters in American literary history had begun. (And it is not over yet.) The story is by turns bizarre and hilarious, and one day some lucky doctoral candidate with the perseverance of a Huizinga or a Hauser will do it justice. I can offer no more than the broadest outline.

After the Second World War, in the late 1940s, American intellectuals began to revive a dream that had glowed briefly in the 1920s. They set out to create a native intelligentsia on the French or English model, an intellectual aristocracy—socially unaffiliated, beyond class distinctions—active in politics and the arts. In the arts, their audience would be the inevitably small minority of truly cultivated people as opposed to the mob, who wished only to be entertained or to be assured they were "cultured." By now, if one need edit, the mob was better known as the middle class.

Among the fashionable European ideas that began to circulate was that of "the death of the novel," by which was meant the realistic novel. Writing in 1948, Lionel Trilling gave this notion a late-Marxist twist that George Steiner and others would elaborate on. The realistic novel, in their gloss, was the literary child of the nineteenth-century industrial bourgeoisie. It was a slice of life, a cross section, that provided a true and powerful picture of individuals and society—as long as the bourgeois order and the old class system were firmly in place. But now that the bourgeoisie was in a state of "crisis and partial rout" (Steiner's phrase) and the old class system was crumbling, the realistic novel was pointless. What could be more futile than a cross section of disintegrating fragments?

The truth was, as Arnold Hauser had gone to great pains to demonstrate in *The Social History of Art*, the intelligentsia have always had contempt for the realistic novel—a form that wallows so enthusiastically in the dirt of everyday life and the dirty secrets of class envy and that, still worse, is so easily understood and obviously relished by the mob, i.e., the middle class. In Victorian England, the intelligentsia regarded Dickens as "the author of the uneducated, undiscriminating public." It required a chasm of time—eighty years, in fact—to separate his work from its vulgar milieu so that Dickens might be canonized in British literary circles. The intelligentsia have always preferred more refined forms of fiction, such as that longtime French intellectual favorite, the psychological novel.

By the early 1960s, the notion of the death of the realistic novel had caught on among young American writers with the force of revelation. This was an extraordinary turnabout. It had been only yesterday, in the 1930s, that the big realistic novel, with its broad social sweep, had put American literature up on the world stage for the first time. In 1930 Sinclair Lewis, a realistic novelist who used reporting techniques as thorough as Zola's, became the first American writer to win the Nobel Prize. In his acceptance speech, he called on his fellow writers to give America "a literature worthy of her vastness," and, indeed, four of the next five Americans to win the Nobel Prize in literature—Pearl Buck, William Faulkner, Ernest Hemingway, and John Steinbeck—were realistic novelists. (The fifth was Eugene O'Neill.) For that matter, the most highly regarded new novelists of the immediate postwar period—James Jones, Norman Mailer, Irwin Shaw, William Styron, Calder Willingham—were all realists.

Yet by 1962, when Steinbeck won the Nobel Prize, young writers, and intellectuals generally, regarded him and his approach to the novel as an embarrassment. Pearl Buck was even worse, and Lewis wasn't much better. Faulkner and Hemingway still commanded respect, but it was the respect you give to old boys who did the best they could with what they knew in their day. They were "squares" (John Gardner's term) who actually thought you could take real life and spread it across the pages of a book. They never comprehended the fact that a novel is a sublime literary game.

All serious young writers—*serious* meaning those who aimed for literary prestige—understood such things, and they were dismantling the realistic novel just as fast as they could think of ways to do it. The dividing line was the year 1960. Writers who went to college after 1960 . . . *understood*. For a serious young writer to stick with realism after 1960 required contrariness and courage.

Writers who had gone to college before 1960, such as Saul Bellow, Robert Stone, and John Updike, found it hard to give up realism, but many others were caught betwixt and between. They didn't know which way to turn. For example, Philip Roth, a 1954 graduate of Bucknell, won the National Book Award in 1960 at the age of twenty-seven for a collection entitled *Goodbye, Columbus*. The title piece was a brilliant novella of manners—brilliant . . . but, alas, highly realistic. By 1961 Roth was having second thoughts. He made a statement that had a terrific impact on other young writers. We now live in an age, he said, in which the imagination of the novelist lies helpless before what he knows he will read in tomorrow morning's newspaper. "The actuality is continually outdoing our talents, and the culture tosses up figures daily that are the envy of any novelist."

Even today—perhaps especially today—anyone, writer or not, can sympathize. What novelist would dare concoct a plot in which, say, a

Southern television evangelist has a tryst in a motel with a church secretary from Babylon, New York—Did you have to make it *Babylon?*—and is ruined to the point where he has to sell all his worldly goods at auction, including his air-conditioned doghouse—*air-conditioned doghouse?*—whereupon he is termed a "decadent pompadour boy" by a second television evangelist, who, we soon learn, has been combing his own rather well-teased blond hair forward over his forehead and wearing headbands in order to disguise himself as he goes into Louisiana waterbed motels with combat-zone prostitutes—Oh, *come on*—prompting a third television evangelist, who is under serious consideration for the Republican presidential nomination, to charge that the damning evidence has been leaked to the press by the Vice President of the United States . . . while, meantime, the aforesaid church secretary has now bared her chest to the photographers and has thereby become an international celebrity and has gone to live happily ever after in a castle known as the Playboy Mansion . . . and her erstwhile tryst mate, evangelist No. 1, was last seen hiding in the fetal position under his lawyer's couch in Charlotte, North Carolina . . .

What novelist would dare dream up such crazy stuff and then ask you to suspend your disbelief?

The lesson that a generation of serious young writers learned from Roth's lament was that it was time to avert their eyes. To attempt a realistic novel with the scope of Balzac, Zola, or Lewis was absurd. By the mid-1960s the conviction was not merely that the realistic novel was no longer possible but that American life itself no longer deserved the term *real*. American life was chaotic, fragmented, random, discontinuous; in a word, *absurd*. Writers in the university creative writing programs had long, phenomenological discussions in which they decided that the act of writing words on a page was the real thing and the so-called real world of America was the fiction, requiring the suspension of disbelief. *The so-called real world* became a favorite phrase.

New types of novels came in waves, each trying to establish an avant-garde position out beyond realism. There was Absurdist novels, Magical Realist novels, and novels of Radical Disjunction (the novelist and critic Robert Towers's phrase) in which plausible events and plausible characters were combined in fantastic or outlandish ways, often resulting in dreadful catastrophes that were played for laughs in the ironic mode. Irony was the attitude supreme, and nowhere more so than in the Puppet-Master novels, a category that often overlapped with the others. The Puppet-Masters were in love with the theory that the novel was, first and foremost, a literary game, words on a page being manipulated by an author. Ronald Sukenick, author of a highly praised 1968 novel called *Up*, would tell you what he looked like while he was writing the words you were at that moment reading. At one point you are informed that he is stark naked. Sometimes he tells you he's crossing out what you've just read and changing it. Then he gives you the new version. In a story called "The Death of the Novel," he keeps saying, à la Samuel Beckett, "I can't go on." Then he exhorts himself, "Go on," and on he goes. At the end of *Up* he tells you that none of the characters was real: "I just make it up as I go along."

The Puppet-Masters took to calling their stories *fictions*, after the manner of Jorge Luis Borges, who spoke of his *ficciones*. Borges, an Argentinian, was one of the gods of the new breed. In keeping with the cosmopolitan yearnings of the native intelligentsia, all gods now came from abroad: Borges, Nabokov, Beckett, Pinter, Kundera, Calvino, García Márquez, and, above all, Kafka; there was a whole rash of stories with characters named H or V or K or T or P (but, for some reason, none named A, B, D, or E). It soon reached the point where a creative writing teacher at Johns Hopkins held up Tolstoy as a master of the novel—and was looked upon by his young charges as rather touchingly old-fashioned. As one of them, Frederick Barthelme, later put it, "He talked Leo Tolstoy when we were up to here with Laurence Sterne, Franz Kafka, Italo Calvino, and Gabriel García Márquez. In fact, Gabriel García Márquez was already *over* by then."

By the 1970s there was a headlong rush to get rid of not only realism but everything associated with it. One of the most highly praised of the new breed, John Hawkes, said: "I began to write fiction on the assumption that the true enemies of the novel were plot, character, setting, and theme." The most radical group, the Neo-Fabulists, decided to go back to the primal origins of fiction, back to a happier time, before realism and all its contaminations, back to myth, fable, and legend. John Gardner and John Irving both started out in this vein, but the peerless leader was John Barth, who wrote a collection of three novellas called *Chimera*, recounting the further adventures of Perseus and Andromeda and other characters from Greek mythology. *Chimera* won the 1972 National Book Award for fiction.

Other Neo-Fabulists wrote modern fables, à la Kafka, in which the action, if any, took place at no specific location. You couldn't even tell what hemisphere it was. It was some nameless, elemental terrain—the desert, the woods, the open sea, the snowy wastes. The characters had no backgrounds. They came from nowhere. They didn't use realistic speech. Nothing they said, did, or possessed indicated any class or ethnic origin. Above all, the Neo-Fabulists avoided all big, obvious sentiments and emotions, which the realistic novel, with its dreadful Little Nell scenes, specialized in. Perfect anesthesia; that was the ticket, even in the death scenes. Anesthetic solitude became one of the great motifs of serious fiction in the 1970s. The Minimalists, also known as the K-Mart Realists, wrote about real situations, but very tiny ones, tiny domestic ones, for the most part, usually in lonely Rustic Septic Tank Rural settings, in a deadpan prose composed of disingenuously short, simple sentences—with the emotions anesthetized, given a shot of novocaine. My favorite Minimalist opening comes from a short story by Robert Coover: "In order to get started, he went to live alone on an island and shot himself."

Many of these writers were brilliant. They were virtuosos. They could do things within the narrow limits they had set for themselves that were more clever and amusing than anyone could have ever imagined. But what was this lonely island they had moved to? After all, they, like me, happened to be alive in what was, for better or for worse, the American century, the century in which we had become the mightiest military power in all history, capable of blowing up the world by turning two cylindrical keys in a missile silo but also capable, once it blew, of escaping to the stars in spaceships. We were alive in the first moment since the dawn of time in which man was able at last to break the bonds of Earth's gravity and explore the rest of the universe. And, on top of that, we had created an affluence that reached clear down to the level of mechanics and tradesmen on a scale that would have made the Sun King blink, so that on any given evening even a Neo-Fabulist's or a Minimalist's electrician or air-conditioner mechanic or burglar-alarm repairman might very well be in Saint Kitts or Barbados or Puerto Vallarta wearing a Harry Belafonte cane-cutter shirt, open to the sternum, the better to reveal the gold chains twinkling in his chest hair, while he and his third wife sit on the terrace and have a little designer water before dinner . . .

What a feast was spread out before every writer in America! How could any writer resist plunging into it? I couldn't.

In 1979, after I had finally completed my book about the astronauts, *The Right Stuff*, I returned at last to the idea of a novel about New York. I now decided the book would not be a nonfiction novel but a fictional one. Part of it, I suppose, was curiosity or, better said, the question that rebuked every writer who had made a point of experimenting with nonfiction over the preceding ten or fifteen years: Are you merely ducking the big challenge— The Novel? Consciously, I wanted to prove a point. I wanted to fulfill a prediction I had made in the introduction to *The New Journalism* in 1973; namely, that the future of the fictional novel would be in a highly detailed realism based on reporting, a realism more thorough than any currently being attempted, a realism that would portray the individual in intimate and inextricable relation to the society around him.

One of the axioms of literary theory in the Seventies was that realism was "just another formal device, not a permanent method for dealing with experience" (in the words of the editor of the *Partisan Review*, William Phillips). I was convinced then—and I am even more strongly convinced now—that precisely the opposite is true. The introduction of realism into literature in the eighteenth century by Richardson, Fielding, and Smollett was like the introduction of electricity into engineering. It was not just another device. The effect on the emotions of an everyday realism such as Richardson's was something that had never been conceived of before. It was realism that created the "absorbing" or "gripping" quality that is peculiar to the novel, the quality that makes the reader feel that he has been pulled not only into the setting of the story but also into the minds and central nervous systems of the characters. No one was ever moved to tears by reading about the unhappy fates of heroes and heroines in Homer, Sophocles, Molière, Racine, Sydney, Spenser, or Shakespeare. Yet even the impeccable Lord Jeffrey, editor of the *Edinburgh Review*, confessed to having cried—blubbered, boohooed, snuffled, and sighed—over the death of Little Nell in *The Old Curiosity Shop*. For writers to give up this power in the quest for a more up-to-date kind of fiction—it is as if an engineer were to set out to develop a more sophisticated machine technology by first of all discarding the principle of electricity, on the grounds that it has been used ad nauseam for a hundred years.

One of the specialties of the realistic novel, from Richardson on, was the demonstration of the influence of society on even the most personal aspects of the life of the individual. Lionel Trilling was right when he said, in 1948, that what produced great characters in the nineteenth-century European novel was the portrayal of "class traits modified by personality." But he went on to argue that the old class structure by now had disintegrated, particularly in the United Sates, rendering the technique useless. Again, I would say that precisely the opposite is the case. If we substitute for *class*, in Trilling's formulation, the broader term *status*, that technique has never been more essential in portraying the innermost life of the individual. This is above all true when the subject is the modern city. It strikes me as folly to believe that you can portray the individual in the city today without also portraying the city itself.

Asked once what three novels he would most recommend to a creative writing student, Faulkner said (or is said to have said): "*Anna Karenina, Anna Karenina,* and *Anna Karenina.*" And what is at the core of not only the private dramas but also the very psychology of *Anna Karenina*? It is Tolstoy's concept of the heart at war with the structure of society. The dramas of Anna, Vronsky, Karenin, Levin, and Kitty would be nothing but slow-moving romances without the panorama of Russian society against which Tolstoy

places them. The characters' electrifying irrational acts are the acts of the
heart brought to a desperate edge by the pressure of society.

If Trilling were here, he would no doubt say, But of course, "class traits
modified by personality." These are substantial characters (*substantial* was
one of Trilling's favorite terms) precisely because Russian society in Tolstoy's
day was so clearly defined by social classes, each with its own distinctive
culture and traditions. Today, in New York, Trilling could argue, Anna would
just move in with Vronsky, and people in their social set would duly note the
change in their Scully & Scully address books; and the arrival of the baby, if
they chose to have it, would occasion no more than a grinning snigger in the
gossip columns. To which I would say, Quite so. The status structure of
society has changed, but it has not disappeared for a moment. It provides an
infinite number of new agonies for the Annas and Vronskys of the Upper
East Side, and, as far as that goes, of Leningrad. Anyone who doubts that
need only get to know them.

American society today is not more or less chaotic, random,
discontinuous or absurd than Russian society or French society or British
society a hundred years ago, no matter how convenient it might be for a
writer to think so. It is merely more varied and complicated and harder to
define. In the prologue to *The Bonfire of the Vanities*, the mayor of New York
delivers a soliloquy in a stream of consciousness as he is being routed from a
stage in Harlem by a group of demonstrators. He thinks of all the rich white
New Yorkers who will be watching this on television from within the
insulation of their cooperative apartments. "Do you really think this is *your*
city any longer? Open your eyes! The greatest city of the twentieth century!
Do you think *money* will keep it yours? Come down from your swell co-ops,
you general partners and merger lawyers! It's the Third World down there!
Puerto Ricans, West Indians, Haitians, Dominicans, Cubans, Colombians,
Hondurans, Koreans, Chinese, Thais, Vietnamese, Ecuadorians,
Panamanians, Filipinos, Albanians, Senegalese, and Afro-Americans! Go
visit the frontiers, you gutless wonders! Morningside Heights, St. Nicholas
Park, Washington Heights, Fort Tryon—*por qué pagar más*! The Bronx—the
Bronx is finished for you!"—and on he goes. New York and practically every
other large city in the United States are undergoing a profound change. The
fourth great wave of immigrants—this one from Asia, North Africa, Latin
America, and the Caribbean—is now pouring in. Within ten years political
power in most major American cities will have passed to the nonwhite
majorities. Does that render these cities incomprehensible, fragmented
beyond the grasp of all logic, absurd, meaningless to gaze upon in a literary
sense? Not in my opinion. It merely makes the task of the writer more
difficult if he wants to know what truly presses upon the heart of the

individual, white or nonwhite, living in the metropolis in the last decade of the twentieth century.

That task, as I see it, inevitably involves reporting, which I regard as the most valuable and least understood resource available to any writer with exalted ambitions, whether the medium is print, film, tape, or the stage. Young writers are constantly told, "Write about what you know." There is nothing wrong with that rule as a starting point, but it seems to get quickly magnified into an unspoken maxim: The only valid experience is personal experience.

Emerson said that every person has a great autobiography to write, if only he understands what is truly his own unique experience. But he didn't say every person had *two* great autobiographies to write. Dickens, Dostoyevski, Balzac, Zola, and Sinclair Lewis *assumed* that the novelist had to go beyond his personal experience and head out into society as a reporter. Zola called it documentation, and his documenting expeditions to the slums, the coal mines, the races, the *folies*, department stores, wholesale food markets, newspaper offices, barnyards, railroad yards, and engine decks, notebook and pen in hand, became legendary. To write *Elmer Gantry*, the great portrait of not only a corrupt evangelist but also the entire Protestant clergy at a time when they still set the moral tone of America, Lewis left his home in New England and moved to Kansas City. He organized Bible study groups for clergymen, delivered sermons from the pulpits of preachers on summer vacation, attended tent meetings and Chautauqua lectures and church conferences and classes at the seminaries, all the while doggedly taking notes on five-by-eight cards.

It was through this process, documentation, that Lewis happened to scoop the Jim Bakker story by sixty years—and to render it totally plausible, historically and psychologically, in fiction. I refer to the last two chapters of *Elmer Gantry*. We see Elmer, the great evangelist, get caught in a tryst with . . . the church secretary (Hettie Dowler is her name) . . . who turns out to be in league with a very foxy lawyer . . . and the two of them present Elmer with a hefty hush-money demand, which he is only too eager to pay. . . . With the help of friends, however, Elmer manages to turn the tables, and is absolved and vindicated in the eyes of humanity and the press. On the final page, we see Elmer on his knees beside the pulpit on Sunday morning before a packed house, with his gaze lifted heavenward and his hands pressed together in Albrecht Dürer mode, tears running down his face, loudly thanking the Lord for delivering him from the vipers. As the book ends, he looks toward the choir and catches a glimpse of a new addition, "a girl with charming ankles and lively eyes . . ."

Was it reporting that made Lewis the most highly regarded American novelist of the 1920s? Certainly not by itself. But it was the material he found through reporting that enabled Lewis to exercise with such rich variety his insights, many of them exceptionally subtle, into the psyches of men and women and into the status structure of society. Having said that, I will now reveal something that practically every writer has experienced—and none, as far as I know, has ever talked about. The young person who decides to become a writer because he has a subject or an issue in mind, because he has "something to say," is a rare bird. Most make that decision because they realize they have a certain musical facility with words. Since poetry is the music of language, outstanding young poets are by no means rare. As he grows older, however, our young genius keeps running into this damnable problem of *material*, of what to write about, since by now he realizes that literature's main arena is prose, whether in fiction or the essay. Even so, he keeps things in proportion. He tells himself that 95 percent of literary genius is the unique talent that is secure inside some sort of crucible in his skull and 5 percent is the material, the clay his talent will mold.

I can remember going through this stage myself. In college, at Washington and Lee, I decided I would write crystalline prose. That was the word: *crystalline*. It would be a prose as ageless, timeless, exquisite, soaring, and transparently dazzling as Scarlatti at his most sublime. It would speak to the twenty-fifth century as lucidly as to my own. (I was, naturally, interested to hear, years later, that Iris Murdoch had dreamed of the same quality and chosen the same word, *crystalline*, at a similar point in her life.) In graduate school at Yale, I came upon the Elizabethan books of rhetoric, which isolated, by my count, 444 figures of speech, covering every conceivable form of wordplay. By analyzing the prose of writers I admired—De Quincey, I remember, was one of them—I tried to come up with the perfect sequences of figures and make notations for them, like musical notes. I would flesh out this perfect skeleton with some material when the time came.

Such experiments don't last very long, of course. The damnable beast, material, keeps getting bigger and more obnoxious. Finally, you realize you have a choice. Either hide from it, wish it away, or wrestle with it. I doubt that there is a writer over forty who does not realize in his heart of hearts that literary genius, in prose, consists of proportions more on the order of 65 percent material and 35 percent the talent in the sacred crucible.

I never doubted for a moment that to write a long piece of fiction about New York City I would have to do the same sort of reporting I had done for *The Right Stuff* or *Radical Chic & Mau-mauing the Flak Catchers*, even though by now I had lived in New York for almost twenty years. By 1981, when I started work in earnest, I could see that Thackeray's *Vanity Fair* would not be an adequate model. *Vanity Fair* deals chiefly with the upper orders of British society. A book about New York in the 1980s would have to deal with New York high and low. So I chose Wall Street as the high end of the scale and the South Bronx as the low. I knew a few more people on Wall Street than in the South Bronx, but both were terrae incognitae as far as my own experience was concerned. I headed forth into I knew not exactly what. Any big book about New York, I figured, should have at least one subway scene. I started riding the subways in the Bronx. One evening I looked across the car and saw someone I knew sitting there in a strange rig. He was a Wall Street broker I hadn't seen for nine or ten years. He was dressed in a business suit, but his pants legs were rolled up three or four hitches, revealing a pair of olive green army surplus socks, two bony lengths of shin, and some decomposing striped orthotic running shoes. On the floor between his feet was an A&P shopping bag made of slippery white polyethylene. He had on a dirty raincoat and a greasy rain hat, and his eyes were darting from one end of the car to the other. I went over, said hello, and learned the following. He and his family lived in the far North Bronx, where there are to this day some lovely, leafy Westchester-style neighborhoods, and he worked on Wall Street. The subways provided fine service, except that lately there had been a problem. Packs of young toughs had taken to roaming the cars. They would pick out a likely prey, close in on his seat, hem him in, and ask for money. They kept their hands in their pockets and never produced weapons, but their leering, menacing looks were usually enough. When this fellow's turn came, he had capitulated, given them all he had—and he'd been a nervous wreck on the subway ever since. He had taken to traveling to and from Wall Street in this pathetic disguise in order to avoid looking worth robbing. In the A&P shopping bag he carried his Wall Street shoes and socks.

I decided I would use such a situation in my book. It was here that I began to run into not Roth's Lament but Muggeridge's Law. While Malcolm Muggeridge was editor of *Punch*, it was announced that Khrushchev and Bulganin were coming to England. Muggeridge hit upon the idea of a mock itinerary, a lineup of the most ludicrous places the two paunchy, pear-shaped little Soviet leaders could possibly be paraded through during the solemn business of a state visit. Shortly before press time, half the feature had to be scrapped. It coincided exactly with the official itinerary, just released, prompting Muggeridge to observe: We live in an age in which it is no longer possible to be funny. There is nothing you can imagine, no matter how ludicrous, that will not promptly be enacted before your very eyes, probably by someone well known.

This immediately became my problem. I first wrote *The Bonfire of the Vanities* serially for *Rolling Stone*, producing a chapter every two weeks with a gun at my temple. In the third chapter, I introduced one of my main characters, a thirty-two-year-old Bronx assistant district attorney named Larry Kramer, sitting in a subway car dressed as my friend had been dressed, his eyes jumping about in a bughouse manner. This was supposed to create unbearable suspense in the readers. What on earth had reduced this otherwise healthy young man to such a pathetic state? This chapter appeared in July of 1984. In an installment scheduled for April of 1985, the readers would learn of his humiliation by a wolfpack, who had taken all his money plus his little district attorney's badge. But it so happened that in December of 1984 a young man named Bernhard Goetz found himself in an identical situation on a subway in New York, hemmed in by four youths who were, in fact, from the South Bronx. Far from caving in, he pulled out a .38-caliber revolver and shot all four of them and became one of the most notorious figures in America. Now, how could I, four months later, in April of 1985, proceed with my plan? People would say, This poor fellow Wolfe, he has no imagination. He reads the newspapers, gets these obvious ideas, and then gives us this wimp Kramer, who caves in. So I abandoned the plan, dropped it altogether. The *Rolling Stone* readers' burning thirst, if any, to know what accounted for Assistant D.A. Kramer's pitiful costume and alarming facial tics was never slaked.

In one area, however, I was well ahead of the news, and this lent the book a curious kind of alter-life. The plot turns on a severe injury to a black youth in an incident involving a white couple in an automobile. While the youth lies in a coma, various forces close in on the case—the press, politicians, prosecutors, real estate brokers, black activists—each eager, for private reasons, to turn the matter into a racial Armageddon. Supreme among them is Reverend Bacon, a Harlem minister, a genius at handling the press who soon has the entire city throbbing to the young man's outrageous fate. In the book, the incident casts its shadow across the upcoming elections and threatens to cost the white mayor City Hall.

The Bonfire of the Vanities reached bookstores in October of 1987, a week before the Wall Street crash. From the start, in the press, there was a certain amount of grumbling, some of it not very nice, about my depiction of Reverend Bacon. He was a grotesque caricature of a black activist, grotesque or worse. Then, barely three months later, the Tawana Brawley case broke. At the forefront of the Brawley case appeared an activist black minister, the Reverend Al Sharpton, who was indeed a genius at handling the press, even when he was in the tightest corners. At one point the New York *Post* got a tip that Sharpton was having his long Byronic hair coiffed at a beauty parlor in Brooklyn. A reporter and photographer waited until he was socketed in under the dryer, then burst in. Far from throwing up his hands and crying out about invasion of privacy, Sharpton nonchalantly beckoned to his stalkers. "Come on in, boys, and bring your cameras. I want you to see how . . . a real man . . . gets his hair done." Just like that!—another Sharpton media triumph, under the heading of "Masculinity to Burn." In fact, Sharpton was so flamboyant, the grumbling about Reverend Bacon swung around 180 degrees. Now I heard people complain, This poor fellow Wolfe, he has no imagination. Here, on the front page of every newspaper, are the real goods—and he gives us this little divinity student, Reverend Bacon.

But I also began to hear and read with increasing frequency that *The Bonfire of the Vanities* was "prophetic." The Brawley case turned out to be only one in a series of racial incidents in which young black people were, or were seen as, the victims of white brutality. And these incidents did, indeed, cast their shadow across the race for mayor in New York City. As in the prologue to the book, the mayor, in real life, was heckled, harassed, and shouted down by demonstrators in Harlem, although he was never forced to flee the podium. And perhaps these incidents were among the factors that cost the white mayor City Hall. But not for a moment did I ever think of *The Bonfire of the Vanities* as prophetic. The book only showed what was obvious to anyone who had done what I did, even as far back as the early Eighties, when I began; anyone who had gone out and looked frankly at the new face of the city and paid attention not only to what the voices said but also to the roar.

This brings me to one last point. It is not merely that reporting is useful in gathering the *petits faits vrais* that create verisimilitude and make a novel gripping or absorbing, although that side of the enterprise is worth paying attention to. My contention is that, especially in an age like this, they are essential for the very greatest effects literature can achieve. In 1884 Zola went down into the mines at Anzin to do the documentation for what was to become the novel *Germinal*. Posing as a secretary for a member of the French Chamber of Deputies, he descended into the pits wearing his city clothes, his frock coat, high stiff collar, and high stiff hat (this appeals to me for reasons I won't delay you with), and carrying a notebook and pen. One day Zola and the miners who were serving as his guides were 150 feet below the ground when Zola noticed an enormous workhorse, a Percheron, pulling a sled piled with coal through a tunnel. Zola asked, "How do you get that animal in and out of the mine every day?" At first the miners thought he was joking. Then they realized he was serious, and one of them said, "Mr. Zola, don't you understand? That horse comes down here *once*, when he's a colt, barely more than a foal, and still able to fit into the buckets that bring *us* down here. That horse grows up down here. He grows blind down here after a year or two, from the lack of light. He hauls coal down here until he can't haul it anymore, and then he dies down here, and his bones are buried down here." When Zola transfers this revelation from the pages of his documentation notebook to the pages of *Germinal*, it makes the hair on your arms stand on end. You realize, without the need of amplification, that the horse is the miners themselves, who descend below the face of the earth as children and dig coal down in the pit until they can dig no more and then are buried, often literally, down there.

The moment of The Horse in *Germinal* is one of the supreme moments in French literature—and it would have been impossible without that peculiar drudgery that Zola called documentation. At this weak, pale, tabescent moment in the history of American literature, we need a battalion, a brigade, of Zolas to head out into this wild, bizarre, unpredictable, Hog-stomping Baroque country of ours and reclaim it as literary property. Philip Roth was absolutely right. The imagination of the novelist is powerless before what he knows he's going to read in tomorrow morning's newspaper. But a generation of American writers has drawn precisely the wrong conclusion from that perfectly valid observation. The answer is not to leave the rude beast, the material, also known as the life around us, to the journalists but to do what journalists do, or are supposed to do, which is to wrestle the beast and bring it to terms.

Of one thing I am sure. If fiction writers do not start facing the obvious, the literary history of the second half of the twentieth century will record that journalists not only took over the richness of American life as their domain but also seized the high ground of literature itself. Any literary person who is willing to look back over the American literary terrain of the past twenty-five years—look back candidly, in the solitude of the study—will admit that in at least four years out of five the best nonfiction books have been *better literature* than the most highly praised books of fiction. Any truly candid observer will go still further. In many years, the most highly praised books of fiction have been overshadowed *in literary terms* by writers whom literary people customarily dismiss as "writers of popular fiction" (a curious epithet) or as genre novelists. I am thinking of novelists such as John le Carré and Joseph Wambaugh. Leaving the question of talent aside, Le Carré and Wambaugh have one enormous advantage over their more literary confreres. They are not only willing to wrestle the beast; they actually love the battle.

In 1973, in *The New Journalism*, I wrote that nonfiction had displaced the novel as American literature's "main event." That was not quite the same as saying that nonfiction had dethroned the novel, but it was close enough. At the time, it was a rash statement, but *como Fidel lo ha dijo*, history will absolve me. Unless some movement occurs in American fiction over the next ten years that is more remarkable than any detectable right now, the pioneering in nonfiction will be recorded as the most important experiment in American literature in the second half of the twentieth century.

I speak as a journalist, with some enthusiasm, as you can detect, a journalist who has tried to capture the beast in long narratives of both nonfiction and fiction. I started writing *The Bonfire of the Vanities* with the supreme confidence available only to a writer who doesn't know quite what he is getting into. I was soon plunged into despair. One very obvious matter I had not reckoned with: In nonfiction you are very conveniently provided with the setting and the characters and the plot. You now have the task—and it is a huge one—of bringing it all alive as convincingly as the best of realistic fiction. But you don't have to concoct the story. Indeed, you can't. I found the sudden freedom of fiction intimidating. It was at least a year before I felt comfortable enough to use that freedom's advantages, which are formidable. The past three decades have been decades of tremendous and at times convulsive social change, especially in large cities, and the tide of the fourth great wave of immigration has made the picture seem all the more chaotic, random, and discontinuous, to use the literary clichés of the recent past. The economy with which realistic fiction can bring the many currents of a city together in a single, fairly simple story was something that I eventually found exhilarating. It is a facility that is not available to the journalist, and it seems more useful with each passing month. Despite all the current talk of "coming together," I see the fast-multiplying factions of the modern cities trying to insulate themselves more diligently than ever before. However brilliant and ambitious, a nonfiction novel about, say, the Tawana Brawley case could not get all of New York in 1989 between two covers. It could illuminate many things, most especially the press and the workings of the justice system, but it would not reach into Wall Street or Park Avenue, precincts even the resourceful Al Sharpton does not frequent. In 1970 the Black Panthers *did* turn up in Leonard Bernstein's living room. Today, there is no chic, radical or otherwise, in mixing colors in the grand salons.

So the doors close and the walls go up! It is merely another open invitation to literature, especially in the form of the novel. And how can any writer, in fiction or nonfiction, resist going to the beano, to the rout! At the end of *Dead Souls*, Gogol asks, "Whither art thou soaring away to, then, Russia? Give me an answer!" Russia gives none but only goes faster, and "the air, rent to shreds, thunders and turns to wind," and Gogol hangs on, breathless, his eyes filled with wonder. America today, in a headlong rush of her own, may or may not truly need a literature worthy of her vastness. But American novelists, without any doubt, truly need, in this neurasthenic hour, the spirit to go along for that wild ride.

RAND RICHARDS COOPER

Tom Wolfe, Material Boy:
Embellishing a Doctrine

Tom Wolfe splashed into the national consciousness in the summer of
1970 with "Radical Chic," his *New York* magazine account of a fund-raising
party for the Black Panthers thrown by Leonard Bernstein and wife in their
Park Avenue duplex. The piece was a *succès de scandale* that impressed by the
impudent cunning of its commando raid on limousine liberalism. Here
indeed was a "new" journalism, freed to be sly, to slander by implication and
the damning detail. When Wolfe described maids serving from "gadrooned
silver platters," and a guest inwardly rhapsodizing over Roquefort *hors
d'oeuvres* ("It's the way the dry sackiness of the nuts tiptoes up against the
dour savor of the cheese . . .") as the Panthers held forth on revolutionary
violence, you didn't need to know what a gadroon was to see that the
Bernsteins and their socialite friends were in trouble. Eavesdropping not
only on conversations, but on minds, Wolfe plumbed an inner ooze-of-
consciousness sticky with self-flattery, covetousness, and other thoughts too
naughtily incorrect (as we say nowadays) to utter. This was a journalism of
the fox let loose in the chicken coop.

Through the 1970s, America's least welcome party guest applied his
Day-Glo conservatism to architecture (*From Bauhaus to Our House*) and art
(*The Painted Word*), witty polemics defending your and my sensible aesthetic
intuitions—that paintings should be beautiful, and houses comfy—against a

From *Commonweal* 126, no 9 (7 May 1999). © 1999 by the Commonweal Foundation.

cabal of modernists bent on our eternal bafflement. Wolfe's shrewd co-optation of hip style in service of a meat-and-potatoes cultural agenda won countless admirers, who hailed him as brilliant satirist with a voice extravagant as America itself. And when inevitably these fans began to wonder what a *novel* by that voice might be like, could anyone blame Wolfe for being tempted? Just think about it: the master, unfettered . . . his wicked intelligence, his vaunted powers of observation . . . unconstrained . . . a big book . . . an *important* book. . . .

Deny it if you will!

Wolfe's plunge into novel writing came accompanied by an eight-thousand-word literary manifesto (in the November 1989 *Harper's*), "Stalking the Billion-Footed Beast." With typical brio, the essay asserted that the raucous complexity of America had overwhelmed a generation of writers. Writing programs across the land were cranking out "young people with serious literary ambitions [who] were no longer interested in the metropolis or any other big, rich slices of contemporary life." Minimalism, metafiction, magical realism, and other innovations were actually safe refuges, *cul de sacs* where our novelists could "avert their eyes" from the roaring challenge of American reality. To rectify the sorry state of affairs, Wolfe looked back for inspiration to the titans of realism—to Sinclair Lewis, and to Balzac and Zola, writers he credited with the novel's highest fulfillment, "a true and powerful picture of individuals in society." If that sounded like the nineteenth century talking, so much the better. Against modernism's emphasis on psychological states, interiority, and the writer-as-creator, Wolfe stressed objectivity, society, and the writer-as-recorder. This last was crucial. Our novelists had to stop dreaming and start . . . interviewing! Conjuring Zola tramping into coal mines and Lewis at Chatauqua meetings, "doggedly taking notes on five-by-eight cards," Wolfe urged "a highly detailed realism based on reporting" that would once again give America "a literature worthy of her vastness." Thus the man who had revived journalism by infusing it with fiction would now save fiction by handing novelists pencil and notebook and shoving them out the door. And when no one volunteered to go first, Wolfe manfully stepped to the plate and took a whack at it himself.

Well, two novels have sailed over the fence so far, and as advertised, they are *big*. *Bonfire of the Vanities* weighed in at 659 pages, and the current opus, *A Man in Full*—another saga of a wealthy overreacher stretched on the rack of modern American life—runs to 742. *A Man in Full* charts the ruin of Charlie Croker, an aging Georgia Tech gridiron-hero-*cum*-highly-leveraged-Atlanta-business-king, beset by creditors eyeing his office tower, jet, *and* twenty-nine-thousand-acre quail-hunting plantation. Wolfe propels toward him the *current* star of Tech's football team, Fareek Fanon, black and poor and soon to be charged with date raping the (rich white) daughter of Croker's best friend, a major player in Atlanta's business elite. The city's (black) mayor, meanwhile, faces reelection worries and a looming race crisis. And *also* meanwhile . . . in distant California, a hard-working Croker Foods employee loses his job and begins a harrowing odyssey that by strange twists of fate will bring him . . . guess where? Toss in assorted trophy wives, scavenging lawyers, and lavish mansions, and away we go. It's a sprawling plot built on headline themes, race *and* sex *and* money *and* politics—a meganovel crammed to bursting with all that is sensational in American life.

As for the promised realistic detail, *A Man in Full* has scads of it: trade terms from "debt defalcation" to "Peel yo cap!"; the demographics of each Atlanta neighborhood; and endless descriptions of décor. Where Balzac believed that rooms reveal their occupants, Wolfe outdoes him, giving us "burled tupelo maple" and "cruciform mullions," "ogee curves" and "white industrial muntins"—architecture as erotica. His reporter's notebook, meanwhile, yields well-researched set pieces, including a wildly technical—and X-rated—scene in which Croker's prize stallion is put to stud before a group of astonished weekend guests. Wolfe's goal was to "take real life and spread it across the pages of a book"; and to the extent that real life means knowing how loan officers choreograph their intimidation of a delinquent $300-million borrower, or how the pickers operate their tuggers in the freezer unit of a food wholesaler, he succeeds brilliantly.

But what of the real, inner lives of men and women? *A Man in Full* displays a repertoire of bravura emotional effects, from the rage of the mighty at finding their power challenged, to the chewy misery of coveting someone else's house, wife, life. But in lull moments, Wolfe's people are made to say—and think—most unlikely things. Listen to the mayor of Atlanta, stumping for civic harmony: "Nothing, least of all a vile canard like that, should be allowed to tear this city asunder. . . ." Or an *arriviste* African-American lawyer dismayed by the excesses of a black college-student party: "Brothers! Sisters! Is *this* why you've become the *jeunesse dorée* of Black America?" French has always served Wolfe as a trusty marker of luxury and pretension. It's one thing to season your essays with piquant *mots justes*, however, and another to have backwoods, Georgia-Cracker Cap'm Charlie Croker thinking them ("Aw, this was *esprit de l'escalier* stuff, as the French say"). Impartially Wolfe spreads around his own pet phrases. Here's Charlie, recalling courting his second wife: "She made him feel like a kid, like a twenty-year-old in the season of the rising sap." Conrad, the Croker Foods employee, ruining an unhappy marriage: "He was only twenty-three! Still in the season of the rising sap!" Coach Buck McNutter on his star's indiscretions: "You get some kid twenty or twenty-one years old, and he's in the season of the rising sap. . . ." Such echoes sound like telltale signs of a writer's impatience at having to differentiate his characters, both from each other and from himself.

Sensational themes and plot, scandals in opulent settings, interchangeable characters—has Wolfe committed a novel that, to borrow a phrase, does not rise to the level of art? Writing in the *New Yorker*, John Updike judged *A Man in Full* "entertainment, not literature," while Norman Mailer, in the *New York Review of Books*, called it an "adroit commercial counterfeit," designed for those who like their heroes pure, their plots sentimental, and their protagonists' thoughts cozily predictable. "Mega-bestseller readers," Mailer observes, "do not want to ponder any truly unexpected revelations. Reality might lie out there, but that is not why they are reading." He accuses Wolfe of cynically dumbing-down his novel—"writing a bestseller with conscious intent."

As an example of how *A Man in Full* can be, to quote Mailer, "so good and so empty all at once," consider Wolfe's treatment of Raymond Peepgass, a loan officer involved in the unraveling of Charlie Croker. His own life in chaos (nasty separation, dead-end career), Raymond concocts a risky, illegal scheme to acquire Croker properties cheap through foreclosure. Eager to enlist Croker's embittered ex-wife, Martha, in funding the scam, he drives out to her lavish house. And what do we get when Wolfe takes us inside his character at this fateful juncture? A catalogue of Martha's wealth, and how agog our man is at it. A "silver tray with gadrooned edges" [!!]; saucers with handles "designed in flamboyant swoops"; the Georg Jensen silverware; and on and on. "Viscerally he could sense how much the sugar bowl, a mere sugar bowl, must have cost, which was in fact $1,250. . . . The luxury of it all coursed through Peepgass's central nervous system. . . ." In Mailer's indictment, this Peepgass-in-paradise bit would seem to be one of those smoking-gun moments when Wolfe opts for entertainment over literature— a mega-bestselling author turning the scene into "Lifestyles of the Rich and Famous" (complete with brand names and price tags) while turning his back, as Mailer charges, to "the real complexity of men and women."

Or maybe . . . Wolfe doesn't believe in that kind of complexity. To be sure, what made fans slaver at the thought of Wolfe-as-novelist was partly a premonition of how well his wicked insights into people would play as fiction. And yet the hilarious sketches tossed off in such essays as "The Me Decade" (Germaine Greer in a London restaurant, setting fire to her hair out of boredom!) were the opposite of novelistic, a kind of blitzkrieg caricature. "The Me Decade" was not fiction, but pop sociology with a satirical thrust. It had a thesis—that American prosperity had exploded old restraints, igniting an indulgent religion of the self—and if certain *techniques* of fiction came into play (irony, interior monologue, vivid description), it was to push the thesis. Similarly, reducing Leonard Bernstein in "Radical Chic" to a mass of liberal contradictions was not a portrayal of a man but a pathology report on the times. Wolfe's satiric/diagnostic reduction of individuals to symptoms made for brilliant cultural criticism. But a novel—especially the old-fashioned realist novel he pledged in his *Harper's* essay to write, that dealt in "what truly presses upon the heart of the individual"—requires the whole person.

Wolfe doesn't write the whole person. Tellingly, his *Harper's* essay proposes "status traits modified by personality" as the key to writing characters: a "technique," he says, for "portraying the innermost life of the individual." The formulation suggests a writer interested less in people themselves than in people illuminated, or revealed, in the light of an idea. Status is Wolfe's great subject, his *raison d'écriver*. It lay behind "Radical Chic" and "The Me Decade"; and his later writings about art and architecture are really exposés of status maneuvers in the *professions* of art and architecture. Indeed, his career has consisted in playing a hundred jazzy variations on the homey theme of keeping up with the Joneses.

No other writer—living or dead—can touch Wolfe on his subject. What his characters wears, what they drive (or wish they drove), where they went to school (or didn't), how much they earn (and why it's never enough), their beer of choice, music of choice, living room furniture of choice: he engages the hermeneutics of status with the crazed comprehensiveness of an *idiot savant* (or a Ph.D. from Yale). So too the narcissism, megalomania, and general churning anxiety that comprise the personal pathology of status. *A Man in Full* begins with Charlie Croker on his plantation on a sunny winter Saturday, breathing in "the resinous air of the pines." Before too many more breaths, his pleasure has yielded to a bolder satisfaction in reflecting that "every square inch of it, every beast that moved on it . . . was his, Cap'm Charlie Croker's." Ineluctably, Wolfe's characters skid toward the bottom line, converting love and beauty, art and nature, into assets in the ceaseless calculus of status. It amuses, it appalls.

But real life spread across the pages of a book?

The nineteenth-century realism Wolfe reveres was partly a revolt against the insipid conventions of romance ("the old trade of make-believe," wrote William Dean Howells, "that pamper[s] our gross appetite for the marvelous"), and partly an attempt to keep pace with the successes of nineteenth-century materialism. Zola's influential 1880 essay, "The Experimental Novel," grounded literary naturalism in diagnosis, casting the writer as an observer of fixed laws of nature and society, rather than a mere poetic mystifier. Human nature was not some free-floating emanation, after all, but an interplay of instinct and environment. This new emphasis sought to bring literature in line with science, dispensing with ladies and lakes and noble Indians in the woods, and clearing the way for serious projects such as Zola's study of five generations of the Rougon-Macquart family. It was an intuition that the hazy fancifying of a Walter Scott or a Fenimore Cooper would not do in the age of Darwin and Marx.

Here Wolfe presents an odd mishmash. Brazenly *A Man in Full* flouts the realist pitch for things to occur in novels—the words are Henry James's— "as they occur in life, where the manner of a great many of them is not to occur at all." In Wolfe, *everything* occurs. (And the more marvelous, the better, including a character sprung from prison by a timely earthquake.) Yet beneath the razzle-dazzle surface lies a relentless naturalism, one that seizes the novel as a forum for illustrating certain theses on human nature and society. Though Wolfe cites Lewis, Balzac, and Zola, the deeper animating presences behind *A Man in Full* are not novelists at all, but scientists— Darwin and, above all, Thorstein Veblen.

That Veblen merits no mention in the *Harper's* essay suggests one of those influences too fundamental to disclose or even, perhaps, to see. Veblen extracted from the function of wealth in modern society a keen and durable insight: acquiring things is not, as was conventionally believed, about consuming them, but rather about showing them. Ownership was a "mark of prowess," he wrote; "visible success . . . an end sought for its own utility as a basis of esteem." And though Howells reviewed *The Theory of the Leisure Class* (1899) as a biting satire of *fin de siècle* wealth, Veblen had something far broader in mind, an evolutionary interpretation of modern life. Social organization was—as ever—tribal and hierarchical, and his terms for it darkly atavistic: "the warrior and the hunter" prowling a "predatory culture" in which "any effort that does not involve an assertion of prowess comes to be unworthy of the man. . . ." Wealth as an assertive show of force was the central drama of modern society.

It's no exaggeration to say that these ideas form a complete blueprint for *A Man in Full*. Wolfe's tone is merry where Veblen's was mordant, but his terms are identical. His novel pursues the predatory-culture argument tirelessly. We are shown Charlie Croker out hunting; relaxing in his Gun House, its walls festooned with shotguns and boars' heads; wrestling a rattlesnake before awed admirers. We observe hierarchy-display behavior, both dominant (Charlie, who "showed the room his omnipotent deltoids and *latissimi dorsi*, which bulged beneath his shirt") and submissive (Martha's milquetoast escort, dissolving when they run into Charlie—"a big submissive grin came over his face, and he began blurting out pleasantries"). And if we still don't get it, characters help out, like teachers at the blackboard, as when Peepgass's scheme sparks in Martha this rumination: "He now seemed . . . more of a man. He was no Charlie, but he had Charlie's passion for the deal, which was perhaps where the contemporary male's passion for battle went these days."

To my ear, this and many similar passages ("A quail shoot was a ritual in which the male of the species acted out his role of hunter, provider, and protector . . .") sound less like the calculated simplicities of a mega-bestseller than the stilted attempts of an evolutionary psychologist moonlighting as novelist. Life is status, and status is (male) power: Wolfe turns his novel into *Gray's Anatomy* to bring this idea home. "He was a mountain of flesh. . . ." "His mighty neck swelled out until it seemed to merge with his trapezii in one continuous slope to the shoulders." "He rolled his massive shoulders, he flexed his neck up and down. . . ." "His neck fanned out wider than his ears and merged with a pair of trapezius muscles that sloped like his native Balkar Dagh Mountains down to his shoulders." "His neck, trapezii, shoulders, and chest, as well as his upper arms, seemed to swell out to a prodigious size. . . ." "He was so massive through the back and shoulders, the seat seemed incapable of containing him." "He was so big, his fingertips reached almost from one end of the couch to the other."

Writing like this has dispensed not merely with "what presses upon the heart of the individual," but with the individual himself—these sentences actually describe *seven different* characters in *A Man in Full* (and can you guess which is a horse?). It suggests that what attracted Wolfe to the idea of realism wasn't "the metropolis" or "the heart of the individual" but a literary determinism, born in nineteenth-century literature's science envy, which turns a novel into a shooting gallery for someone armed, as he is, with an all-encompassing thesis about what makes people tick. For while Wolfe—to borrow Isaiah Berlin's famous distinction—may look like the fox, sly and quick and knowing many things, secretly he's a hedgehog of a novelist, burrowing ever deeper into his One Big Idea. "He leaned forward with his huge forearms on the table and the testosterone flowing." "They sat with their thighs ajar in an athletic sprawl, as if they were bulging with so much testosterone they couldn't have closed their legs if they tried." *A Man in Full* is the production of an extravagant, radical materialism. Deeper and deeper Wolfe digs, implacably—almost desperately—reducing his characters: to the things they own and covet, the things they wear, and finally to the muscle and hormones that they are.

Two-thirds of the way through *Bonfire of the Vanities*, Wolfe inserted a revealing philosophical aside about an Amazon tribe who believe that "there is no such thing as a private self."

The Bororos regard the mind as an open cavity . . . in which the entire village dwells and the jungle grows. In 1969 José M. R. Delgado, the eminent Spanish brain physiologist, pronounced the Bororos correct. For nearly three millennia, Western philosophers had viewed the self as something unique, something encased inside each person's skull, so to speak. . . . At the core of one's self there was presumed to be something irreducible and inviolate. No so, said Delgado. "Each person is a transitory composite of materials borrowed from the environment." . . . He cited experiments in which healthy college students lying on beds in well-lit but soundproofed chambers, wearing gloves to reduce the sense of touch and translucent goggles to block out specific sights, began to hallucinate within hours. Without the entire village, the whole jungle, occupying the cavity, they had no minds left.

What is the innermost life of the individual when the individual has, by definition, no inner life? As it turns out, the "empty" quality of *A Man in Full* is not, as Mailer argued, a sell-out, but a philosophical position. If we begin to get the stealthily dreary feeling that Wolfe's characters are not individuals but types, whose complexity lies largely in what they wear, buy, and covet, it's because Wolfe himself believes it. Believing it may make him a perfect writer for our time and place—the ultimate Material Boy for an America where invisible, databank-sifting marketers craft enticements tailored to your "personal" and "individual" desires. Who is this "you" they seem to know so well? He's a Tom Wolfe character.

Finally, it's tantalizing to consider that the mega-bestseller may issue not from cynical or mindless pandering, but rather the opposite, with its ideal author a covertly ideological one, in dedicated thrall to an idea. In Hollywood, the term for narratives pitchable in a single sentence and characters reducible to a single motivation is "high-concept." But doesn't that also describe Wolfe's fiction, this novelization of Veblen and Darwin, in which writing is a matter of "technique" driven by a theory, and characters who might develop interesting resistances to an author's intentions are nowhere to be found?

In this light Wolfe himself seems an evolutionary marvel. A closet ideologue with a lively voice and rollicking sense of humor—that's a killer adaptation in an environment where screenplays and film rights deliver maximum long-term push to your gene pool. In *A Man in Full* it makes for darkly manic comedy, but also a surprising heavy-handedness, and an underlying take on human possibility bleak enough that even a chuckling reader might leave the novel wishing for an author whose black bag held not just status yardstick but stethoscope, to take the pulse of characters forlornly crying, Where's the rest of me?

JOSHUA J. MASTERS

Race and the Infernal City in Tom Wolfe's Bonfire of the Vanities

> And you, O slaves, worthless in your vileness, for now you may continue to besmirch yourselves. Let your bellies be filled with wine, your kidneys be rotted with excess, and your hands be stained with the blood of the poor, for this is your portion and your lot. But know that your bodies and your souls are in my hands and soon your bodies will be worn out by the scourges and your souls I will hand over to the eternal fire.
>
> —Savonarola *Compendium Revelationum*

> Thus I say to you, Florence, that this is the time to build the new house of God and to renew your city.
>
> —Savonarola, Sermon of December 14, 1494

In the late fifteenth century, Savonarola, a preacher of repentance and a prophet of doom, exhorted the citizens of Florence to cast off their vain personal ornaments and objects of vice—their cosmetics, cards, dice, books, and pornographic pictures—and throw them into symbolic bonfires that would purge them of their sins. Yet while Savonarola preached his message of fire, envisioning Florence as both the infernal city and the city of sin, he always imagined the possibility of redemption and renewal, that in these baptisms of fire Florence would become the new city, the City of God. Thus

From *JNT: Journal of Narrative Theory* 29, no. 2 (Spring 1999). © 1999 by *JNT: Journal of Narrative Theory*.

just as Christian 'man' is figured as half angel and half beast, Savonarola's Florence is at once Jerusalem and Sodom, the City of God and Babylon, utopia and dystopia.

The title of Tom Wolfe's 1987 novel, *The Bonfire of the Vanities*, undoubtedly refers to the urban pyrotechnic rituals that Savonarola inspired during the Italian Renaissance. This would suggest that his novel shares a similar prophetic vision of the city, one capable of illuminating the corruption and decay of contemporary American values, beliefs, and practices. However, Savonarola's message of renewal and rebirth is conspicuously absent from Wolfe's novel, for in it he denies the Christian teleology that entertains apocalypse as the prelude to utopia. Instead, we find the collapse of Christianity's "grand narrative" and the absolute triumph of the apocalyptic city: the city as Sodom, Babylon, Wasteland, necropolis, and kakatopia—the city of shit. For unlike Savonarola's Florentine bonfires fed by the "vanities" the bourgeois citizens themselves chose to contribute, the bonfires in Wolfe's novel threaten from without, having been set by the jealous masses. In the first description of the McCoy's Park Avenue apartment, this infernal thematic becomes clear: "It was the sort of apartment the mere thought of which ignites the flames of greed and covetousness under people all over New York and, for that matter, all over the world." According to this formulation, the "world" is dominated only by the Veblenian desire for social recognition via "pecuniary emulation" and "conspicuous consumption"; thus, the "flames" in this passage are neither redemptive nor baptismal, and instead symbolize the "greed" of the undeserving, who desire, but cannot obtain, the fruits of the blessed.

In typical American fashion, Wolfe rewrites class struggle as the agonistic conflict between wealthy Anglo-Americans and an increasingly racialized Other, and it is this conflict that dominates the way city-space is both imaged and imagined in the novel. To be sure, *Bonfire* satirizes every sector of New York society: the self-satisfied egotism and excess of the upper class, the maudlin envy of the bourgeoisie, the dogged but witless tenacity of the working class, and the brute animality of the so-called "underclass." What interests me is the way the novel naturalizes these class tensions through its incessant, and at times gratuitous, deployment of racial stereotypes, stabilizing the fictive categories of "racial" difference and ultimately fetishizing whiteness. In order to unmask and assess the novel's racialization of the infernal city, a place for the "miserable and the damned," my paper begins with an examination of Wolfe's narrative technique in terms of both his methodological assumptions and his limited narratorial perspective. I then consider the way this narrative technique underwrites the novel's racial satire, which depends upon the conflicted deployment of several tropes common to colonial discourse: the "jungle," the "cannibal," and the dirty/bestial "races." I conclude with an examination of Wolfe's denigration of radical resistance and his elevation of the protagonist, Sherman McCoy, as the great "white" warrior, a familiar figure in narratives of urban decay.

My discussion of *Bonfire*'s narrative technique focuses on the following questions: What is it to *know* the city in Wolfe's text? How is city-space registered, how is it disciplined, and what values and ideologies are attached to the form of the narrative? In terms of the novel's formal arrangement, most critics agree that Wolfe attempts to adapt the stylistics of the New Journalism, a brand of reportage he is generally credited with inventing, to the exigencies of the realist novel. Robert Sommer describes the New Journalism as a "subjective, impressionistic, and highly personal brand of reportage . . . whose strengths lie in a lively, intimate writing style and extensive participant observation to identify physical details and subjective responses of individuals." New Journalism's will to truth, then, lies in two concomitant strategies: its *"impressionistic* reportage" lays claim to a philosophical realism, in that the world *presses in* upon the mind, while its ethnographic methodology of "participant observation" connotes a scientific or empirical truth claim. Significantly, the novel's empirical eye is exclusively "white," "seeing" and registering the city through the eyes of five Anglo, male characters: the protagonist Sherman McCoy, the assistant district attorney Lawrence Kramer, the reporter Peter Fallow, the Episcopal minister Edward Fiske III, and the Mayor. Thus rather than facilitating a clearer understanding of the city, *Bonfire*'s narrative perspective severely limits the range and scope of what can be known about it. First, the complete absence of a woman's perspective in the novel constructs urban space as unproblematically masculine. Second, despite the absence of a fully realized African-American subjectivity, the novel pretends to a layered examination of racial conflict. Finally, our view of the city is essentially microscopic rather than macrocosmic, and Wolfe offers little insight into the larger social and economic processes determining the organization of urban space.

In order to illuminate the implicit epistemology of the novel's narrative perspective, we might consider a statement District Attorney Abe Weiss makes about the city, one which seems to capture the essence of Wolfe's own novelistic method. Weiss states (or rather shouts), "This is the laboratory of human relations! This is the experiment in urban living!" The argument here is quite obvious: the city can be known and understood only from an elevated perspective, presumably that of a disinterested, dislocated, and class-less cultural observer. And despite Wolfe's ironic treatment of the character's liberal social scientific discourse, he casts himself in precisely this depoliticized role, utilizing Weiss's ethnographic and anthropological trope which transforms real space into the controlled, "experimental" space of the "laboratory." Wolfe, then, is the disinterested social scientist who *knows* the city through his subjects' experiences and perceptions of it. Like the Realist and Naturalist novelists Wolfe embraced in his essay "Stalking the Billion-footed Beast" (1989), such as Zola, Balzac, Norris, and Dreiser, Wolfe also plays the part of the scientist testing the effects of the environment on human behavior. Wolfe's self-fashioning as a social realist is somewhat curious, however, for he shares neither the Naturalists' progressive political vision nor the Realist interest in developing characters in relation to complex, authentic social conditions.

The most notable effect of the novel's use of free indirect discourse, in which the city and its inhabitants are known through the phenomenological registers of five "white" male subjects, is the construction of human differences as "racial" characteristics. And while the five narrative personae are at times distinguishable only in the range and sophistication of their racial, ethnic, and gendered fixations, we experience them as fully conscious characters despite their absurdities. The rest of the characters are always filtered through the five male subjects' rich archive of chauvinistic stereotypes (gendered and racial), and therefore they are denied a conscious response of their own to the city. Thus, while the novel satirically exposes the way individuals substitute myths for authentic understanding, it does so only to further its dystopic vision of human society and human relations, for the possibility of seeing through or beyond racial schemas is never seriously entertained.

There is a singular instance in which Wolfe's narrator at least imagines the possibility of seeing through the eyes of an Othered character, however. This occurs early in the first chapter, when Sherman has a paranoid encounter with a "black youth" while standing at a public telephone. As usual, we are made privy to his conscious response: "Well, let him come! I'm not budging! It's my territory! I'm not giving way for any street punks!" After the "youth" crosses the street and the perceived danger is averted, the narrative suddenly takes its unprecedented turn, pulling back from the subject's viewpoint and turning him into the object of study:

> Not once did it dawn on Sherman McCoy that what the boy had seen was a thirty-eight-year-old white man, soaking wet, dressed in some sort of military-looking raincoat full of snaps and buckles, holding a violently lurching animal in his arms, staring, bug-eyed, and talking to himself.

In this one moment, the narrator distances himself from the "white" subject's perspective and suggests that other points of view do in fact exist, that the Other might have his or her own perceptions of the city and its inhabitants. This performance is never repeated, which only further concretizes the primacy and normalcy of the "white" male point of view; however, it does reveal what the novel *might have been* had it diversified its range of viewpoints.

But because the novel insists on a narrow, privileged, masculinist perspective, the "minority" characters are consistently registered by way of their perceived racial and ethnic differences, while the "white" middle and upper class characters, generally of English descent, are described by way of their class standing and status symbols. We see this pattern begin to emerge in a description of Pollard Browning, the president of Sherman's building:

> He was only forty but had looked fifty for the past twenty years. His hair was combed back smoothly over his round skull. He wore an immaculate navy suit, a white shirt, a shepherd's check necktie, and no raincoat.

A former classmate of Kramer's, Andy Heller, is depicted in a similar manner:

> [He] was a young man, almost babyish in appearance, with a round face and dark hair, neatly combed back. He was wearing a covert cloth Chesterfield topcoat with a golden brown velvet collar and carrying one of those burgundy leather attaché cases that come from Mädler or T. Anthony on Park Avenue and have a buttery smoothness that announces: "I cost $500."

These "white" characters appear to exist outside of racial and ethnic categories, demarcated instead by their grooming habits, deportment, style, status symbols, and clothing. These seemingly race-neutral descriptions stand in direct contrast to those that are determined by "race" and ethnicity. For example, the owner of a restaurant is described as "[a] glum flat-faced Asian . . . his eyes darting this way and that"; the "Hasidic Jew," Winter, is described as "grossly fat but powerfully built, bulging out of his liverish skin like a length of bratwurst"; and perhaps most telling is the description of three "shackled" African American males as "germs."

In *The Wretched of the Earth*, Frantz Fanon analyzes the oppressive Manichean psychology informing precisely this form of racial discourse. He argues that the European colonizer imagines himself (or herself) as the model of perfection, as sublime beauty itself, and thus has no qualitative differences, while the colonized are the manifestation of the grotesque, the locus of evil and fifth. He writes:

> At times this Manicheism goes to its logical conclusion and dehumanizes the native, or to speak plainly, it turns him into an animal. In fact, the terms the settler uses when he mentions the native are zoological terms. He speaks of the yellow man's reptilian motions, of the stink of the native quarter, of breeding swarms, of foulness, of spawn, of gesticulations. When the settler seeks to describe the native fully in exact terms he constantly refers to the bestiary.

This Manichean aesthetic emerges quite clearly in Wolfe's narrative, for while characters like Browning and Heller are defined by a semiotics of dress, the "minority" characters are defined by a semiotics of the body which translates physical differences into moral and intellectual signifiers.

In *Race, Colonialism, and the City*, John Rex analyzes the politics behind these racialized social divisions and representational practices. He states:

> Inter-ethnic conflict never arises solely and simply because of perceived ethnic or physical difference. Such perceived differences may, it is true, be the basis on which individuals within any society are assigned to social positions, but the positions themselves already exist and, by virtue of having to fill them, members of differing ethnic groups find that the conflicts between their groups become exacerbated.

Wolfe's narrative technique, based on his fictional subjects' perceptions of "difference," plays out the logic of racial oppression in that the marginalized characters appear to "fill" their racial and ethnic roles (e.g. "pimp," "thug," "hustler," "dealer") "naturally," without regard for the material conditions creating those roles. The argument that such a narrative constitutes a realistic depiction of the way most people tend to 'see,' which seems to be Wolfe's point (and that of many other social scientists), strikes Rex as particularly impoverished. He works against sociological theories which "categorize a situation as racial if the people whom we are studying think it to be so. This is a solution which commends itself to all those who adopt a subjective phenomenological approach to sociology." I should add that it is a solution which also leads to much of the novel's ideological distortion: because the narrative subjects' phenomenological registers are dominated by categories of race and ethnicity, differences are ultimately naturalized.

The naturalization of difference, then, significantly shapes and maintains the dystopic visions of Wolfe's three main subjects, Kramer, Sherman, and Fallow, for all three project the failure of the city onto the racially demonized masses. In the novel, "New York" becomes the ultimate site of human failure, thereby creating an anxious relationship between the individual and the built environment. As Burton Pike states in *The Image of the Modern City in Literature*:

> The city has been used as a rhetorical topos throughout the history of Western culture. But it has another aspect as well, whose referent seems to be a deep-seated anxiety about man's relation to his created world. The city crystallizes those conscious and unconscious tensions which have from the beginning characterized the city in Western culture.

In *Bonfire*, as in any number of novels and movies set in the city, the city itself becomes the displaced source of anxiety rather than the institutions responsible for both the realization and construction of the city, such as the intertwined structures of capitalism, racism, and imperialism. This anxiety is articulated in Kramer's vision of the city as a failed Jerusalem, Sherman's vision of the city as the fallen Rome, and Fallow's vision of the city as Gothic nightmare.

Lawrence Kramer's conception of the city's failure is perhaps the most racially oriented, based in part on the historical tensions between Jewish and African American communities competing for scarce urban resources. As he surveys the Bronx from the summit of 161st Street, he longs for the "golden Jewish hills of long ago!", but his pastoral imaginings soon degenerate. The "Jewish dream of the new Canaan" is no longer attainable, for "the Grand Hotel of the Jewish dream was now a welfare hotel, and the Bronx, the Promised Land, was 70 percent black and Puerto Rican." In other words, the foul-mouthed, "baleful blacks and Latins" have transformed the "golden dream of an Apollonian future" into the Tower of Babel. While Kramer's vision of the fallen city is defined by its failure as the New Jerusalem, Sherman sees the city in much more secular terms, imagining New York as the city of the New Empire: "There it was, the Rome, the Paris, the London of the twentieth century, the city of ambition, the dense magnetic rock, the irresistible destination of all those who insist on being *where things are happening*—and he was among the victors! Sherman's experiences in the urban "jungle," and the subsequent persecution he endures while in the hands of his racialized antagonists, will later defile this image, as he comes to imagine himself in the very "bowels" of hell.

Fallow's vision of the infernal city is steeped in Gothic allegory, and in the Gothic notion that the isolated, alienated individual cannot trust the mind and its sensory registers to interpret and translate the natural world accurately. An alcoholic, Fallow perceives his waking mind as separate and dissociated from his body, for in his debauched state he is blind to the actions of "the beast" (his body), with its phallic "filthy snout." His anxiety, then, stems from the mind's dislocation from the body's experience of urban space. This rupture between mind and body leads Fallow to conflate Gothic analogies of the city—as an unholy, unknowable place—with the realities of the city as a lived environment. We see this in his experience of the New York subway:

> Heading down the stairs of the City Hall subway station with these dark shabby people was like descending, voluntarily, into a dungeon, a very dirty noisy dungeon. Grimy concrete and black bars were everywhere, cage after cage, level upon level, a delirium seen through black bars in every direction.

Fallow imagines the city as a Gothic "dungeon," projecting onto the city itself the "delirium" of the "insane." Fallow's own deranged mental condition is thus an extension of the city's personified pathology, while the moral corruption of his body is an extension of the corrupt, "shabby" body politic.

And while Fallow's infernal, "insane" city underplays issues of "race," his vision of America as a crass, Gothic nightmare is often laced with latent racist tropes. For instance, consider the following description of a trendy and "grotesque" nightclub Fallow visits while feeling "unusually witty, drunk, and charming":

> The place was practically ringed by black youths wearing enormous sneakers and perching on the old iron church fence, eyeing the drunks and heads going in and out of the door.

The qualifier "practically" immediately establishes the imaginative qualities of the description, for it creates the impression that Fallow's conceptual schemas, which have been informed by Gothic analogues, are filling in the blanks felt by his sensory perceptions. Fallow's imagination thus constructs a scene with implicit boundaries and seemingly natural insiders and outsiders. While the favored, "white" elect make their way into one of the city's inner sanctums, the stigmatized, "black" degenerates threaten from the periphery. He goes on to interpret these outsiders as "*perching* on an old iron church fence," thus transforming them into monstrous gargoyles awaiting the opportunity to victimize (and perhaps cannibalize) what they can only see as disembodied "heads." This scene is exemplary, both of Wolfe's narrative technique and the novel's subtle racist subtext, a subtext I examine more closely below.

I have attempted to demonstrate that the "white," male subject's dystopic vision of the city is predicated on the existence of a racialized "underclass" and its "culture of poverty." Underpinning the realization of this vision is a very specific collection of racial and ethnic tropes deeply rooted in colonial discourse. The novel's prologue, during which the Mayor is verbally assaulted by an assembly of "Reverend Bacon's people" while making a speech, immediately establishes the racist symbology that will dominate the novel. The mayor experiences this act of defiance as a contrived, calculated, and inauthentic media ploy designed by "Parasites! The lice of public life!" When the Mayor registers a woman's voice as "one of those ungodly contralto cackles," and when he later sees his bodyguard grab "some big devil," the symbolic resonance is particularly acute. The "black people" are transformed into "ungodly" or godless heathens, inhuman "devils," witches with sinister "cackles."

The predominance of two racial tropes in particular, the "cannibal" and the "jungle," becomes central to this demonization of the Other in the novel. Built into these tropes, of course, is the colonialist ideology constructing the Other as savage, godless, inhumane, and inhuman. In the chapter entitled "King of the Jungle," Sherman and his lusty concubine, Maria, find themselves lost and disoriented in the labyrinth of the Bronx, a space in which is transformed into both the Wasteland and Necropolis in the following passage:

> It was as if he had fallen into a junkyard. He seemed to be underneath the expressway. In the blackness he could make out a cyclone fence over on the left . . . something was caught in it . . . A woman's head! . . . No, it was a chair with three legs and a burnt seat with the charred stuffing hanging out in great wads, rammed halfway through a cyclone fence.

In this "goddamned jungle," as Sherman later calls it, a "fallen" world into which he descends, he imagines that the primitive forces of darkness have triumphed, and thus his reality is shaped and informed by a B-movie version of the savage locale (in which human heads are regularly impaled on fence posts). During this descent into hell, the terrorizing prospect of being incorporated into the body of the Other is foremost in Sherman's imagination; thus, he attaches particular significance to a billboard which reads:

TOPS IN THE BRONX
MEAT WAREHOUSE

Sherman's ethnocentric fear of this unfamiliar space transforms his body into "meat" desired by the heathen, which, along with too many episodes of *Tarzan*, would explain his initial interpretation of the "black," "brute" Roland as "Hunter! Predator!" And like *Tarzan* and similar adventure narratives, the threat of rape and miscegenation underscores the action in this scene, for in it the "white" male is called upon to rescue the "white" woman from the savage, libidinal energies of the "jungle."

Yet the "jungle" is only one of many city-metaphors Wolfe utilizes in the novel. At other times his fictional city is imaged as "the third world," "Indian country" the Wild West, the frontier, and the "wasteland"; thus, Wolfe's New York is an over-determined space, the excessive metaphors writing over the realities of the city as a place where people live and work. These narrative impositions ultimately displace the city's population from their material conditions, transforming categories of history into categories of nature. If I read Wolfe correctly, he is satirizing our self-deceptive conviction that the modern, "civilized" world has triumphed over the forces of nature, but his satire succeeds only if we accept the premise that "nature" (i.e. "The Wild West" and "Indian Country") is racialized space.

Wolfe's critique of "white" social institutions fails for similar reasons. Initially, the novel appears to satirize Sherman's fear of being cannibalized by exposing a criminal justice system designed and operated by privileged "white" males "feeding" on the poor and people of color. Thus Kramer imagines judicial processes as a "maw" consuming vans full of "the usual . . . blacks and Latins," also referred to as "the chow." This metaphor recurs several times in the novel. For instance, Kramer later imagines lawyers and judges "shoveling the chow into the gullet of the criminal justice system." Like Savonarola, who depicted class domination as a form of cannibalistic gluttony by linking the corpulent bodies of the wealthy to "the blood of the poor," Wolfe seems to suggest that judiciary retribution is a form of capitalist aggression. By reversing the conventional trajectory of cannibalism, Wolfe could be confirming Peter Hulme's assertion that "boundaries of community are often created by accusing those outside the boundary of the very practice on which the integrity of that community is founded." In other words, the fear of being devoured masks the actual desire to devour the Other. Thus Sherman, the great devourer of "crumbs," has transformed his gluttonous desires into a fear of being ingested and incorporated.

Unfortunately, the satire deteriorates when we realize that the judicial "maw" means to feed on Sherman's sacred white flesh, that his is the unpolluted "meat" actually desired by the "system." During his brief incarceration in "the pens," the predominant metaphor of the slaughterhouse constructs Sherman's body as food to be incorporated into the body of the city, as in the following description of his journey to the courtroom:

> The corridor was airless. There were no windows. It was filled with a fluorescent haze and the heat and stench of too many bodies. The meat spigot! The chute to the abattoir! Going . . . where? . . . The courtroom! At the end of the chute was the courtroom!

If we were to read the "courtroom" as a space dominated by "white," capitalist society, the potential for a powerful commentary on the nature of a "system" which cannibalizes its own would still seem possible, though certainly problematic in its own right. However, when we consider that this cannibalistic judiciary "system" is, in fact, the political instrument of the "Jew," Abe Weiss, and that Weiss is a political instrument in the "black" Reverend Bacon's quest for capitalist domination, we discover that Wolfe has subtly re-inverted the trope of cannibalism. As a "black" male, Bacon's cannibalistic ancestry dates back to the earliest African imperial narratives—Henry Stanley's travel writing, H. Rider Haggard's *She*, Conrad's *Heart of Darkness*—while Weiss, in his devotion to and hunger for the "Great White Defendant," has two significant literary precursors. He is, of course, Ahab, as we are often reminded, but he is also Shylock, craving his pound of privileged, "white" flesh.

Wolfe's use of the cannibal trope thus strikes me as particularly convoluted, conflicted, and finally elusive. He begins by satirizing the "white" fear of "black" savagery, then suggests that "whites" are actually cannibalizing "blacks and Latins," but then finally confirms Sherman's original, culturally constructed fear of "black" (and "Jewish") cannibals desiring his body as "meat." What I now want to argue is that in order to fully realize his vision of the city and its social institutions (now operated by "Jews" and "blacks"), Wolfe must maintain the primacy of Sherman's body *as* "meat." Thus, he differentiates Sherman's body from those of his fellow prisoners: theirs become representative of various waste products, while his becomes the divine, sacred flesh desired for a perverse, "savage" communion.

As the novel progresses, "waste," "garbage," and "shit" become powerful metaphors dominating the imaging of "black" and "Latino" bodies. In *Wasting Away*, Kevin Lynch provides a comprehensive definition of "waste," one which illuminates *Bonfire*'s excremental symbology:

> Waste is what is worthless or unused for human purpose. It is a lessening of something without an apparently useful result; it is loss and abandonment, decline, separation, and death. It is the spent and valueless material left after some act of production or consumption, but can also refer to any used thing: garbage, trash, litter, junk, impurity, and dirt. As we have seen, there are waste things, waste lands, waste time, and wasted lives.

Thus "waste" products, as registered in the popular imagination, must be contained and regulated using any number of available methods: collection and consolidation (town dumps), burial (landfills), dispersal (sewage systems), or purification (treatment facilities). This representational schema has proven invaluable in the rhetoric of urban planners. In "'Polluting the Body Politic': Racist Discourse and Urban Location," David Theo Goldberg argues that the practice of stigmatizing the racially oppressed by associating them with "waste," and thus the functions of the lower body, provides a powerful rationale in urban planning. Like Fanon, Goldberg reasons that blacks are made "dirty" so that they may be "cleansed" by specific urban policies. He states, "This 'sanitation syndrome' caught hold of the colonial imagination as a general social metaphor for the pollution by blacks of urban space."

We can trace the novel's use of waste imagery to Kramer's initial contact with the "black and Latin" "chow," who verbally assault him from the confines of a police van. Their collective voice is registered as "a chorus! A rain of garbage! A *Rigoletto* from the sewer, from the rancid gullet of the Bronx!" Not only are their words imagined as "garbage" in their moment of production, simultaneously consumed and excreted by Kramer's ears, but their bodies' origins are relegated to the realm of "the sewer." The metaphor recurs when Kramer reflects on his role in the trial of a Muslim murder defendant, Herbert 92X: "To prosecute such cases was to be part of the garbage-collection service, necessary and honorable, plodding and anonymous." And throughout the novel, numerous court cases (and presumably the defendants being tried in the cases) are referred to by the term "piece of shit." And if Wolfe hasn't made the parallel between prisoners and excrement clear enough for his readers, he offers the following description of one of Sherman's fellow-inmates in "the pens": "There was only one person inside [the cell], the tall man, slumped on a ledge. There was a brown mess on the floor. The odor of excrement was overpowering." Like Wolfe's cannibalism metaphor, his displacement of "waste" onto "black and Latin" bodies is conflicted and contradictory, for the bodies that are originally imagined as "the chow" have become "shit" before they are even processed by the judicial system. It is Sherman, then, the sublime manifestation of consumption (he barely makes ends meet on a million dollars a year, after all), who becomes the only suitable food for "the maw," for his flesh, simultaneously despised and desired, is elevated by the very category of "whiteness."

These loaded representational categories, "black" (or "colored") and "white," ultimately situate the novel's convoluted plot in a specific field of conflict. The novel's story is an old one, as Peter Fallow reminds us in one of his tabloid masquerades; it is "A Tale of Two Cities," the struggle between the rich and the poor, the masters and slaves, the "whites" and everyone else. But the novel suggests that this agonistic tension is irresolvable, that the City of God is out of reach, out of sight, and, most importantly, out of mind. Revolution is depicted as an empty possibility, the liberal notion of 'give and take' offers too little too late, and all gestures of resistance or discontent prove to be artificial media hoaxes. Finally, the novel leaves us with little more than a puerile racial struggle for the control of capitalist machinery.

Earlier, I suggested that Wolfe's apocalyptic vision of the city refuses the possibility of redemption or salvation. However, Sherman McCoy, after enduring his trial by fire, is renewed, becomes, in fact, a "new incarnation": "he had died and been reborn." And despite Wolfe's satiric treatment of Sherman, ultimately we are asked to identify with him. After all, he is the only character who enjoys an authentic, genuine emotion in the entire novel, which we discover in his "fears and his love" for his daughter, the innocent Campbell. Sherman is also the only character whose consciousness undergoes any sort of transformation or exhibits any signs of growth. He will eventually develop "the heart for this shit," a quality Detective Martin sees as initially lacking in him. His new status as "The Great White Defendant," in fact, enhances his understanding of the city, and like a prophet, he begins to see "the things of everyday life, more clearly." It is this vision, the vision of the "realist," which ultimately commands our respect.

Sherman, then, becomes an authentic and authenticating symbol of resistance in the novel, which is perhaps most poignantly registered in his appropriation of "the Black Power salute." Looking back on his former life, Sherman recognizes this salute as the empty gesture of someone who had given his "heart and soul" to Wall Street. But in his new incarnation, this gesture takes on meaning which presumably the "blacks" themselves never understood. According to the newspaper report in the epilogue, "At one point, Mr. McCoy looked toward his wife, smiled slightly, and raised his left hand in a clenched-fist salute." Thus Sherman's desire for power, domination, and authority is legitimized; he is the new revolutionary ready to reclaim the "birthright" that Bacon and Weiss (the "black" and the "Jew") have usurped. But in this act, Sherman has "gone native," as it were. He has become the savage Other he once feared, appropriating the savage's brutish, violent behavior and embracing the law of the "Jungle." This then, is the final achievement of the novel: both the realization and the stabilization of the racialized, infernal city.

By the novel's end, Sherman has learned how to answer the questions posed by the Mayor in the novel's prologue:

> Do you really think this is *your* city any longer? Open your eyes! The greatest city of the twentieth century! Do you think *money* will keep it yours? . . . It's the Third World down here! Puerto Ricans, West Indians, Haitians, Dominicans, Cubans, Colombians, Hondurans, Koreans, Chinese, Thais, Vietnamese, Ecuadorians, Panamanians, Filipinos, Albanians, Senegalese, and Afro-Americans!"

Like the mayor, Sherman adopts a world view dominated by ethnic and racial categories, thereby defining the forces against which he must struggle. Sherman has been persecuted and "lynched" by his oppressors, but in the process, Wolfe suggests, he has learned to fight back. In his struggle to reclaim his "birthright" from the "ungodly" hordes, Sherman becomes a symbol of the new "white" warrior. This announces, I think, the most dangerous message in this apocalyptic novel, which is by no means a new one. As Burton Pike explains, "The general malaise which accompanied the sense of doom of a civilization and the longing for a new order doubtless had much to do with the appeal of Fascism and Nazism in the 1920s and 1930s; both were notably urban phenomena." Sherman, The Great White Defendant rising phoenix-like from the ashes of the smoldering city, evokes a similar longing for a "new order" of stronger, fiercer white males willing to accept the urban apocalypse as a utopian field of battle. Thus, while the novel announces the end to an era of "white" supremacy, it also marks the beginning of a new urban struggle, sure to be just as terrifying as the last.

Chronology

1931   Born on March 2 in Richmond, Virginia, to Helen Hughes and Thomas Kennerly Wolfe.

1947   Adopts various pen names, such as "Tekay Wolfe" and "T. K. Wolfe," in his writings while attending Washington and Lee University, Lexington, Virginia. Writes three short stories as an undergraduate, but primarily is a sportswriter for the university's student newspaper.

1951   Wolfe graduates from Washington and Lee University with honors.

1951–56   Attends Yale University for degree in American Studies Department, but leaves before completing work on Ph.D. dissertation.

1956   Works briefly as truck loader and then joins staff of the *Springfield Union* in Massachusetts as a general assignment reporter.

1957   Completes dissertation "The League of American Writers: Communist Activity among American Writers, 1929–1942" and is awarded doctorate.

1959–62   Joins the "City Life" staff of the *Washington Post*. Wins Washington Newspaper Guild Award for his coverage of Cuba in 1960.

1962   Leaves *Washington Post* for the *New York Herald-Tribune*. While at the *Herald-Tribune*, Wolfe writes for its Sunday supplement, *New York*, which later becomes an independent magazine.

1963   Writes "There Goes (Varoom! Varoom!) That Kandy-Kolored Tangerine-Flake Streamline Baby" for *Esquire*.

1964   Covers the arrival of the Beatles for the *Herald-Tribune*.

1965   "The Kandy-Kolored Tangerine-Flake Streamline Baby" is published. His drawing are exhibited at the Maynard Walker Gallery in New York. Also publishes a two-part series of articles about *The New Yorker* magazine, "Tiny Mummies! The True Story of the Ruler of 43rd Street's Land of the Walking Dead" and "Lost in the Whichy Thicket."

1966–67   Researches and writes extended piece on the fugitive novelist Ken Kesey. Regular contributor to *Esquire* and the *Herald-Tribune's* Sunday magazine, *New York*.

1968   Publishes *The Electric Kool-Aid Acid Test*, his book about Ken Kesey, and a second collection of magazine articles, *The Pump House Gang*, on the same day. *The World Journal Tribune*, successor to the *Herald-Tribune*, goes out of business, although its Sunday supplement, *New York*, lives on. Wolfe becomes a contributing editor to *New York*.

1970   Publishes *Radical Chic and Mau-Mauing the Flak Catchers*.

1971   Receives honorary doctorate from Minneapolis College of Art.

1973   Series on the astronauts appears in *Rolling Stone*. Wins Frank Luther Mort Award for research in journalism.

1974   One-man show of drawings exhibited at the Tunnel Gallery in New York. Receives honorary doctor of letters degree from Washington and Lee University.

1975   *The Painted Word* is published.

1976   *Mauve Gloves and Madmen, Clutter and Vine, and Other Stories, Sketches, and Essays* is published. His phrase characterizing the 1970s, the "Me Decade," becomes incorporated into the language.

1977   Named Virginia Laureate for Literature.

1978   Marries Sheila Berger, a magazine art director, on May 27.

1979   *The Right Stuff* is published.

1980   *In Our Time*, a collection of drawings, verse, and short prose is published. Wins Harold D. Vursell Memorial Award for Excellence in Literature from the American Institute of Arts and Letters. Daughter Alexandra is born.

1981   Publishes *From Bauhaus to Our House* and *Underneath the I-Beam: Sequel to The Painted Word*.

1983   Film version of *The Right Stuff* is released. Awarded honorary doctorate from Virginia Commonwealth University.

1984   Begins serializing his long-discussed novel *The Bonfire of the Vanities* in *Rolling Stone*.

1985   Son Thomas is born.

1986   Awarded the Washington Irving Medal for Literary Excellence from the Nicholas Society.

1987   *The Bonfire of the Vanities* is published and receives enormous critical acclaim.

1989   Video recording, *Crisis of Democracy*, released by Mystic Fire Video, Public Affairs Television, in which both Wolfe and linguist-philosopher Noam Chomsky debate political and economic assumptions.

1990   Film version of *The Bonfire of the Vanities* is released.

1994   *Frederick Hart: Sculptor* is published.

1998   *A Man in Full: A Novel* is published.

Contributors

HAROLD BLOOM is Sterling Professor of the Humanities at Yale University and Henry W. and Albert A. Berg Professor of English at the New York University Graduate School. He is the author of over 20 books, including *Shelley's Mythmaking* (1959), *The Visionary Company* (1961), *Blake's Apocalypse* (1963), *Yeats* (1970), *A Map of Misreading* (1975), *Kabbalah and Criticism* (1975), *Agon: Toward a Theory of Revisionism* (1982), *The American Religion* (1992), *The Western Canon* (1994), and *Omens of Millennium: The Gnosis of Angels, Dreams, and Resurrection* (1996). *The Anxiety of Influence* (1973) sets forth Professor Bloom's provocative theory of the literary relationships between the great writers and their predecessors. His most recent books include *Shakespeare: The Invention of the Human*, a 1998 National Book Award finalist, and *How to Read and Why*, which was published in 2000. In 1999, Professor Bloom received the prestigious American Academy of Arts and Letters Gold Medal for Criticism.

RONALD WEBER is a professor of American Studies at the University of Notre Dame. He is the author of *The Midwestern Ascendancy in American Writing* (1992) and *Hired Pens: Professional Writers in America's Golden Age of Print* (1997).

MAS'UD ZAVARZADEH is a professor of English at Syracuse University. He is the author of *Seeing Films Politically* (1991) and *Theory as Resistance: Politics and Culture after (Post)structuralism* (1994).

A. CARL BREDAHL is a professor of English at the University of Florida, Gainesville. His works include *The Body as Matrix: Narrative Pattern in "The Green Hills of Africa"* (1987) and *Valuing Surface* (1989).

RICHARD A. KALLAN is a professor in the Communication Arts Department at California State Polytechnic University, Pomona, California. He is the co-author of *Semi-Aesthetic Detachment: The Fusing of Fictional and External Worlds in the Situational Literature of Leon Uris* (1982).

THOMAS L. HARTSHORNE is a professor of history at Cleveland State University. He is the author of *From* Catch-22 *to* Slaughterhouse-Five: *The Decline of the Political Mode* (1979).

BARBARA LOUNSBERRY is a professor of English at the University of Northern Iowa. She is the author of *The Diaries vs. the Letters: Continuities and Contradictions* (1996) and *Virginia Woolf and the Community of Diarists* (1999).

JAMES F. SMITH is on the faculty of the American Studies Program at Penn State University, Ogontz campus.

JAMES STULL teaches at Iowa State University in Ames. His major areas of interest are American literature and 20th century culture.

ED COHEN is a professor of English at Rutgers University. He is the author of *The Double Lives of Man: Narration and Identification in Late Nineteenth Century Representation of Ec-Centric Masculinities* (1993) and *Posing the Question: Wilde, Wit, and the Ways of Man* (1996).

RAND RICHARDS COOPER is a regular contributor to the *New York Times Book Review*. He is the author of *Charming Alice: A Unique Voice in American Fiction* (1998) and *Living in the Gap* (1998).

JOSHUA J. MASTERS is a graduate student at the University of Connecticut. His essays have appeared in *The Journal of Narrative Theory*, *Critique: Studies in Contemporary Fiction*, and *The MAWA Review*.

Bibliography

Aldridge, John. *The American Novel and the Way We Live Now*. New York: Oxford University Press, 1983.

Anderson, Chris, ed. *Literary Nonfiction: Theory, Criticism, Pedagogy*. Carbondale and Edwardsville: Southern Illinois University Press, 1989.

Bellamy, Joe David. *The New Fiction: Interviews with Innovative American Writers*. Urbana: University of Illinois Press, 1974.

Dennis, Everette E., and William L. Rivers. *Other Voices: The New Journalism in America*. San Francisco: Canfield Press, 1974.

Dickstein, Morris. *Gates of Eden: American Culture in the Sixties*. New York: Basic Books, 1977.

Epstein, Joseph. "Tom Wolfe's Vanities," *The New Criterion* 6, no. 6 (February 1988).

Felman, Shoshana, and Dori Laub. *Testimony: Crises of Witnessing in Literature, Psychoanalysis, and History*. New York: Routledge, 1992.

Fetterley, Judith. *The Resisting Reader: A Feminist Approach to American Fiction*. Bloomington: Indiana University Press, 1978.

Fishkin, Shelley Fisher. *From Fact to Fiction: Journalism and Imaginative Writing in America*. Baltimore: Johns Hopkins University Press, 1985.

Fletcher, Angus, ed. *The Literature of Fact*. New York: Columbia University Press, 1976.

Frus, Phyllis. *The Politics and Poetics of Journalistic Narrative*. New York: Cambridge University Press, 1994.

Graff, Gerald. *Literature Against Itself: Literary Ideas in Modern Society*. Chicago: University of Chicago Press, 1979.

Hellmann, John. *Fables of Fact: The New Journalism As New Fiction*. Urbana and Chicago: University of Illinois Press, 1981.

Hollowell, John. *Fact and Fiction: The New Journalism and the Nonfiction Novel*. Chapel Hill: University of North Carolina Press, 1977.

Johnson, Michael L. *The New Journalism: The Underground Press, the Artists of Nonfiction, and Changes in the Established Media*. Lawrence: University of Kansas, 1971.

Kolb, Harold H. *The Illusion of Life: American Realism As a Literary Form.* Charlottesville: University of Virginia, 1969.

Lounsberry, Barbara. *The Art of Fact: Contemporary Artists of Nonfiction.* Connecticut: Greenwood Press, Inc., 1990.

Macdonald, Dwight. "Parajournalism, or Tom Wolfe and His Magic Writing Machine." *The New York Review of Books*, 26 August 1965.

Murphy, James E. "The New Journalism: A Critical Perspective." *Journalism Monographs* 34 (May 1974)

Newman, Charles. *The Post-Modern Aura: The Act of Fiction in an Age of Inflation.* Evanston, Ill.: Northwestern University Press, 1985.

O'Donnell, Patrick and Robert Con Davis, eds. *Intertextuality and Contemporary American Fiction.* Baltimore: Johns Hopkins University Press, 1985.

Pike, Burton. *The Image of the City in Modern Literature.* Princeton, N.J.: Princeton University Press, 1981.

Poirier, Richard. *The Performing Self: Compositions and Decompositions in the Languages of Contemporary Life.* New York: Oxford University Press, 1971.

Renbar, Charles. *The Law of the Land: The Evolution of Our Legal System.* New York: Harper and Row, 1989.

Ross, Charles S. "The Rhetoric of 'the Right Stuff.'" *Journal of General Education* 33 (Summer 1981).

Salamon, Julie. *The Devil's Candy: "The Bonfire of the Vanities" Goes to Hollywood.* Boston: Houghton Mifflin, 1991.

Schwartz, Tony. "Tom Wolfe: The Great Gadfly." *New York Times Magazine* (20 December 1981).

Scura, Dorothy, ed. *Conversations with Tom Wolfe.* Jackson: University Press of Mississippi, 1990.

Sims, Norman, ed. *Literary Journalism in the Twentieth Century.* New York: Oxford University Press, 1990.

———, ed. *The Literary Journalists.* New York: Ballantine, 1984.

Tanner, Tony. *City of Words: American Fiction, 1950–1970.* New York: Harper and Row, 1971.

Varsava, Jerry A. *Contingent Meanings: Postmodern Fiction, Mimesis, and the Reader.* Tallahassee: Florida State University Press, 1990.

Webb, Joseph M. "Historical Perspective on New Journalism." *Journalism History* 1 (Summer 1974).

Weber, Ronald. *The Literature of Fact.* Athens: Ohio University Press, 1980.

———. *The Reporter As Artist: A Look at the New Journalism Controversy.* New York: Hastings House, 1974.

Wolfe, Tom and E. W. Johnson, eds. *The New Journalism.* New York: Harper and Row, 1973.

Zavarzadeh, Mas'ud. *Mythopoeic Reality: The Postwar American Nonfiction Novel.* Urbana: University of Ilinois Press, 1976.

Acknowledgments

"Tom Wolfe's Happiness Explosion" by Ronald Weber. From *Journal of Popular Culture* 8, no. 1 (Summer 1974): 71–79. © 1974 by Ray B. Browne/Bowling Green State University. Reprinted with permission.

"The Contingent *Donnée:* The Testimonial Nonfiction Novel" by Mas'ud Zavarzadeh. From *The Mythopoeic Reality: The Postwar American Nonfiction Novel* by Mas'ud Zavarzadeh. © 1976 by Mas'ud Zavarzadeh. Reprinted with permission.

"An Exploration of Power: Tom Wolfe's Acid Test" by A. Carl Bredahl. From *Critique: Studies in Modern Fiction* 23, no. 2 (Winter 1981–82): 67–84. Published by Heldref Publications, 1319 Eighteenth Street NW, Washington, DC 20036-18020. © 1981 by The Helen Dwight Reid Educational Foundation. Reprinted with permission.

"Style and the New Journalism: A Rhetorical Analysis of Tom Wolfe" by Richard A. Kallan. From *Communication Monographs* 46 (March 1979): 52–62. © 1979 by the National Communication Association. Reprinted with permission.

"Tom Wolfe on the 1960's" by Thomas L. Hartshorne. From *Midwest Quarterly: A Journal of Contemporary Thought* 23, no. 2 (Winter 1982): 144–163. © 1982 by Pittsburg State University. Reprinted with permission.

Index